Another Face of Empire

A book in the series

LATIN AMERICA OTHERWISE: LANGUAGES, EMPIRES, NATIONS

SERIES EDITORS:

Walter D. Mignolo, *Duke University*
Irene Silverblatt, *Duke University*
Sonia Saldívar-Hull, *University of California, Los Angeles*

ANOTHER FACE OF EMPIRE

Bartolomé de Las Casas, Indigenous Rights,
and Ecclesiastical Imperialism

Daniel Castro

Duke University Press
DURHAM & LONDON 2007

© 2007 Duke University Press
All rights reserved
Printed in the United States of America on acid-free paper ∞

Designed by Jennifer Hill
Typeset in Granjon by Keystone Typesetting, Inc.

Duke University Press gratefully acknowledges the support of the
Program for Cultural Cooperation between Spain's Ministry of Culture
and United States Universities.

Library of Congress Cataloging-in-Publication Data appear
on the last printed page of this book.

This book is dedicated to
Mariella Ruiz-Castro
who made it possible

Contents

About the Series ix

Acknowledgments xi

Introduction I
Bartolomé de Las Casas,
Savior of Indoamerica?

Chapter One 17
Defining and Possessing

Chapter Two 40
American Crucible

Chapter Three 63
Conversions, Utopias,
and Ecclesiastical Imperialism

Chapter Four 105
Theory and Praxis

Chapter Five 135
Toward a Restoration of the Indies

Chapter Six 150
The Legacy of Las Casas

Conclusion 177

Notes 187

Bibliography 215

Index 229

About the Series

The words and deeds of Father Bartolomé de Las Casas have invited recurrent interpretations for nearly half a millennium. He has been portrayed as the saintly conscience of Spanish imperialism and adopted as the father of Latin American liberation theology. In *Another Face of Empire*, Daniel Castro seeks to complicate the picture of Las Casas created by his hagiographers. Castro draws on Las Casas's own extensive writings and reappraises the consequences of the friar's advocacy to provide a nuanced portrayal of Las Casas as a historical agent. He also addresses what few scholars have emphasized—the ways in which the Indians themselves confronted Spanish domination and abuses. *Another Face of Empire* highlights these strategies of resistance while showing how Spanish imperial policies undermined attempts at reform.

Despite his strenuous efforts on the Indians' behalf, Las Casas failed to grasp the difficulties and contradictions in imposing an alien religious belief, Christianity, on a people who already had their own highly developed religious beliefs, as well as forms of social, economic, and political organization. By carefully critiquing Las Casas's ethnocentrism and benevolent paternalism, Castro illuminates contemporary struggles against injustice in Latin America.

❧ Acknowledgments ☙

ALTHOUGH IN MOST CASES it is only one person who receives credit for the production of a book, nothing could be further from the truth. A book is rarely a solitary endeavor; it is the result of a collective effort and a willingness to create.

This modest undertaking might have never materialized without the patience, cooperation, support, and understanding of many people and institutions. I would like to thank the administration of Southwestern University which graciously extended its support in the form of grants of funds and time. I have also received support from Gene and Trudy Yeager in the form of invitations to lecture and the opportunity to do additional research at the Howard Tilton Library.

I want to single out and thank Sara Castro-Klarén, who encouraged me to present my work publicly at a symposium on human rights at Johns Hopkins University. She read the original manuscript and made invaluable suggestions about its content and its potential for publication. I also want to acknowledge the help and support I received from one of the maestros of Indoamerican colonial history from the inception of this project, Colin Mac-Lachlan of Tulane University.

At different times, I have received support and critical suggestions from Richard E. Greenleaf, James Boyden at Tulane, Ida Altman at the University of New Orleans, and Peter Klarén at George Washington University.

I have contracted a profound debt of gratitude with Walter D. Mignolo of Duke University, who is one of the editors of the Latin America Otherwise series at Duke University Press, for taking a chance and offering me the opportunity to submit the original manuscript for evaluation. I feel fortunate to have this work published by Duke University Press and I am particularly indebted to my editor, Valerie Millholland, who has graciously guided me through the task of preparing the manuscript and navigating this delicate process. I would also like to thank Duke's assistant editor Miriam Angress for her support and cooperation. I am indebted to Lynn Walterick, my copyeditor, and to Katharine Baker, who, as assistant managing editor, helped me to navigate the complex editorial process. My appreciation also goes to the critical readers of the manuscript for their valuable suggestions, which have contributed to make it a better work.

Along the way, I have received invaluable support and encouragement from my colleagues at Southwestern, in particular Jan Dawson, Thom Mc-Clendon, Elisabeth Piedmont-Marton, and Jim Hunt. I would like to thank Amy Wink for her editorial suggestions and for preparing the index. I have also benefited from constructive evaluations received in conferences and symposia, in particular the advice offered by Judith Ewell, Mark Burk-holder, and Vincent Peloso, among others.

Last, but not least, I want to thank and dedicate this modest effort to Mariella Ruiz-Castro, my untiring *compañera,* spouse, and best friend. Words will never capture my debt of appreciation to her for her unqualified support through the years, and for always being there with the right question and the right word. I dedicate this book to her because of her love of justice and her support for those who struggle for a better life.

Introduction

Bartolomé de Las Casas:
Savior of Indoamerica?

*The early discourse of the New World then is full of questions that
cannot be asked or answers that cannot be understood.*
— Stephen Greenblatt, *Marvelous Possessions*

*I am Indian: Because of the ignorance of the white men who arrived
to the lands ruled by my grandparents. I am Indian: Now I am not
ashamed to be called this way, because I know of the historical
mistake of the Whites.*
— Natalio Hernández, *Canto nuevo de Anahuac*

CHRISTOPHER COLUMBUS'S fortuitous landing on the island of Guana-
haní, the morning of October 12, 1492, marked the irreversible demise of
one world, the expansion of another, and the birth of a third and unique
creature, Indoamerica.[1] This was a "New World" shaped by the collision
and fusion of conquerors and conquered, the forced encounter of Europe
and the wondrous "an other world" (*un otro mundo*) encountered by the
Genoese adventurer.[2] From its inception Indoamerica became a world
shaped by the intense, and often violent and cruel, interaction between
colonizers and colonized.

America, as the new continent was baptized, created boundless opportunities and unexpected challenges for the Europeans and their attempt to
impose their way of life on the newly discovered territory and its inhabitants.[3] The dialectics of creation and destruction so evident in the birth of
this New World, a world so radically different from both progenitors, was
defined by the hegemonic domination of the Europeans, and the subser-

vience and decline of the natives, or Indians, a term used by Columbus to describe the inhabitants of the newly encountered territories.[4]

In the absence of legal mechanisms to safeguard the integrity of the natives against the predatory exploitation of the newcomers, the responsibility for protecting them fell to the members of the religious orders present in the new territory. The Dominican order, under the leadership of Antonio Montesinos and Pedro de Córdoba, led the group of reformers emerging as defenders of indigenous human rights in America.[5] In those early years of imperial expansion, these reformers became the main intercessors between the natives and the Spanish crown. By the end of the second decade of occupation, the leadership of the "indianist" movement, as the reformers were collectively identified, was transferred to one of the latest converts to their cause: a "champion of rightful and lost causes," the earlier cleric-*encomendero*, prolific writer, historian, activist, and enduring symbol of the reformers' struggle for the protection of the natives, Fray Bartolomé de Las Casas.[6] The American historian Lewis Hanke, one of his most fervent admirers and a sympathetic biographer, describes him thus:

> A reformer in the Spanish court, failed colonizer in Venezuela, friar in Española, obstructer of unjust wars in Nicaragua, fighter for justice for the Indians in acrid debates with the Mexican ecclesiastics, sponsor of a plan to Christianize the Indians in Chiapa and Guatemala exclusively by peaceful means, fortunate agitator in the Court of Charles V in favor of the New Laws and bishop of Chiapa.[7]

Bartolomé de Las Casas emerges in contraposition and opposition to the large number of antiheroes and villains during Spain's early years in the Americas, the likes of Nuño de Guzmán, Pedro de Alvarado, Pedrarias de Ávila, Fernando Cortés, or Lope de Aguirre, among innumerable others. Of all these personages, it is Bartolomé de Las Casas, the tireless activist, who is remembered as a paradigm of virtue and as a larger-than-life archetypal hero. In a void created by the absence of autochthonous heroes, Las Casas and his work become a powerful symbolic presence, a palliative to counter the ills that afflicted, and continue to afflict, Indoamerica from the time of that fateful first encounter to the present.

At the same time, few participants in the imperial expansion of Spain into the New World have generated as much controversy, been so demonized, become the object of such uninhibited hagiographic adoration and derision, or received so much attention from contemporaries and from modern students of the Indoamerican colonial period as Bartolomé de Las Casas.[8]

Because of the vitriolic denunciation of the abuses committed by his compatriots against the Indians, Las Casas earned the dubious distinction of being identified as the progenitor of the "Black Legend" of the Spanish conquest, published in bookform. The slim tract was originally written in 1542 and published in 1552 under the title *Brevísima relación de la destruición de las Indias* (often translated into English as *A Short Account of the Destruction of the Indies*). The book was widely read throughout Europe and provided Spain's enemies with a unique opportunity to attack the Spanish venture in the Americas. Despite its close association with Las Casas, the Black Legend "has a history much older than the term itself," going back to the Italians' anti-Spanish stance in the fourteenth century and extending as well to the unfavorable opinion of Spaniards held by the Germans and the Dutch in the sixteenth century.[9]

As Spanish power declined in Europe and the Americas at the end of the eighteenth century, Spaniards became less tolerant of criticism, and many mainstream intellectual and political figures assumed the responsibility of dispelling the negative images conjured by the Black Legend. This attempt to exalt the virtues of Spain is known as the *leyenda aurea* (Golden Legend). Unlike Spain and its former domains, where the proponents of the Golden Legend were almost uniformly conservative, in the United States, where the legend is identified as the White Legend, adherents included moderate, conservative, and pro-Spanish historical revisionists. These historians, most of them writing in the first three quarters of the twentieth century, took a favorable view of Spanish exploits in the Americas during the dark time of the conquest and settlement of the New World.[10] Nevertheless, if the term "Black Legend" is used to refer to the dark period of the conquest of the Americas, then its opposite is not so much a luminous interpretation of historical events as a conscious effort to retouch the darkest events of that traumatic period, to cover up the seamier side of imperialist Spanish occupation beneath a glittering mythical patina destined to create a "gilded legend."[11] Unfortunately, the fact that the creation of the Black Legend is credited almost exclusively to Las Casas tends to limit all interpretations of the friar within the parameters of the Black Legend–White Legend dichotomy.

Over the last four centuries, Las Casas and his historical persona have been adopted by a multifaceted multitude of people to validate their creeds at different times and for different purposes. At first, it was the Dominicans who used him as a spearhead of the reformist movement in their dealings with the crown. In the last years of his life he was used to validate the fairness of the Council of the Indies by acting as consultant for that body in all matters dealing with the Americas while serving, at the same time, as a representative of Indian interests to be argued before the courts. In the nineteenth century, precursors of Indoamerican independence like Simón Bolívar in Venezuela and Fray Servando Teresa y Mier in Mexico often invoked his work as a paradigm of struggle and resistance to be emulated. In the first half of the twentieth century, he was appropriated as a symbol by defenders and opponents of the Black Legend to argue their cases about Spain's "true" role in the creation of the New World. In the second half of the century, the friar became an inspiration for the transforming power of Christian reformist thought propounded by some of the standard bearers of the Theology of Liberation movement.[12]

As with all mythological figures, the characterizations of Father Las Casas cover a broad spectrum of tendencies and definitions depending on geography, historical period, or where one's sympathies lie on any given issue. He is variously seen as an apostolic prototype of love, a noble protector of the Indians, or, as some have called him, the "father of America." In 1935, in a bit of hyperbolic enthusiasm, the participants in the Congreso de Americanistas in Seville anointed him as the "authentic expression of the true Spanish conscience."[13]

At the opposite pole, his detractors have characterized him as a pious fanatic, the father of the infamous Black Legend, and even a court gadfly.[14] One of his most vitriolic critics, the modern Spanish historian Ramón Menéndez Pidal, went as far as to challenge the friar's sanity by claiming that "[Las Casas] was not a saint, nor an impostor, nor was he evil nor crazy, he was simply a paranoiac."[15] It seems that Menéndez's overtly nationalistic perception of Las Casas as a tool of Spain's enemies prompted this extreme, and unwarranted, attack. In addition to the political inspiration for the attack, the historian's intense dislike is largely based on the friar's denunciation of the crimes committed by his country in the New World. Further, the attack seems to have been fueled by a need to sanitize Spain's image in the aftermath of the Civil War. Despite Menéndez's solipsistic reliance on a multitude of value-laden psychological typologies, he never did build a strong case to substantiate his charges, beyond the name-calling.

Most of the characterizations of the Dominican, perhaps with the single exception of the one by Menéndez Pidal, appear to have some basis in truth, and they have contributed to the creation of a mythical Las Casas used to mobilize peoples and ideas. Most of Las Casas's mythical reputation, with its accomplishments and implicit although unmentioned shortcomings, rests on a vociferous activism surrounding the treatment of the American natives. Ironically, while Las Casas's work is largely measured in terms of his praxis, there is little mention made of the fact that his praxis seldom resulted in improving the lives of the natives, and often his main accomplishment was to keep himself in the political and social limelight. Las Casas was an activist, and as such, he was measured by the results he obtained, but this did not always result in long-range beneficial outcomes for the oppressed natives, and often his utopian proposals had the opposite result of what he intended. His inability to act outside the totality of the royally sanctioned legal system, and his unwillingness to dialogue with the encomenderos (the colonialists), or to empower the natives to do so, made the success of his self-appointed mission to help the Indians a largely formalistic endeavor. Although he claimed to act for the oppressed, he rarely acted with them, and there is no evidence that at any time he worked with the natives to transform them from passive objects into active subjects responsible for transforming their own fate.

In the case of Las Casas, as in the cases of other legendary figures, it is difficult if not impossible to separate historical reality from myth. A reinterpretation of Las Casas must necessarily move beyond the mythological dimensions of his legacy, and beyond the multiple-legend construct, in an attempt to define him in light of his participation in the dialectical reality of the construction of a new world built on the ruins of another.

Given the relative paucity of texts detailing the Dominican's life and work, and perhaps with the exception of some extremely critical tracts written by some of his contemporaries, we have only his own texts by which to examine his life and the significance of his work. That is, the main source of information about Las Casas is the subject himself. Conscious of his role as a vital protagonist in the history of the New World, the friar never shied away from recognizing the impact of his participation in the colonial drama. As Anthony Pagden writes, "Since his project was to establish the unique status of his voice, most of his writings are, implicitly or explicitly, autobiographical. No historian of America is so tirelessly self-referential."[16]

The absence of external sources of information presents some insurmountable difficulties in reevaluating the legacy of the reformer. Consequently, the only way of gaining a critical appreciation of Las Casas is to dissect and deconstruct his own written work and recorded deeds against the background of established historical events, including the perceptions of his contemporary and later admirers and detractors.

Although the reputation of Bartolomé de Las Casas rests on his widely reported struggle to gain better treatment for the Indians, there has rarely been a concerted effort to evaluate the practical outcome of this work vis-à-vis the natives and their day-to-day well-being. This results largely from the fact that "neither his biographers nor the historians of America have to date subjected the plans of Las Casas to methodical analysis."[17] Little or no attention has been paid to the immediate and long-range application and consequences of his proposals or legislative efforts on behalf of the natives, who, from Las Casas's perspective, become the unseen protagonists of a drama that could not exist without them.

The list of Las Casas's accomplishments disseminated by his supporters is endless. It includes the creation of a native sanctuary of sorts in Paria (present-day Venezuela), the pacification of Tuzulutlán, the land of war, rebaptized as Verapaz in present-day Guatemala, the paternity of the New Laws, his petition to abolish the encomienda in Peru, and the *Ordenanzas para descubrimientos* (Ordinances for Discoveries). The ordinances were issued by Philip II years after the friar's death. Yet even the most cursory examination of these "accomplishments" will reveal that almost invariably these efforts were unimplemented and in most cases ended in failure; they rarely translated into tangible gains for the natives.

What is often overlooked in the exaltation of Las Casas is his overriding concern to convert the inhabitants of the Americas to Christianity, if not directly, at least through different missionary agents.[18] Despite the contradictions implicit in proselytism, many of the Dominican's admirers still view this vocation as virtuous and worthy of praise instead of as an act of ecclesiastic imperialism. In an attempt to justify Las Casas's vocation to convert the Indians to Christianity, his advocates point out that, in his case, conversion is acceptable and desirable, insofar as it is done by peaceful means and to implement assimilation to the dominant culture. At the same time there is no rationale offered to justify an imposition from the perspective of the Spaniards, other than the tenuous argument that conversion implies spiritual salvation. This important motivation underlying the friar's relationship with the natives is evident in his written works and deeds, as this observation from the *Historia de las Indias* demonstrates: "[T]here are no people in the world, no matter how barbaric or inhuman they are, nor can a nation be found that being indoctrinated and taught, in *the manner required by the natural condition of men, mostly through the doctrine of faith*, will not produce as a reasonable fruit the very best of men."[19]

While not advocating the overt subjugation of the natives, he nevertheless leaves open the way for the possessors of the "doctrine of faith" to justify territorial usurpation and the exploitation of the inhabitants of the occupied territory in order to produce "as a reasonable fruit the very best of men." All this under the guise of indoctrinating and teaching in "the manner required by the natural condition of men." From his writings and practice it is apparent that as a Spaniard he fully shared his compatriots' belief that the dissemination of the Christian faith was their divinely ordained mission. This acceptance of Spain's ascendancy over the Americas implies his tacit recognition of the "salvific" role assigned to himself and his compatriots in the divine apportionment of duties. As Gustavo Gutierrez points out in his examination of Las Casas and his Christian mission in the Americas: "From the beginning of his struggle in defense of the Indian, Las Casas considers that the only thing that can justify the presence of Christians in the Indies is the announcement of the Gospel of Jesus Christ."[20] That is, as long as the Spaniards intended to preach the Christian Gospel among the indigenous infidels, then their presence should be tolerated and welcomed. Such a consideration is a capitulation to a form of pseudo-humanism that only partially recognizes the humanity of the subjected indigenous people.[21]

Judging from the actions of the participants in the colonization of America, there was never any doubt among the early colonizers about their moral imperative to bring the "true faith" to these remote regions of the world, and Las Casas seems to have fully shared these aspirations. The same zeal that fueled the *Reconquista* of Spain from the Moors was transferred to the conquest and settlement of the Americas. This essential component of the cultural conquest of the Americas is found at the core of the primer for conversion, *The Only Way [to Attract All People to the True Faith]*, where Las Casas states his belief in his, and his nation's, mandate to win the natives over to the "true faith":

> It was due to the will and work of Christ . . . that God's chosen should be called, should be culled *from every race, every tribe, every language, every corner of the world . . . no race, no nation in this entire globe would be left totally untouched by the free gift of divine grace*. Some among them be they few or many are to be taken into eternal life. We must hold this to be true also of our Indian nations.[22]

While criticizing the manner in which his religious brethren went about converting the natives en masse through the wholesale dispensation of baptisms and other sacraments, Las Casas attempted to differentiate himself from the others in the methods for catechization that he proposed. Essentially, his disagreements with the others were more concerned with form while leaving the essence of the cultural onslaught untouched. It was simply a case of peaceful versus forceful conversion to Christianity, and his proposals offered a different form of implementing the same goal of converting the natives to attain the ultimate objective of the colonization of consciousness.

If the difference between Las Casas and his compatriots was one of form and not of essence, then rather than viewing him as the ultimate champion of indigenous causes, we must see the Dominican friar as the incarnation of a more benevolent, paternalistic form of ecclesiastical, political, cultural, and economic imperialism rather than as a unique paradigmatic figure. In this context, he must be reevaluated as a representative of another face of Spanish ecclesiastical imperialism, albeit a more benevolent form of imperialism than the one offered by the traditional colonists.

In the historical context of the time, his role as a proponent of imperialism was tempered by his calls for reform in defense of the rights of the natives, at least on paper. Nevertheless, this defense seems to have ensued from the forms that domination assumed, rather than from a wholehearted opposition to the motives behind the practice. Nor did his defense seem to come from a feeling of sympathy or empathy with the natives but from a preoccupation to implement a more humane form of exploitation. In effect, given his active and willing participation in the imperialist venture, the friar was little more than another member of the occupying forces. What differentiates him from the rest is his willingness to reach out to offer temporary succor to those being victimized so they could be benevolently converted, peacefully exploited, and successfully incorporated as members of a new subject-colony where existence depended on the dictates of the king in the imperial capital.

Father Las Casas's reputation as a reformer is based on his advocacy of Indian freedom, but in the earlier years of his practice as a reformer, the liberty he envisioned for the natives was little more than a liberty conditioned by the economic and political needs of the motherland. This is patently evident in his first list of *remedios* (remedies) for the Indians of Cuba. In this list, prepared in 1516 as a complement to his memorial of grievances presented to the acting crown regent, Cardinal Ximénez de Cisneros, he refrained from calling for the abolition of the practice of assigning grants of tribute-paying Indians to a conquistador as a reward for services rendered to the crown, the infamous *encomienda*.[23] He limited himself to call for the amelioration of the tasks imposed on the natives so they could survive the ordeal:

> While Your Highness orders an investigation and determines what must be done in those [Caribbean] islands . . . it should be ordered that all Indians from all islands should cease working and serving in all capacities . . . . because the little idle time they have will serve [the Indians] to recover their strength, to have some leisure time and to have the chance to put on some weight or become stronger, so when they return to work, they will be able to bear it[24]

9

Later in his life, the condemnation of the encomienda became more pointed and vociferous, but this transformation came well after the conquest of the whole continent had been accomplished and the establishment of irreversible exploitative practices had been validated and enforced, if not by law, by force of habit.

Las Casas's and the other religious reformers' paternalistic benevolence toward the Indians set them apart from most participants in the settlement of the New World. They provided a humanitarian element absent among ordinary conquistadores, but at the same time they could not escape their roles as advocates of the "true" faith and as integral components of the vanguard of an imperialist church striving to impose its beliefs and aspirations on other peoples. They were part, whether willingly or unwillingly, of the shock troops of the "faithful" heralding the triumph of the City of God over the terrestrial countryside of sin inhabited by the pagans. Paradoxically, Las Casas never appeared to have grasped the contradiction implied in the act of imposing an alien religious belief, like Christianity, on a people who already had well-defined theological beliefs and carefully constructed cosmogonies. The only explanation for such behavior must be found in his overriding conviction of the innate superiority of his religious beliefs over those of the Native Americans he so wanted to protect.

The accelerated and unregulated imperialist expansion of Spain placed Las Casas at the heart of a multi-tiered conflict pitting the centralized aspirations of the crown against the semi-feudal aspirations of the colonists, who, driven by their desire for immediate rewards, had brought the natives to the verge of extinction. Experience taught Las Casas that his visions of a gentler, kinder imperialism could be accomplished by appealing directly to the king and his advisors rather than the colonists. Until the end of his days he appeared convinced that all the Spanish monarch needed to do to set things right in his kingdom was to be informed, "[for] it follows that the simple knowledge that something is wrong in his kingdom is quite sufficient to ensure that [the king] will see that it is corrected, for he will not tolerate any such evil for a moment longer than it takes him to right it."[25] King Charles V, aware of the benefits of the friar's role as an active defender of the centralized government against the feudal and aristocratic aspirations of the conquistadores, not only allowed Las Casas to express his critical views of the Spanish colonizers but encouraged him to do so at every possible turn.[26] Ironically, modern historians, most prominently the proponents of the Golden Legend, often choose this one instance as an illustration of sixteenth-century Spanish toleration and freedom of speech.[27]

Aside from his claims for legislative reform, the single most important contribution of Bartolomé de Las Casas to the history of Indoamerica was to provide an ongoing record of the events associated with the first half-century of Spanish domination. He, unlike most of his contemporaries, seems to have internalized the horror of the conquest and resolved to bear witness for posterity. If Columbus, through a daring and momentous act, lessened the geographic and cultural distances between two worlds, it fell to Las Casas, a man driven by profound Christian beliefs and untamed humanism, to attempt to bridge the informational gap created by the forced incorporation of America into the Spanish empire. Working from the medieval perspective that the Spanish occupation of the Indies had "destroyed" them, Las Casas dedicated the best and most productive years of his life to attempting to "restore" them to a new grandeur under the aegis of Spain.

Another frequently overlooked fact about Las Casas's history, as a fighter for the rights of the American Indian, is that his most effective praxis was carried out in the context of the Spanish court, not in American territory. It was at court where he uninhibitedly played out his complex role as the "universal protector of all the Indians of America" (*protector universal de todos los indios de América*), a title he had received from Cardinal Ximénez de Cisneros during the latter's tenure as regent of Spain. From early on the friar understood that the best alternative to influence the political landscape of the time was to remain at courtside as much as possible. It was there where he could be more visible, have direct access to the monarch, and be ostensibly more effective in his work.

Despite all impressions to the contrary, his contact with the objects of his affection, the American Indians, was minimal. Despite his good intentions and his supporters' claims to the contrary, it is apparent that the reformer was never able to bridge the cultural gulf that separated him, a Spanish *letrado* and a dweller of "the lettered city," from the inhabitants of that "stone-age" illiterate countryside where a New World was being forcefully erected.[28] This divorce from the indigenous people and their culture is partially evident in his apparent lack of interest in learning native languages. One of his most fervent critics, the Franciscan missionary Toribio de Benavente, Motolinía, provides testimony about this aspect of his work, a fact that is also evident in the friar's own testimony.[29] This ignorance of native languages forced him to rely on intermediaries to communicate with the natives, rendering him impotent to reduce the cultural gap between himself and his beloved "charges."

The America that Las Casas knew and inhabited for different periods was a static continuum where two worlds existed in a permanent state of conflict. He often seemed incapable of grasping the dynamic dialectical process whereby a political, economic, cultural, and racial "New World" was being born in the midst of violence, exploitation, and neglect. While he appears to have been aware of the demographic disaster that befell the natives and the extent of the human genocide obtaining in this emerging world, he either could not see or chose to ignore the cultural genocide. He seems to have been unaware, unconcerned, and unmoved by the progressive emergence of a new hybrid culture and all the complexities accompanying its origins. It is as if for him the collision of the two worlds never moved beyond its original Caribbean stage.

A label that is also attached to Las Casas is that of "anti-colonialist." This perception understandably pertains to his opposition to the manner in which the colonialists exploited the New World and its inhabitants. Las Casas's characterization as an anti-colonialist arises from his opposition to the creation of semi-autonomous colonies, collections of private fiefs, headed by encomenderos in America, but this perceived anti-colonialism does not necessarily translate into anti-imperialism. It was not until the waning years of his life that his deeds and words raised the possibility of Spain's withdrawal or the renunciation of its possessions in the New World. While he called for the removal of the encomenderos as intermediaries between the crown and its Indian subjects, he suggested that their role should be taken over by the crown directly, implying only a change of masters, from a private one, the encomenderos, to a public one, the state.[30]

On the contrary, his compulsion to find a counterbalance to the pretensions of the conquistador-colonizers propelled him to increasingly embrace the alternatives offered by the imperial demands of king and church as the only acceptable sources of authority and justice.

Las Casas's career abounds with instances in which his quest to improve the conditions of the natives contributed to the consolidation of the crown's control over both colonists and natives, but this is rarely acknowledged. Looking beyond the sound, fury, and pyrotechnics of Las Casas's *Brevísima*, and the idea that the king used it as an authoritative source of information to justify the passage of the New Laws, we find that those very laws afforded Charles a unique opportunity to check the growing ambition of the encomenderos. By limiting the scope of the encomienda and its conditions of heritability, he was in effect stripping them of their only bargaining tool to support their claims.

Another one of the deeds most celebrated by Las Casas's admirers is his participation in the debates of Valladolid in 1550–51. The debate pitting Las Casas against the humanist and royal chronicler Juan Ginés de Sepúlveda centered on the issue of using force to convert the indigenous people of the New World to the Christian faith. It also aimed to invalidate the claim that Sepúlveda shared with other Spanish intellectuals of the time and, naturally, the encomenderos, that the Indians were "slaves by nature," thus inferior to the Spanish conquerors and subject to being enslaved. The ambivalent outcome of Valladolid established that the waging of war against the American "infidels" was unacceptable, but at the same time it retained for the crown the moral and religious obligation of carrying out the evangelization of the natives by peaceful means. In this manner Spain's right to be in America was justified in terms of the expectations that it would fulfill its duty as a Christian nation to disseminate the true faith and to assume the tutelage of the infidels while taking over their temporal possessions. Significantly, after Valladolid the question of whether Spain had the right to have dominion over the New World was never raised again.

In the aftermath of the debate against Sepúlveda, royal authority was further reaffirmed with the emergence of the issue of perpetuity pitting the encomenderos against the reformers and the Peruvian Indian elite. By accepting the king's absolute authority on all matters pertaining to the Indies, Las Casas's intervention in the debates about perpetuity, like his participation in Valladolid, helped in no small way to consolidate the power of the imperial center and the values that it represented in the New World.

The life and work of Bartolomé de Las Casas remains an invaluable source for understanding the gestation and development of the alluring, mysterious, and contradictory Indoamerican continent, but any analysis of Las Casas and his work must diverge from the distortions of mythmaking, mystification, and hagiography if it is to be illuminating. The heroic-mythical image of Las Casas has satisfied too many people for far too long. Yet, despite the impossibility of producing a truly objective reinterpretation, a reevaluation of the man and his work becomes mandatory if we want to have an accurate interpretation of a real living, complex man and his time rather than the inert comfortable myth with which we have become so familiar. A reinterpretation of Las Casas within the contradictory context of the complexities of the formative century of Indoamerica is also necessary in order to get rid of prevailing utopian fictions surrounding the historical origins of the New World. Such a reevaluation is necessary because Las Casas—who without doubt is one of the most significant historical figures to emerge out of the collision and merger of Spain and America in the sixteenth century—must be subject to the same unsparing examination that less celebrated personages receive.

13

In the process of reinterpreting the Dominican's role, we must strip and discard the layer of adjectives under which he has been artificially preserved. Titles like "apostle" or "father of the Indians" only cloud the true nature of his accomplishments or lack of them. That is, an apostle, by definition, is an individual who performs an active person-to-person evangelizing role attempting to convert unbelievers to his or her own faith, but as I will show, Las Casas rarely had direct contact with the indigenous people. Las Casas's roles as organizer of missions and missionaries and as a theoretician and tactician of ecclesiastical imperialism, in addition to his driving compulsion to convert all American "infidels" to Christianity, are mistakenly construed as apostolic work.[31] The depiction of Las Casas as "father of America" is also a somewhat distorted and overenthusiastic characterization, given that paternity implies a high level of responsibility for an offspring, but the America Las Casas abandoned in 1547 was neither his creation nor in any way his responsibility.

Furthermore, there seems to be a slight confusion between paternity, which implies profound responsibility and a dialogical relationship, with the more one-sided quality of paternalism, where the dichotomy protector-victim acquires primacy. In almost every respect Las Casas's work with and for the Indians is more paternalistic than paternal, more sympathetic than empathetic. This should not be surprising since the attitude is in keeping with the Europeans' belief in their hegemonic ascendancy, which imbued them with a deeply seated belief in their "positional" superiority.[32] This fine differentiation between charitable paternalism and paternity is unavoidable in an examination of Las Casas and his legacy.

As one of the most admired and celebrated participants in the imperialist venture of his country, Las Casas must also be recognized as one of the most vociferous critics of the Spanish colonization project, and as one of the most prolific writers of treatises, histories, and countless other documents about colonial Indoamerica. His theoretical contributions to the scholarly corpus of information about Indoamerica notwithstanding, when we probe further into the results of his praxis on behalf of the natives, we will discover that, ultimately, he brought little or no improvements to their material well-being. As Paulo Freire indicates:

> Political action on the side of the oppressed must be pedagogical action in the authentic sense of the word, and therefore, action *with* the oppressed. Those who work for liberation must not take advantage of the emotional dependence of the oppressed—dependence that is the fruit of the concrete situation of domination which surrounds them and which engendered their view of the world.[33]

From this perspective, Las Casas's work develops not *with* the oppressed, the indigenous people, but within the context of the society of Spanish letrados, the imperial hegemonic culture, working to maintain the oppressive edifice represented by the occupiers. While the amount of legislation that he managed to exact from the crown is an outstanding example of tenacity and erudition, ultimately, it did little to alter the fate of the natives he professed to love. Many of Las Casas's admirers often see the Dominican's role as a lobbyist and advocate of legislation in favor of American Indians as evidence of his being a paradigm of rebelliousness and revolutionary fervor.

It is precisely because of the yearning to recuperate some positive elements from the conquest that Las Casas is singled out from his contemporaries. While the passage of legislation in favor of the natives is one of his single most recognizable accomplishments, legislation without implementation in favor of those it is supposed to benefit is futile. Las Casas will always be remembered by the amount of laws he influenced, but this should not cloud the perception that throughout his career he was unable, or unwilling, to get close to the natives beyond his self-appointed role of providential protector of the colonized. In this context it is worth recalling that his massive *Apologética historia sumaria* was largely an intellectual exercise to disprove the charges brought by Sepúlveda that the Indians were slaves by nature. In this work the natives are viewed more from the perspective of a social scientist analyzing an inert subject to prove a thesis than from that of a loving, empathetic person trying to come close to his subject. Further, Las Casas's attempt to demonstrate that the Indians were not natural slaves, in clear refutation of Aristotle, responds to a desperate attempt to fit and conform what he knew about America to other events in both ancient Greco-Roman culture and his own European experience. Rather than an attempt to find new ways of understanding and interpreting the unique world he inhabited, he was content to rely on traditional methods of disquisition.

15

To take the true measure of any individual can be a daunting task, and in the case of Bartolomé de Las Casas, even more so. Nevertheless, no historical figure is immune to the light of analysis and reevaluation, especially if the intention is nothing more than an attempt to recapture the individual historical figure from a less customary and unadorned perspective than the most widely accepted ones. In this particular case, the intention is to reevaluate the Dominican friar as a significant and dynamic historical agent with marked flaws and attributes, and to define his role as a benevolent agent of Spanish political and ecclesiastical imperialism, not as the abstract, heroic, and mythological figure that he has become.

To gain a close approximation of the Dominican, it will be necessary to analyze the context within which he worked and evolved. It is only from this perspective that we can gain a true sense of him. Through this process I hope we will gain a new and more accurate understanding of Las Casas's role in the complex context of that violent and dynamic intersection of time and people resulting in the traumatizing and dramatic birth of our New World.

One

Defining and Possessing

The colonization of America, trade with the colonies, the increase in the means of exchange and in commodities generally, gave to commerce, to navigation, to industry, an impulse never before known.
—Marx and Engels, *The Communist Manifesto*

AFTER COLUMBUS'S ORIGINAL encounter with the new continent, the priority of the Spanish crown was to define its rights of possession and its political jurisdiction. Equally important was the imperative to define the nature of the inhabitants of the new territories to enable the crown to develop a plan of action concerning the roles to be ascribed to the different participants. Lacking a frame of reference to interpret the portents they had found, European intellectuals, near and far, took their cue from Columbus, who interpreted the new continent through the principle of attachment, of "translating varieties of experiences from an alien world into the practices of his own."[1] The newness of the world the Europeans encountered forced them to search deep into their past and to retrieve the concepts and values with which they were familiar in order to apply them to the land and the people they were attempting to define and possess.

Interpreting an "Other World"

The practice of attachment, and its limitations, became evident in Columbus's earliest communication to the Catholic Sovereigns announcing the discovery of the "New World," where he wrote that "in whatever land I traveled, [the natives] believed and believe that I, together with these ships and people, came from heaven, and they greeted me with such veneration."[2]

The admiral did not hesitate to "attach" specific attitudes and perceptions to the natives despite his total ignorance of native languages and the people he encountered. What the statement reflects is not so much a perception of the natives but Columbus's response to a new situation that reflected and illustrated his own cultural milieu, his time, and his own deeply rooted messianic conviction rather than the reality of the world he had encountered.

Columbus, like other colonizing pioneers, assessed his encounter with the New World in the terms he knew best, religion and profit. Not only was there the possibility of immeasurable riches but also a vast captive audience of natives waiting to be converted to his faith, as he noted in the same letter:

> Most powerful sovereigns: all of Christendom should hold great celebrations, and especially God's Church, for the finding of such a multitude of such friendly peoples, which with very little effort will be converted to our Holy Faith, and *so many lands filled with so many goods, very necessary to us in which all Christians will have comfort and profits.*[3]

Faith and profit had become an indissoluble whole for those who, leaping into the void, had followed the admiral. Even though they knew they had found "an other" world, they could only understand it within the parameters of their limited perspective and experience. Thus their urgency to translate the wonders they encountered into material and spiritual terms they could understand. Columbus, our earliest reference in acquainting Europe with the New World, interpreted everything he saw and learned through the filter of what was familiar to him, as, for example, his interpreting the Tainos' practice of fasting and abstaining from sex for twenty days before seeking gold as equivalent to Christian practices to obtain grace, which in effect, according to Anthony Pagden, was nothing more than attempting to conflate two different experiences.

> European and Amerindian sacred rites are not said as many later commentators would say *often to be similar*, the one either a diabolic inversion or a residual memory of the other. Indeed the supposed effectiveness of the rituals of the "bestial Indians: excludes the possibility of any such claims. Instead what is familiar, abstention and self-denial, is employed to *"attach" one unfamiliar action to another familiar one.*[4]

Lacking any point of reference for the new practices they encountered, Columbus and his fellow Europeans were at a loss to assess the incalculable magnitude of encountering *terra incognita*. Perhaps it was ignorance paired with the newly gained sense of arrogance and belief in their innate superiority that might help explain the inhuman treatment of the natives by the earliest Spanish settlers and their successors. According to Stephen Greenblatt, the lives of the natives were of little importance to the Europeans because the latter approached the new continent as members of a group whose "culture was characterized by immense confidence in its own centrality, by *a political organization based on practices of command and submission, by a willingness to use coercive violence on both strangers and fellow countrymen*, and by a religious ideology centered on the endlessly proliferated representation of a tortured and murdered god of love."[5] Thus from the beginning a hegemonic relationship was established with the Spaniards occupying the position of commanding masters, and the natives that of abject subjects.

As would be expected, the interpretive tools used by the Spaniards were the same ones that had served as the foundations upon which their nation had built its complex legal, political, and cultural apparatus of domination. Rooted in a strong Greco-Roman tradition colored by seven hundred years of struggle against the Arab "infidel," they were transferred unchanged and applied without regard for their nuanced consequences in their new setting.

The newcomers saw America from a perspective influenced by their most recent historical experience, "through a filter of war with the Moors: a complex mixture of religion, heroic discovery, gold, and the self-justified conquest of infidels, a sort of *jihad*, or Holy War."[6] The religious aspect of the exploration and conquest of the new territory lent to the enterprise an otherworldly dimension as it became "the irresistible march of Catholic civilization brought to the heathen by God's new Chosen People."[7] Yet, soon after they took possession of the new territories and its inhabitants, they were chagrined to discover that even their vast knowledge of the classics and their reliance on their religious traditions were not sufficient to define the world they so wanted to dominate.

Incapable of finding suitable terminology to express the magnitude of the event, the Spanish chroniclers of the time resorted to superlatives and grandiose proclamations. These ranged from Columbus's and Las Casas's exalted and enthusiastic description of the land and its inhabitants to Francisco López de Gómara's pronouncement that "the greatest thing, after the creation of the world, with the exception of the incarnation and death of its Creator, is the discovery of the Indies; so called the New World."[8]

According to Las Casas, the ability to capture and describe this phenomenon was a privilege reserved for those whose authority was derived from first-hand experience. This "appeal to the authority of the eyewitness" is what Pagden has identified as the autoptic imagination.[9] And it was the act of bearing witness to the new reality that became the ultimate validation of interpretation, as Las Casas indicated in the *Brevísima*:

> Everything that has happened since the marvelous discovery of the Americas— from the short-lived initial attempts of the Spanish to settle there, right down to the present day—has been so extraordinary that *the whole story remains quite incredible to anyone who has not experienced it at first hand.*[10]

The vertiginous speed of unfolding events exacerbated the urgency of the demand to undertake the complex task of defining, organizing, and controlling a world encountered under such abrupt and unique circumstances. The unnamed continent offered the Iberians the unique opportunity to recreate it in their own image through the imposition of their sociopolitical and cultural norms and beliefs on the inhabitants of the new territories.[11] Nevertheless, the absence of a referential framework to define and understand the New World posed complex and unparalleled challenges for the empire and its future colonies for the administration of the land and its people.

The transfer of institutions and beliefs from Europe to the New World was substantially justified by the deeply seated belief among Spaniards that after the *Reconquista* (Reconquest) they had become the vanguard of the chosen called on to conquer and to convert infidels wherever they were. To win converts to the "one true faith," Christianity, and save them from perdition had become an overriding priority and an integral component of their task. Columbus, although not a Spaniard by birth, fully identified with the Spanish messianic mission, thereby becoming one of the most important purveyors of the transfer of religious beliefs from Europe to America. Why else, if not by divine intervention, and intention, could the Creator have chosen Spain, and by extension Columbus himself, to carry out his gospel to illuminate the heathen in those faraway lands?

No other region of the world could offer the legions of avid Spanish evangelizers the innumerable candidates for salvation represented by those Amerindians being consumed by the infernal flames of idolatry and polytheism. The vanguard of the faithful, one of the dominant components in this equation of power, felt fully justified in its quest to colonize the poor forgotten souls dwelling in darkness. This ecclesiastical imperialism was fueled by the messianic zeal of the mendicant orders, and above all by a growing belief in the miraculous quality of their religious symbols and a quest for personal, national, and universal salvation.[12]

Dividing the Spoils

Columbus's extraordinary feat of doubling the size of the known world, almost overnight, inaugurated a new age for Castile and the rest of the European world, an age of new and vital imperial expansion. The original difficulties that Columbus had encountered in filling even the most essential positions required for safe navigation before his first voyage were absent in the second one. He had the luxury of selecting more than twelve hundred individuals, all of them lured by the promises of unbound opportunity offered by the new territory. Ultimately, the unnamed continent was physically conquered and colonized by the sheer driving power of a small group of enterprising conquistadores, but "force alone could not construct an empire, royal regulation of the most important socio-political aspects of the new possessions became mandatory."[13]

By the time the admiral found the new continent, Castile was already in full control of the Canary Islands, providing the nation with a springboard to the New World.[14] Nevertheless, the Canaries had come at a high price. The Treaty of Alcaçovas, signed in 1479, required that in exchange for the islands, Spain would be forced to recognize Portugal's rights to the Azores, Cape Verde, Madeira, and the African Coast.[15]

The concessions made by Spain at Alcaçovas only confirmed previous donations made to Portugal by popes Eugene IV and Nicholas V. Along with the territorial donations, the popes granted the Portuguese the possession of captured "Negroes" to convert them to the Catholic faith, marking in effect the beginning of the slave trade.[16] The conversion clause eventually became the cornerstone of Spanish imperial practices in the New World, except that in America, the term "Negroes" was tacitly substituted by the term "Indians." The Spanish, vying for Iberian hegemony, saw with unease the papal donations to the Portuguese, which explains Spain's urgency to obtain an imperial charter from the papacy, the fountainhead of universal authority.

Like most other political practices of the time, the reliance on the papacy to grant temporal kingdoms was rooted in medieval practice, specifically the "Donation of Constantine" that surfaced for the first time in mid-eighth century. At the time of Charlemagne's coronation and proclamation as emperor of the Holy Roman Empire, 800 C.E., the *Donatio Constantini* was being quoted by jurists and theologians, who continued to use it as an authoritative source even though by the end of the medieval period it had been found to be apocryphal.[17]

The overlap of authority between church and state, so evident in medieval times, was still in effect at the time of Spain's colonization of the New World.[18] In the temporal-ecclesiastical equation, the balance of power leaned toward the primacy of spiritual power, allowing the papacy the authority to grant rights of conquest and territorial expansion while forcing the temporal authorities to request the approval of the papacy in order to carry out their imperialist designs.[19]

From a moral and legal perspective Spain's "most holy march of civilization," having just concluded its first phase with the retaking of Granada in January of 1492, had to be regulated to conform to both international and domestic necessities. Consequently, as soon as Columbus returned from his first trip to the Indies, the Catholic Monarchs petitioned the Valencia-born pope Alexander VI to issue a proclamation granting them possession of the Indies.[20]

In early May 1493, the Spanish pope obligingly issued two bulls of demarcation granting Ferdinand and Isabella's request:[21]

[Christopher Columbus] discovered most remote islands and mainlands, until then unknown . . . taking into consideration the propagation of the Catholic faith . . . you have determined with the help of God to subdue and bring to the dominion of our faith the inhabitants of the aforementioned islands and lands . . . [Authorized] by the fullness of Apostolic power, we give, grant and assign to you and to your heirs and successors each and all the lands and islands discovered *or to be discovered, as long as they are not subject to the actual temporal dominion of a Christian prince.*[22]

The first bull, *Inter Caetera*, gave the monarchs possession of the Indies and charged them with the responsibility of converting the infidels to Christianity and sending learned men and religious experts to carry out such designs.[23] Further, it granted Spain possession of "all the islands and mainlands, found and discovered," beyond an imaginary line one hundred leagues west of the Azores Islands. This bull has been characterized by John H. Parry as the "juridical charter of Spanish imperialism, and its chief theoretical defence against intruders from abroad and against interfering humanitarians at home."[24]

The second bull, *Eximiae Devotionis*, issued by Alexander only a day later, confirmed the privileges granted to Spain in the first. In addition, it granted "the Catholic Monarchs each and every one of the graces, privileges, exemptions faculties and liberties, immunities and indulgences previously conceded to the king of Portugal on the East Indies."[25] A third bull, *Dudum Siquidem*, made public in September of that same year, further confirmed the donations made by the previous bulls while guaranteeing Spain's right to defend them against all challengers as well as conferring absolute dominion over these possessions. The Catholic Monarchs or their representatives were thus enabled to take material possession of all new lands and to retain them in perpetuity. Finally, the monarchs were given the option of defending them as they saw fit while granting others permission to colonize or visit the territory under their control.[26]

The Catholic Monarchs extracted from the papacy more than any sovereign could have hoped for, but despite their transparent promise to act as evangelizing agents, their main concern was ultimately centered on the material exploitation of the newly discovered world.[27] As expected, the almost absolute rights granted to Spain by the pope were unacceptable to other European rulers, and the king of Portugal set out to curb the sphere of Spanish influence. Under pressure from Portugal, Spain negotiated the Treaty of Tordesillas in 1494. Although the treaty pushed the lines of demarcation to make slightly greater territorial concessions to Portugal, it intended for Spain's actual and projected possessions in the Indies to remain virtually unaffected, although future explorations demonstrated the contrary.[28]

The Spanish Matrix

After defining the boundaries of its new territorial additions, Spain's main priority became the possession of the land and its resources, but the question of dominion over the infidels remained a thorny issue that demanded answers from all parties involved, the crown, the church, and the colonizers. The crown, aware that the guarantees provided by the bulls offered a rather tenuous legal and theological basis for possession, continued to seek legitimacy for its imperial claims wherever it could find it. Despite their specificity on territorial questions, the bulls still allowed a certain ambiguity about the exact nature of the power granted to Spain, and its claims came under the scrutiny of diverse groups of letrados and men of the cloth.

A group of prominent Dominican friars in both continents, among whose numbers could be counted Francisco de Vitoria, Pedro de Córdoba, Domingo de Soto, and Bartolomé de Las Casas, maintained that the bulls only allowed the Spanish sovereigns the right to preach and convert the Indians, requiring them to protect the natives after conversion. However, this provision still left open the question of the crown's right to deprive the Indians of their possessions or lordships if they committed excesses against their subjects, or the new faith being imposed on them. At the same time, a larger group of letrados, from different backgrounds and positions, maintained that the papal donations granted the monarchs absolute dominion and jurisdiction over all discovered territory of the New World and its inhabitants.[29]

The Spanish quest for legality evolved within the context of a complex moral, theological, and legal web in a nation that had gained preeminence in juridical science at the time.[30] Spain's need responded to a desire to justify imperial action: "Although America had been 'donated' to the Spanish Monarchs in 1493 by Pope Alexander VI, King Ferdinand II, partly in order to shake off the authority of Rome, partly to soothe 'su real conciencia,' felt obliged to commission his jurists with clarifying the legal basis of the colonial enterprise."[31]

As part of its quest for legality, the crown commissioned the formation of juntas made up of representatives of "the three branches of learning which had some claim to authority in moral issues, theology, civil law and moral law," which would naturally function under the supervision of representatives chosen from the leading religious orders of the day.[32]

The function of the juntas was not to pass judgment but to act in an advisory capacity and to legitimize. Not surprisingly the junta called by

Ferdinand in 1504 to discuss the legitimacy of Spanish occupation found that the "Indians should be given [to the Spaniards] and that this was in agreement with human and divine law."[33] Yet the findings of any one junta, no matter how learned, were never sufficient to assure the legitimacy of dominion. In addition to the emerging contrary opinions, there existed numerous precedents where the prerogative of the pope to grant temporal powers had been challenged. More than two centuries before the donation of Alexander, none other than Dante Alighieri had ventured the opinion that "the Church's foundation is Christ. . . The Empire's foundation is human right. So, I claim that, if the Church may not leave its foundation— but must always rest on it," and this being the case, "then neither may the Empire do anything contrary to human right."[34] For his efforts, Dante was condemned to spend the last third of his life banished from his native Florence, but his example soon spread all across Europe and was often cited in the Spanish debate.

The challenge to papal authority on temporal matters became a point of contention in Spain at the time when the nation was just beginning to colonize its American possessions. The quest for answers gave rise to interminable and passionate debates dealing with fundamental issues concerning the nature of the natives, of the New World, and the role that the crown and the church should play in this context.

For the letrados, jurists, and men of the cloth touched by the immensity of events surrounding the emergence of a New World, the imperative to establish the legitimacy of the Spanish imperial enterprise remained paramount. While theologians and jurists wanted to define the role of the empire in the spread of Christianity, others, including the Spanish government, were solely concerned with establishing political and economic dominance over the New World. Still another faction, the original investors in Columbus's exploratory forays, expected quick returns for their investments and demanded a prompt and satisfactory solution to the legal difficulties they encountered with respect to the exploitation of the Indians and their land.

Since Spanish imperialism was not a monolithic enterprise, the vertiginous pace of colonization produced at least four distinct schools of thought to justify, define, and challenge the terms of Spain's dominion over the New World. The first current represented the position of the crown defined by the findings of the junta of 1504. This school of thought was mostly concerned with finding a legal justification for taking possession of the Indies, and it found one in the writings of the Scottish Dominican John Major

(Mair or Maior). The friar had stated in 1510 that the kingdom of Christ was not of this world and challenged the pope's right to grant temporal monarchies since his vicariate was confined to the spiritual realm.[35]

Since Major did not accept papal authority in the temporal realm, the best rationale he could offer to justify the occupation of America by Spain was the acceptance of the *"prevalence of the divine right of faith,"* for converting and baptizing the Indians, by whatever means necessary.[36] These means included the construction of fortresses so the native infidels could become accustomed to the presence of the Europeans and thus facilitate the evangelizing labor of the missionaries.[37]

As an additional justification of Spain's dominion over the Indians, Major simply resorted to the traditional Aristotelian argument that "some men were free by nature and others servile. In the natural order of things the qualities of some men are such that, in their own interests, it is right and just that they should serve while others living freely, exercise their natural authority and command."[38] This particular conclusion, echoed almost a half-century later by Ginés de Sepúlveda, enabled many of the participants in the colonizing enterprise, who felt "free by nature" to justify the naked and inhuman exploitation of the naturally "servile" indigenous inhabitants of the new colonies.

Major's recognition of Spain's right of dominion over the American territories and its inhabitants was found in the work of Spanish letrados such as the Dominican Matías de Paz and the civil jurist Juan López de Palacios Rubios. Although both coincided in recognizing the Indians as rational beings and naturally free, they, unlike Major, held firm to the medieval belief in papal primacy but, like the Scotsman, found justification in the preeminence of the divine right of faith. Ultimately they advocated and justified a Spanish imperialism suffused with humanitarian overtones for dealing with the infidels.

A second school of thought was represented by the advocates of unregulated colonialism who sought a higher degree of autonomy for the semi-feudal encomenderos in the New World. This school was championed by a rhetorician and member of Charles's court, Juan Ginés de Sepúlveda, a humanist trained in Italy, who, like Major, adopted the Aristotelian position that the Indians were not rational and therefore subject to being natural slaves of the superior civilization represented by Spain and the Spanish. In Sepúlveda's view, natural law was equal to the law of nations, but it could only be applicable to nations of civilized people. Consequently, since the

Indians were not civilized, they had no rights and could not be participants in the law of nations.[39] To grant equal rights to the Indians seemed to him

> a very absurd thing, for *there is nothing more contrary to distributive justice than to grant equal rights to unequal things*. . . For the barbarians or those who possess scant reasoning and humanity, the best rule is that of the master [for] either they are natural slaves, like the ones born in certain regions and climates of the world, or because of the depravity of their acts or due to other causes [they] cannot be made to conform to acceptable modes of behavior."[40]

From this perspective, Sepúlveda argued that Spain was not usurping the rights of the barbarians in assuming territorial and jurisdictional dominion over the Indians, for they clearly fell into the category of natural slaves. Furthermore, natural law, which in Sepúlveda's view coincided with divine law and the law of nations, "gave to the Spaniards a well-defined chain of rights of conquest and colonisation in the New World."[41] In the last instance, Sepúlveda could always resort to the text of Alexander's donation to find legitimacy for the empire. His position enjoyed a great deal of support among influential members of Spanish society, who supported him in his famous disputation with Las Casas in Valladolid.[42]

The complex process of Spanish imperialist expansion into the New World extended beyond the definition and clarification of mere legal principles, or the interests and justifications of any single group, and even beyond the elaboration of juridical treatises produced at the request of the crown. The debate about the justice of conquest and the rights of proprietorship over the Indies, which began in earnest in 1512 and went on for nearly a half-century, became the focus of a third school of thought comprising the best theological minds of the time, the prestigious "School of Salamanca."[43] Members of the school such as Melchor Cano, Domingo de Soto, and, perhaps its most famous exponent, the Dominican Francisco de Vitoria, sought to establish a religious and juridical rationale for explaining Spain's presence in the Indies.

Using his position as professor of the prestigious University of Salamanca, Francisco de Vitoria lectured on the topic of Spain's right to be in the Indies.[44] His probing led him to challenge the validity of the temporal grants of power made by the pope to different monarchs, but, at the same time, he left open the option of papal intervention in temporal affairs in times of crisis.[45] Vitoria recognized the political dominion and proprietary rights of the Indians in their own land, but unlike Major and his followers, he categorically opposed the Aristotelian argument in favor of natural slavery. While he recognized the proprietary right of the infidels, Vitoria, like the Scottish Dominican, also recognized the right of the Christian monarchs to attempt to convert them to Christianity. Despite the superficial similarities between Major and the Spanish theologians on the question of the right of temporal rulers to intervene in territories controlled by infidels, they diverged radically in their intentions. While Major "wrote as a theologian and a theorist Vitoria, on the other hand, was concerned with the moral and practical problem—a problem of international relations."[46]

Vitoria's interest in the question of Spain's American possessions dated back to his period at the Colegio de San Gregorio, Valladolid, between 1523 and 1526. While there he had had the opportunity to come in contact with the affairs of the court in general and the president of the Council of the Indies, the fellow Dominican García de Loaysa. Although he denied any direct participation in the deliberation on the affairs of the Indies, it is evident that the inspiration for his *Relecciones* owed a great deal to the Dominicans, in both Spain and the New World.[47]

Vitoria, following the traditional method of scholastic argumentation, began his *Relectio* by posing a question: "whether it was licit to baptize the children of the infidels against the will of their parents." He reasoned that the question had become relevant because the barbarians of the New World "who [were] formerly unknown in our world, have come into the possession of the Spaniards in the past forty years."[48] The original assumption made by Vitoria with respect to the possession of the Indians by the Spaniards is worthy of note, since Vitoria seemed to accept Spain's right of possession in the Indies as a given. The conclusions derived from the theologian's argument only confirmed said possession and provided a justification for the basic reasons whereby the Spaniards claimed dominion over the Indians.

Spain's assumption of dominion of the land and its inhabitants gave rise to the question of whether or not the barbarians were true owners and lords of the continent before the Spaniards came. To this Vitoria answered that they were. In the process of answering this question, not only did he deal with the issue of prior dominion but he managed to establish the importance of theology in deciding any points of questionable legitimacy by stating,

I must point out that this disquisition does not belong to the jurists, at least exclusively . . . [these] things should not be examined by human, but by divine laws, in which the jurists are not competent enough to be able to define by themselves such important questions.

And since it is something that falls within the realms of the conscience, it is for the priest, that is, the Church, to decide.[49]

By allowing that the argument concerning the Indians was not exclusively a juridical one, the theologian reaffirmed the pivotal role that the church reserved for itself in the debate about the Indies.

Having established that the Indians were publicly and privately true lords of their persons and territories, Vitoria conceded that said condition changed with the coming of the Spaniards. According to him, the Spaniards had not come to usurp; acting under divine inspiration, it had become incumbent upon them to take the Indians under their tutelage as an act of charity.[50]

At the core of Vitoria's and his followers' argument was the definition and implications of *dominium*, which differed from possession. While the possessor is limited to the act of physical possession, those having dominium have the right to exclude others from sharing. As Pagden further explains

The term (*dominium*) is dense and the meaning it was made to bear changed very considerably . . . for the Spanish scholastics, men could be said to have dominium not only over their private property, their goods (*bona*), but also over their actions, their liberty, and even—with certain important qualifications— their own bodies.[51]

Accordingly, the second part of Vitoria's *Relectio* was concerned with defining what constituted dominium, and defining it as a function of inviolable natural law. According to natural law the Spaniards, like all other men of good faith, had the right to travel and trade in the newly discovered territories and to remain there as long as they did not harm the barbarians. This was based on the principle of the right of nations (*iure gentium*), for "in all nations, it is considered inhuman to mistreat or to greet travelers badly and without just cause for such behavior, on the contrary, it is humane and courteous to treat foreigners kindly."[52] Vitoria argued, from a theoretical perspective, that the natives were expected to extend to the Spaniards (the foreigners) the courtesy of the international right of nations. But in practice, the discoverers and conquistadores, by not extending any courtesies to their hosts—on the contrary by reciprocating the native's welcome with injury—did not behave in accordance with the laws of nations. Nevertheless, since the natives, the main subjects of the discussion, lacked representation and a voice in the debates, this fact was overlooked.

The colonizers rationalized away the contradictions implicit in the unequal apportionment of rights in the collision of the two worlds by drawing from the segment of Vitoria's lectures where he examined the principles of the doctrine of just war. In keeping with the scholastic tradition, the Dominican lecturer recognized as a valid principle the existence of a state of just war in cases where very strict criteria pertained. For a war to be just, it had to be declared by a lawful ruler, never by a usurper, and it had to have a valid cause, such as saving people from being injured, or protecting the defenseless from aggressors, as in the case of cannibals or those seeking them for human sacrifices. Under such circumstances, the prince or ruler of the barbarians could ask his subjects to abandon these practices. However, if the barbarians refused to abandon their sinful ways, it was within the power of another sovereign, in this case the Christian sovereign, to force the infidels, if they were his subjects, to abandon those sins and rituals that went against natural and divine law. If they refused, a just war could be waged to remedy the situation.[53]

It was only when a Christian sovereign captured his enemies as a result of a just war that this sovereign could impose his beliefs on the former aggressor; otherwise, Vitoria considered it illicit to force members of any one group to be forcefully converted to the faith:

> if the pagans came willingly, that is, spontaneously, to submit to the power and jurisdiction of a Christian prince, [and] if they had put as a condition their not being forced to believe in the Christian religion, the sovereign could not licitly force them to convert; but he is forced, and is under the obligation not to force them to receive the faith, although, he is allowed to ask them to convert . . . once [the barbarians] spontaneously subject themselves to a ruler of whom they were not subjects before, the promises made must not be broken, but rather, they must be respected.[54]

By asserting the barbarians' right to refuse conversion, Vitoria recognized their dominion and the right to be respected because of natural law and the *ius gentium*. At first glance, Vitoria's pronouncements could not be taken as supportive, tacitly or otherwise, of Spanish colonization. Nor could they be interpreted as providing support for the brutality of the conquest under the guise of just war. Nevertheless, as the colonization and economic exploitation of America gained momentum, Vitoria's argument became more important in terms of providing a viable rationale for Spanish domination. It superceded the arguments put forth by Matías de Paz and Palacios Rubios in support of Spain's right of dominion, the papal grants, and the concept of natural slavery could not avoid microscopic theological scrutiny by Vitoria and his Salamanca followers, but the resulting new arguments, aside from increasing the complexity of the disputation, tacitly placed a seal of approval on Spain's claims, if not legally, at least theologically.

Vitoria's and his successors' arguments provided Spain with a tenuous jurisdictional hold on the Indians. In addition to the arguments addressing the question of natural law, Vitoria left Spain no choice but to assume tutelage of the natives, given their inability to manage their affairs adequately: "These Indians, although not entirely irrational [*amentes*], as we have said, are nevertheless not too far from being so, thus, they are not capable of constituting, nor of administering, a legitimate and ordered republic in human and civil terms."[55] By establishing that the Indians had in many respects a reasoning process only slightly above that of children, and because their deficient education left them incapable of fully rational behavior, Spain's role in assuming guardianship became the fulfillment of a moral imperative rather than an act of pity and charity.[56]

Vitoria's argument in favor of Spain's dominium must not be construed as offering support for the encomienda or the encomenderos; on the contrary, he maintained that once the "barbarians 'had been converted' it would not be convenient or licit for the King *to abandon the administration and the government of those territories.*"[57] While recognizing the proprietary right of the infidels, Vitoria also allowed the right of the Christian monarchs to attempt to Christianize them, but ultimately he demonstrated a marked preference for an empire based on the principles of peaceful relations rather than on the rights of conquest. Throughout his life, Vitoria avoided rendering a definite opinion on the Indian debate, answering to those who questioned him that he did not fully understand all the complex issues involved and that there were others who were more qualified than he was.[58]

It might be reasonably assumed that perhaps in time, under the influence of his brethren operating in the New World, and despite his resistance to taking sides, Vitoria could have well taken the side of the reformers, as J. H. Parry claims.[59]

Vitoria's opinions, as expressed in his *Relectio*, must have caused Charles some unease, prompting him to write the theologian and his immediate superior, in 1539, to ask, but in effect to order, him to refrain from any discussion of the Indies unless he, as the monarch, had approved the topic beforehand.[60] Charles's response to the theologian seems to undermine the much vaunted "sixteenth-century freedom of expression" that some of the proponents of the Golden Legend of Spanish domination herald as one of the most salient characteristics of Spain's rule in the early phases of establishing imperial rule in the Americas.[61] Quite to the contrary, Charles's personal intervention seems indicative of the king's profound preoccupation with the challenge to the monarch's absolute power, and the far-reaching consequences of the debates generated by the question of Spain's dominion of the New World. It also reflects the unwillingness of the sovereign to allow the free discussion of the matter to flourish. With the passage of time, and as the king of Spain consolidated his imperialist domination of the New World, the theological and juridical authorities in the motherland were relegated to a secondary position. As Pagden, one of the most acute observers and analysts of sixteenth-century Spain, has noted, the *pareceres*, or written opinions of the theologians and the juntas, "vanished, in all probability unread, into the gaping maw of Spanish bureaucracy."[62]

A fourth and final current participating in the debate about the Indies was defined less by complex academic postulates than by its empirical participation in the struggle in defense of the Indians. This school was largely constituted by the group of religious reformers in America, the "indianists," who were led in their earliest stages by an array of Dominicans on the islands of the Caribbean. In later years, the leadership of this movement on the American mainland and in Spain was taken over by Bartolomé de Las Casas and his followers. These reformers had been deeply affected by witnessing first-hand the wanton destruction of the natives by the greed of the conquistadores who refused to see the value of Indians as human beings of equal worth as themselves.

The View from America

The vital, and often violent and destructive, dialectical process intervening in the birth of the New World set the stage where the drama and the tragedy of the encounter were played out. Yet despite being one of the two essential components in the equation of Spain's imperial scheme, American natives were deprived of the ability to express even their most basic demands, much less their opinions about the disquisitions concerning the nature of their very existence and their expected response to the colonizers.

As in most relationships of power and domination where the occupying power is the dominant force, the relationship of the Spanish state with the colonized was essentially a repressive one.[63] As expected in such an imperialist venture, it was the occupiers who defined the parameters of governance of the subject world. The natives lost their dominium and their collective voice, in the process of dispossession. Under the circumstances of conquest, they lost their ability to express even their most basic expectations and aspirations and the right to defend their own lives in the new hierarchical structures of domination created by the invader. Consequently, it fell to a few men of the cloth, as their self-appointed defenders, to speak for them and to attempt to inform the crown about their desperate condition. At the same time, these defenders also tried to obtain some measure of relief to ameliorate the harsh exploitative conditions under which the natives were being exterminated in the process of creating wealth for their new masters.

The natives remained voiceless, years after the original onslaught, but thanks to the concerns of individual missionaries, some lay chroniclers, and a handful of religious reformers, their stories and some of their most basic aspirations began to be expressed and communicated to the centers of power and to the outside world.[64]

Those among the Spaniards who chose to defend the natives considered it their religious duty to protect them from inhuman exploitation while converting them to Christianity; however in the process of conversion, they adopted, at times, some of the same behaviors they condemned in their compatriots. The indigenous people were rarely, if ever, consulted or allowed to express their opinion about matters that concerned them. Lacking a meaningful voice to express their needs and expectations, the natives were largely subject to the interpretations of their Spanish protectors.

The reformers embraced their self-appointed role as the saviors of the indigenous people. In this one-sided relationship, the well-intentioned reformers interpreted the desires and aspirations of the indigenous people from their own, foreign perspective, allowing their own conception of fairness and justice to cloud the real issues involved. Although they lacked that "vigorous give-and-take between those who exercise power and those who resist it, the outcome [was] always some measure of consent."[65] The enforced silence of the natives owed largely to their ignorance of the occupier's language and the fear of reprisal, which made meaningful communication difficult. Faced with this silence, the reformers often assumed the natives' voicelessness as a form of tacit approval of the practices on their behalf.

There is little doubt that the well-meaning efforts of the reformers, including those of Las Casas, were prompted by real preoccupations with native welfare, but while they played a significant role in the partial easing of the painful oppressor-oppressed relationships, the voice heard throughout the New World and the mother country was but a distorted echo of reality.

The absence of meaningfully enforced legislation, and their own disconnection from the indigenous masses, limited the indianists' effectiveness. In a sense, they were like the privileged wardens of Plato's Cave, recognizing that the natives were people like themselves, but, in an odd inversion of roles, only being able to see the natives as two-dimensional projections speaking with distorted voices.[66] Because of this distortion, more often than not the reformers ended up serving the interests of the crown against the aspirations of the colonists while being satisfied with the promises of new legislation ostensibly enacted to protect the natives.

Aside from the political and social tasks of lobbying to obtain new protective measures for the natives, the reformers were also engaged in an ongoing attempt to define the nature of the Indians. In the absence of a conceptual understanding of that nature, they were forced to rely on the often biased reports making their way to Spain from across the sea. As Juan Friede explains:

These reports, at a time when modern methods of anthropological investigation were lacking, were often carried out in good faith, but they were so inexact and so disorienting that they could not constitute the basis for a rational indigenous policy, even admitting sincerity and a true desire to protect the Indians. On the contrary, they could only cause confusion and are greatly responsible for the illusory, and at times openly contradictory legislation with which the problem of the Indian in the sixteenth century was going to be solved.[67]

And there were deep-seated misconceptions concerning the "nature" of the Indians among all participants in the "great enterprise of the Indies." Chroniclers of the stature of Gonzalo Fernández de Oviedo contributed to this conception with his portrayal of the Indians as outlandish beings less than human and prone to vile inclinations and perversions:

> [T]hese Indians, the majority of them, are a nation far from capable of understanding the Catholic faith . . . they do not have heads like everyone else, they have such thick helmet-like skulls, that when Christians fight with them, [they] must be forewarned not to strike them on the head because their swords shatter. . . And just as thick as their skulls is their bestial and evil inclination.[68]

Fernandez de Oviedo was not the only chronicler who contributed to this conceptual distortion. The chronicler López de Gómara added his voice to the chorus depicting the Indians as promiscuous beings who " with the greatest ease couple with women like crows or vipers, or even worse; not to mention the fact that they are great sodomites, lazy, liars, ingrates, shifty and mean."[69] By stripping the natives of any positive human quality, the colonists found ample justification for the destructive acts committed against them.

To counter these negative perceptions of the Indians, Father Las Casas found it necessary to exaggerate and idealize the Indians' spiritual and physical virtues to emphasize the differences from their abusive exploiters. Like Columbus, who had sought to idealize the natives to further enhance the significance of his feat, Las Casas, through his descriptions of them, turned the natives into paradigms of perfection, anticipating by centuries the Enlightenment's concept of the "noble savage": "And it seems that the first universal causation, which is heavenly influence, *favors greatly these our Indian peoples to be intelligent, ingenious and quite able, they have thus had the good fortune of receiving from God good and noble souls."*[70] Furthermore, Las Casas affirmed that the Indians did not only possess extraordinary mental and spiritual qualities but were also blessed with extraordinary physiques and dispositions in addition to being excellent warriors.[71] This portrayal of the American Indians was largely prompted by the imperative need to provide a positive representation of the natives. The image he created thus was one that could compete with and supersede the negative portrayal and conceptions so prevalent among his compatriots in their discourse about the New World and its inhabitants.

Defining and Possessing

However, in the process of exalting the Indians, Las Casas in fact stripped them of their human qualities and objectified the very subjects he was trying to protect. He manufactured utopian, nonexistent, otherworldly beings who bore no resemblance to the abject workers who represented the only means of obtaining income and wealth for the Spaniards in the New World. By idealizing the Indians, the friar ultimately transformed them into symbolic objects devoid of volition, much as Columbus had done before him. Instead of human beings the Indians became mere ethereal objects disconnected from the day-to-day reality of existence. From this perspective the natives become beautiful, helpless victims deserving only of pity, and only capable of attaining full humanity and cultural autonomy through the intercession of chosen members of the dominant group.

The indianists, unlike the proponents of other currents of thought in Spain, had the benefit of on-site experience. They had had the opportunity to witness some of the most dramatic collisions between the two opposing classes emerging in colonial society. They were both witnesses to and partici-pants in the historical drama unfolding in the New World. What they saw and experienced was a radical and disconcerting reality different from any-thing they could have imagined from their theoretical perspectives at home. Las Casas, more than other reformers, derived his authority from long experience and knowledge of the intricate contradictions arising in the New World between Indians and encomenderos. His experience "of more than fifty years,"[72] his "autoptic imagination," granted him, at least from his own perspective, the moral authority to speak with certainty since his denuncia-tion of the crimes of his compatriots could be shored up by firsthand experi-ence, for he possessed

> the privileged understanding which those present at an event have over those who have only read or been told about it . . . In America this was to dominate the long and bitter struggle over the nature, representation and status of the New World and of its inhabitants . . . Inevitably, it was also to sharpen the boundary, which divided the Old World from the New and the "them" from the "us."[73]

Conscious of the value and power of his immediate experience, Las Casas invariably returned to his years in America as support for the validity of his arguments and to invest his texts with incontrovertible authority, as if time and circumstances had remained ecstatic and unchanged.

As one of a multitude of indianists, Bartolomé de Las Casas might have gone unnoticed, an undistinguishable member of a multifaceted group, but the sheer volume of his written work, his vehemence, and his dogged, single-minded dedication to the cause of legal rights turned him into the preeminent leader of the movement.[74] During his long life, Las Casas underwent various transformations, both in his worldview and his approach to governmental power. Yet despite the multifaceted complexity of the nature of his concerns, Las Casas rarely questioned the royal rights of political power, nor did he engage in profound disquisitions on the topic. Hanke confirms this tendency when he points out that "Las Casas who was a Christian apologist more than a systematic theoretician, never wrote a treatise exclusively dedicated to the study of the origins of government."[75] This absence of questioning of the imperial government raises a multitude of questions concerning his interpretation of the role of the crown, and his own role in relation to it. Was he unwilling to challenge the absolute power of the king? Was he satisfied with the way in which power had been codified by the Spanish state? Or was he so involved in his day-to-day lobbying efforts that he had no time available to challenge the crown? Considering his voluminous literary output, his silence concerning the origins and functioning of the state is oddly disconcerting, and we can only speculate about the motives for it.

From the time he became an advocate of Indian causes, Las Casas never wavered in his conviction that the natives were to be treated as equal subjects of the crown and not as slaves. This principle, he claimed, was based on the belief that slavery was an accidental phenomenon, which made the penurious condition of the Indians a result of accident and luck rather than a preordained condition. This was the position he assumed late in life as part of an effort to convince Philip II not to sell encomiendas in perpetuity to the encomenderos in the colonies. He argued that slavery was contrary to natural law, for it deprived people of individual liberty which was a right conceived by God as an essential attribute of human beings, and since that was the natural state of man, then slavery had to be an aberration.[76] This position was in diametric opposition to the one he had adopted in his early years as a reformer when he had advocated the use of black slaves imported from Africa as part of a general scheme to stimulate Spanish migration to the colonies and to avoid the massive death of indigenous people from overwork and neglect.[77] In the autumn of his existence Las Casas invested great energy and time to renounce his earlier propositions and to attack the form and essence of slavery.

Unlike the members of the School of Salamanca, who raised objections to the papal privileges implicit in the Alexandrian bulls of donation, Las Casas did not spend much time questioning the pope's prerogative to grant temporal powers over peoples and property, but at the same time, he did not accept papal power unqualifiedly. He reasoned that even if the pope was the absolute leader of the Christian world, the head prelate, and the factual and potential shepherd of all infidels, this jurisdiction was only voluntary but not coercive. Consequently, since the pope had granted the kings of Spain privileges over the Indies and its inhabitants, it was incumbent upon the sovereigns to adhere to the restrictions implicit in the voluntary, noncoercive nature of their jurisdiction.[78]

Like other reformers of the day, both lay and religious, Las Casas never questioned the morality of converting the Indians to Christianity. The theme of conversion had been a cornerstone of the bulls of donation, and a primordial argument wielded by Columbus and those who came in his wake. The issue of conversion was also central to the question of dominion and sovereignty.

This claim was evident in the Genoese's letter announcing the discovery of America and joyfully celebrating the possibility of massive conversions. Often it appears as if Las Casas had found in Columbus the fulfillment of a millenarian aspiration to bring light to those in darkness, and if anyone was to be the chosen one, it was Columbus, whose very name, Cristoforo, had preordained him as savior of half of humanity. The navigator, as Las Casas explains, was named after Saint Christopher, "*Christum ferens*, which means carrier, or bearer of Christ."[79] The significance of the name was not lost on Columbus; on the contrary, it helped fuel a belief in his destiny as the bearer of Christ to the rest of the world. This belief, which only intensified with the passage of time, led him to regard himself as the "chosen messenger of God," and to be regarded as such by Las Casas.[80] Nevertheless, when Columbus set foot in the New World, he was already serving two equally important masters, God and his terrestrial financial backers.

Like Columbus, Las Casas served two masters, God and the state, but religious conversion was never far from his every thought and action, and in this respect Las Casas was indistinguishable from his compatriots. Conversion became both a form of rewarding the natives for good behavior and a viable justification for the Spaniards to conquer. This had been evident in the instructions given to Nicolás de Ovando, who, upon being appointed to replace Columbus as governor of Española, was enjoined by Queen Isabel to make sure that "said Indians be converted to our Holy Catholic Faith [and] see to it that [the Indians] are well treated, *those who become Christians better than the others.*"[81]

Conversion thus became the mantle that lent moral legitimacy to all acts practiced by the Spaniards in the New World, as evidenced in Fernando Cortés's first letter to Charles, in which the conqueror of Mexico never loses the opportunity to emphasize his belief in the irreversible and redeeming power of converting the inhabitants of the mainland to the "True Faith":

> And we believe that it is not without cause that Our Good Lord God has been pleased that these parts be discovered in the name of Your Royal Highnesses, so that your Majesties may gain much merit and reward in the sight of God by commanding that these barbarous people be instructed, and brought to the True Faith by Your hands.[82]

Since the conquistadores believed that it was God who had been behind the original success of the Spanish venture in the New World, they also found that the willingness to spread His word provided the Spanish invaders with the excuse they needed to resort to cruelty in the conquest and mistreatment of the Indians whenever they resisted the holy march of Christian civilization. Unable to stem the tide of cruelty on their own, Las Casas and his collaborators turned their eyes toward the sovereign, for they claimed that it was the king who had to ensure that no injustices were committed against his other American subjects, the Indians. By recognizing the almost absolute power of the sovereigns, Las Casas helped to undermine the emergence of foci of resistance among the encomenderos in the colonies, including the rebellion of Gonzalo Pizarro in Peru and a multitude of imitators throughout South America. However, in the process of reaffirming the power of the centralized imperial authority, he alienated the colonists, precluding meaningful dialogue with them and consequently eliminating any chance of bringing about improvement in their treatment of the Indians.

Two

American Crucible

With a very few exceptions, Europeans felt powerfully superior to all the peoples they encountered, even those like the Aztecs who had technological and organizational skills that Europeans could recognize and greatly admire.

—Stephen Greenblatt, *Marvelous Possessions*

The Arab conquest of Spain, occurring at the same time as the conquest of Sind, marked Spain. Eight hundred years later, in the New World, the Spanish conquistadores were like Arabs in their faith, fanaticism, toughness, poverty and greed.

—V. S. Naipaul, *Among the Believers*

IN HIS CHRONICLE of the conquest of Mexico, Bernal Díaz del Castillo, a participant and eyewitness, writing from the perspective of the "ordinary" foot soldier, captured some of the most significant aspirations of those who took part in the conquest and colonization. His vivid account of the event moves beyond providing a version of the events as they unfolded and serves as a unique source enabling us to reconstruct and analyze the motivations, expectations, accomplishments, and failures of the conquistadores. A prime example of his own objectives, as well as those of his compatriots, is evident in his eulogy to their fallen comrades: "As far as I can figure, their names should be engraved in gold letters, for they died the cruelest of deaths in the service of God and his Majesty and [trying] to bring light to those who were in darkness and to acquire wealth, which all of us came to find."[1]

Rarely has anyone summed up so eloquently and honestly the conquistadores' motivations to settle the New World: to serve king and God, to bring light to the heathen in the form of the true faith, and almost as an afterthought, rather than a primary motivation, to "acquire wealth." As in the case of Columbus and his expedition, for Díaz's comrades, piety and the desire for profit became primary motives for their venture and remained a spur to the conquistadores even under the most trying of circumstances. Despite their willingness and readiness, attempting to advance their expectations was a more trying and tortuous process than the conquistadores had expected. While Díaz left no doubt about his and his comrades' satisfaction with their military and political exploits, his writings also made clear that there was always an element of bitterness caused by the feeling that the material rewards derived from the conquest did not measure up to what the Spaniards thought they deserved.

Bernal Díaz was not alone in his lamentations; Columbus and Cortés had also been involved in painful and drawn-out litigation about territorial and proprietary rights to the New World until the time of their deaths. Also, many of the original conquerors returning to Spain to reclaim what they perceived as their just due faced similar situations.

Unhappiness over failed expectations surfaces toward the end of Díaz's work, but it makes its appearance early on in the diary kept by Columbus. Driven by his desire to justify to the monarchs and his other backers the profitability of his expedition, the admiral exaggerated the ubiquity of gold in the New World. The diary of his first voyage is filled with repeated references to the metal and its place of "birth," as if gold should flow like a river born in the entrails of the earth.[2] This insistence on the presence and availability of gold responded to a very practical responsibility to his backers, who required him to provide proof of the profitability of the expedition, and "since the journal Columbus keeps is largely intended for external consumption, signs of the presence of gold must appear on every page (lacking gold itself)."[3]

Masters

One of Columbus's main arguments to gain the support of the Catholic Sovereigns for his exploratory endeavors had been the possibility of finding a route to the Indies that would enable Spain to participate in the spice trade monopolized by Egyptians and Venetians. Yet, upon his arrival in the New World, Columbus was hard pressed to find the spices he believed to abound in the territory where he had landed. Gold, pearls, and other precious metals and stones served as a welcome substitute for spices to reward the investors and participants for the expenses and travails of that first journey. The potential to exploit the natural resources that Columbus had discovered for his Spanish masters necessitated an intensive use of labor to ensure profit, and the natives offered a virtually inexhaustible source of it.

As Columbus and his followers discovered, much to their chagrin, the amount of readily available riches was finite. As he ventured further into the unknown and came upon the mainland that he defined as "an other world," he grew convinced that he had found the Earthly Paradise.[4] However, not even paradise on earth could obviate the more practical considerations of exploiting the vast territorial expanses he had discovered and continued to discover, incorporating them as Spanish possessions, as he went along.

Although gold, realistically and figuratively, played a primary role in the discovery and conquest of America, the quest for it was relatively short lived and gave way to more pragmatic considerations, as James Lockhart writes, disposing of some of the most prevalent myths concerning the alleged idealistic, romantic, and impractical Spanish worldview: "In a way, it must be accounted a shame that Latin American history got its start with the extravagant language and often chimerical notions of the Italian Columbus. Actually, a strong realism and an active search for and exploitation of every economic possibility were the norm for the Spaniards."[5]

The pragmatism of the colonists was also spurred by other considerations that drove them to seek new lives in America. Fundamental among them was that America, for the newcomers, offered an outlet for the aristocratic ambition they could not fulfill at home.[6] Although most Spaniards coming to America were not members of the nobility, the few nobles who migrated served as models to be emulated by those who had come seeking wealth and status.[7] Given that for the Spaniards of the Golden Age a life of fame was more desirable, "more enduring and more glorious than temporal life," coming to America became the cherished dream of those who sought to remake their lives in a new mold, a panacea that freed them from the mounting travails of urban decay, rural poverty, and the anonymity they faced in the motherland.[8] The colonies provided them with a unique opportunity to join the ranks of the nobility from which they had been excluded at home.[9]

In the process of conquest and colonization, America was the stage where the dramatic contradictions resulting from the clash of the colonists' expectations and the native reality they encountered unfolded. The concepts of privilege, rank, lineage, honor, and duty can be viewed today as picturesque, frivolous, unjust, or hypocritical artifacts. Even if most of these concepts are difficult to reconcile with pragmatism, economic dynamism, and social flexibility, all these factors coexisted and are evident in the movement of Spaniards to the New World.[10]

Although pragmatism and the idealized aspirations of the colonists co-existed, the resulting contradictions produced significant social, political, ideological, cultural, and economic turmoil within the confines of the emergent Spanish empire in the Americas. Unwilling to abandon their pretensions to nobility, and unwilling to demean themselves through the performance of menial occupational tasks, which they considered beneath their newly acquired, or perceived, station, the colonists depended unconditionally on the virtually unhampered access to Indian labor, as Lewis Hanke points out: "The idea that someone else should do the hard manual work of the world appealed strongly to sixteenth-century Spaniards, *who inherited a taste for martial glory and religious conquest and a distaste for physical labour* from their medieval forefathers who had struggled for centuries to free Spain from the Moslems."[11]

This attitude and its destructive potential became an integral component of the foundation upon which the edifice of the New World was built, and it was never more evident than when "Columbus, impatient to get things done, drafted some gentlemen volunteers for the hard labor, which caused great indignation; *they had come out to fight or get gold, not to do menial work. If they refused, they got no rations, and that was considered an abominable way to treat a Castilian hidalgo.*"[12]

These depictions of the first Spanish colonizers are not intended to ridicule them. They are simply the testimony of chroniclers of the time, including Las Casas and Fernández de Oviedo, men who, like the others, had come to the New World in search of a different life from the one they had known in their own world, but, at the same time, could detach themselves from their compatriots and evaluate them critically:

> And it was laughable to see their pretentiousness and the vanity with which they ordered [others] around, they, who did not even have a shirt of Castile linen to wear, and no cape nor coat or stockings, but only a cotton shirt on top of a Castilian one, if they could afford it, if not that, only a cotton shirt worn bare-legged, and instead of shoes and buskins, hemp-soled sandals and gaiters.[13]

The misguided pretensions of the colonizers were complicated by their complex and at times contradictory attitudes and personalities. One of the most revealing characterizations of sixteenth-century Spaniards is provided by Luis de Ortiz, one of Philip's advisors, who claimed that "Spaniards are ready to die for their religion and their king. If they cannot find a foreign war, they will fight among themselves, for the majority are by nature choleric and proud."[14] Their choleric and proud characteristics, combined with their autarkic bent, created a volatile, dangerous, and treacherous situation. Every colonizer had brought with him his own *patria chica* (miniature motherland), a place he wanted to recreate, to call his own, to subject, and to protect against real and imaginary enemies, as Fernández de Oviedo explained:

> The discord that existed among the Christians in the past was promoted by the Spaniards, who would rather make war than lay about. If they have no outside enemies they will look for them among themselves. . . because they do not take well to suffering privations . . . although the ones who came were vassals of the Spanish Kings. Who can make the Biscayan get along with the Catalan? Since they come from such different provinces and speak such different languages? How will the Andalusian get along with the Valencian, or the one from Perpignan with the one from Córdoba? Not all the vassals of Spain are alike in habit or tongue. Particularly since at the beginning for each noble man of pureblood who went [to the Indies], ten ill-behaved ones, of lowly and obscure lineage would follow. This is why it ended up that way.[15]

The discord and anarchy existing in the early Spanish settlements precluded the possibility of establishing a well-organized system to maximize the productivity of the land and to care for the natives and other resources. The difficulties encountered in the exploitation of the colonies were further compounded by the fact that many of the early colonists were far from being paradigms of virtue and morality.

Faced with the need to populate the new territory as expeditiously as possible, the sovereigns offered numerous incentives to those who dared venture to the new continent. Those willing to mine gold were guaranteed one third of the metal extracted while the other two thirds went to the crown; further, they were only expected to pay the customary *diezmo* on all other revenues. But these incentives and salaries failed to attract the desired number of people, so a suitable recruiting alternative was found: the commutation of prison sentences. Those charged with capital offenses involving the death of another person had their sentences commuted to two years servitude in Española. Lesser crimes not involving a person's death were reduced to one year of servitude.[16]

The need to prevent a massive exodus back to the motherland forced the crown to reach into the bowels of its society to produce a suitable number of colonists. The unfulfilled expectations of those who had come, the influx of convicted felons, the tension involved in everyday dealing with the Amerindians, and the refusal of many colonists to take orders from foreign-born individuals like the Columbus brothers created an extremely tense atmosphere in the early days of the imperial venture. In one of the greatest historical ironies, the Spaniards, who so resented being ruled by people other than their own, never understood the natives' reasons for refusing to readily accept the imposition of a foreign yoke.

Further contributing to the traumatizing and uneasy birth of the New World were the vast geographical distance separating the two worlds and the absence of established administrative institutions and the technological advantages of the mother country. Faced with increasing anarchy and multiple rebellions by impatient and disenchanted colonists, the sovereigns were forced to take prompt and effective measures to accelerate the productive and profitable exploitation of the new territories.

In 1502, the Catholic Monarchs began to implement what they saw as a rational and productive system of administration of the colonies. To this end they appointed as governor of the island of Española and the rest of the Indies the illustrious *Comendador de Lares*, a member of the Order of Alcántara, Fray Nicolás de Ovando. Significantly enough, the fleet that limped upriver into the safe-harbor of Santo Domingo in the closing days of April 1502 carried in it some of the most important individuals responsible for initiating, in earnest, the military, religious, and bureaucratic conquest of the New World. The fleet carried not only the governor and the future Dominican activist Las Casas but also the Franciscan missionaries known as "The Twelve" who would be largely responsible for the spiritual conquest of Mexico. It also brought the future conqueror of Peru, Francisco Pizarro, and more than two thousand other people.[17]

The appointment of Ovando, so closely identified with the interests of the crown, put the colonists on notice that Ferdinand and Isabel were not inclined to tolerate any type of insubordination or challenges to the authority of the central government.[18] Fresh from their relative success in centralizing the government at home, the Catholic Monarchs could not afford to relax their grip in their newly acquired territories. To empower their governor, they granted him sweeping powers to investigate and to mete out justice to all Spanish subjects in the new continent, whenever and wherever this was necessary. This mandate was clearly specified in their instructions to Ovando:

By the powers conferred on you, you shall make all neighbors and inhabitants of said Islands and *Tierra-Firme*, comply and obey you as *Our Governor in all things* that you, in our name shall order. And be always very careful *that all people exist always in peace, harmony, and justice*, administering [justice] to everyone equally, without exception, appointing for this purpose good ministers and officials, punishing all that must be justly punished.[19]

Ovando's appointment also required taking inventory of those things believed to belong to the sovereigns, including the ones misappropriated by previous officials. His instructions included provisions concerning the protection of the Indians, as well as the return of their women taken by the Spaniards as concubines. The pragmatism that characterized Ferdinand and Isabel's decrees was particularly evident during the very early years of colonization. In addition to the accustomed recommendations that accompanied all official documents, Ovando was instructed to begin collecting tribute immediately and to compel the Indians to work in the extraction of gold for the monarchs. Consequently, one of his earliest tasks was to

inform the Caciques and other *principales* that we want the Indians to be treated well, like all our faithful subjects and vassals, and that no one should dare do ill or harm them; and so you must have it proclaimed in our name; and if from now on, someone were to harm or do them wrong, or take by force what belongs to them you will be informed so you can punish [those responsible], so from now on, no one will dare to harm or wrong them with impunity.[20]

The instructions, like most legislation enacted to "protect" the natives through the centuries of colonization, abounded with promises and good will, and no one reading them could have doubted the good intentions of the monarchs. Together with the provisions for protecting the natives, there were also requests to collect revenues from them:

Because it is our desire and will that the Indians pay us tribute and royalties, just like our neighboring subjects in Our Kingdoms and Dominions do . . . you will talk to the caciques and with the other principales and to all other Indians that you might find necessary, and you will work out with them the amount each one of them will pay to us every year; all this must be said in such a manner so they will know that no injustice is being committed.[21]

Immediately upon his arrival, the governor set out to implement his instructions as thoroughly and expediently as he could under the circumstances. During his second year in office, Ovando requested and received official sanction from the queen to make official the payment of tribute by the Indians to the king and the other colonizers. In December 1503, Isabel signed a decree whereby tribute-paying Indians could be "entrusted" to the Spaniards in the traditional Spanish institution of the encomienda.[22]

In theory, the encomienda, which derives its name from the Spanish verb *encomendar*, to entrust someone with the responsibility of caring for something or someone, stipulated that in exchange for tribute collected from the Indians, the encomenderos assumed the responsibility of providing care and protection for their charges while assuming total responsibility for their spiritual well-being.[23]

Following the established practices of the Spanish Reconquista, it was Columbus who transplanted the institution to the province of Cibao, Española, in 1495. There he ordered that all Indians over fourteen years of age who lived in the settlement of Cibao or near the mines should pay the sovereigns a hawk's bell full of gold every three months. For those who lived away from the mines, tribute consisted of an *arroba* (twenty-five pounds) of cotton per person.[24] To quell discontent among the Spaniards, Columbus began assigning Indians to work for them in the fields and mines, so the new masters could benefit from the fruits of native tribute.[25] His temporary successor, Francisco de Bobadilla, conscious of the need to gain the loyalty of the three hundred or so Spaniards remaining with him, further increased the workload of the Indians by forcing them to labor for the Spaniards, who were expected to pay a tribute of one gold peso for every eleven they extracted.[26] Within a short time of its institution, the encomienda, paired with European diseases brought by the settlers, devastated the native population, bringing about an unparalleled demographic disaster.

Ostensibly, the encomienda as an institution sanctioned by the crown was developed to meet two needs: the production of food to fend off famine among the colonists and the exploitation of gold.[27] It availed the colonists with their best available option to fulfill the most important elements of colonial economy: "the utilization of the forced labor of the Indian with which the conquistador exploited the natural resources of the New World (mines, pearls, agriculture, animal farming, etc.), and the appropriation of his goods (land, gold, slavery, tributes, etc.), which would reimburse him for the expenses incurred in the conquest."[28] The colonists were eager to receive compensation for the risks they had run and to begin amassing the fortunes of which they had dreamed in the Old World. The sovereigns, who were also eager for a return on their investment, wanted to do the same but without upsetting the colonists' claims. This explains, somewhat, the alacrity with which the queen responded to the governor's suggestion of making official the payment of Indian tribute through the encomienda.

Isabel's response, contained in a *cédula real*, was a clever, carefully worded piece of legislation justifying the virtual enslavement of the Indians while disguising its true intentions under a mantle of royal righteousness and legalistic jargon. The document began with the usual affirmation of the crown's well-meaning intentions for the Indians and then proceeded to enumerate the reasons why it was necessary for the Indians to work for the colonists and the crown. While at first sight the cédula appears to be an inoffensive request for Indian help, a careful reading reveals a document riddled with numerous contradictions and platitudes. The contradictory and crafty nature of the document led Lesley Byrd Simpson to identify it as an "amazing piece of sophistry [that] clearly legalized forced labor."[29] This system of labor, known as the *repartimiento* in the Caribbean and Meso-america, was called *mita* in South America, and in addition to the payment of tribute it involved the drafting of indigenous people for forced tours of labor of varying lengths.

Isabel's cédula, in effect, delivered the American natives into the hands of the Spanish colonists like so much chattel or merchandise to be had at will, while at the same time it justified the monarch's good intentions by pretending to act in favor of the Indians. The sheer sophistry of its claims defines the cédula as one of the most notorious testaments to infamy ever prepared by one group of people against another, and it is worth quoting at length:

> Whereas, the King my Lord and I agreed . . . that the Indian inhabitants of the island of Española are free and not subject to servitude. . . and whereas I am now informed that because of the excessive liberty enjoyed by said Indians they avoid

talking and communing with the Spaniards to such a degree that they will not work even for wages. . . and whereas we desire that the said Indians be converted to our Holy Catholic Faith and be indoctrinated in its principles; and whereas this can better be done by having the Indians live in community with the Christians and go among them and associate with them, by which means they will help each other to cultivate settle and reap the fruits of the island, and extract the gold which may be there, and bring profit to my kingdom and subjects . . . [For this reason] I command you [Don Nicolás de Ovando] that from the day in which you receive my letter you will compel and force said Indians to associate with the Christians of the island and to work on their buildings and to gather and mine the gold and other metals, and to till the fields and produce food for the Christian inhabitants . . . and you are to have each one paid for the workday the wages and maintenance which you deem appropriate. . . This the Indians shall perform as free people, which they are, and not as slaves.[30]

The queen's written approval of the repartimiento and encomienda became the model for all future legislation concerning the Indians. Despite the usual protestations about the welfare of its Indian subjects, there was no viable way in which the crown could have enforced its wishes concerning the care of the natives, nor did it seem to have any concern as long as they were Christianized and profits kept streaming in.

As noted earlier, the public officials in charge of administering the affairs of the crown, like the colonizers, brought with them a conception of the Indians as vice-ridden beings whose propensities rendered them not much different from lowly animals and thus incapable of working.[31] This conception of the Indians was necessary to assuage any pang of conscience that Spaniards might have felt while exploiting them. Unsurprisingly it was during Ovando's "brutal regime," and very likely as a direct result of the encomienda, that the Indians "diminished rapidly."[32]

As the number of Indians declined, the colonists insisted in their request that the king allow them to obtain slaves from other islands. Their wish was granted, as long as the slaves were obtained from the so-called useless islands, the ones that did not produce either gold or other valuable commodities. It was precisely the journeying west in search of new laborers that eventually led to the Spanish discovery and exploration of Mesoamerica and the territories in the southern mainland.

The exploitation of Indian labor in the Antilles, officially sanctioned by the infamous cédula, became the basis of all future colonial enterprises in the mainland, and despite the perception of the natives as biologically inferior, the Spaniards were dependent on their labor for the success of the colonial venture. Without the work of the Indians, the land would have remained fallow and the mines abandoned; at the same time, in order to fulfill their most basic aspirations and needs, the Spaniards had no qualms about displacing the Indians from their land and using them as beasts of burden.[33] The cost of building roads to accommodate the traffic of mules, donkeys, or horses represented a considerable investment that the Spaniards were either unwilling or unable to make. It was much easier to use Indians instead of animals: the cost of a horse was prohibitive, while the price of an Indian did not register even at the lower end of the economic scale.[34]

From its inception the encomienda was the most significant and controversial social and economic institution transplanted to the New World by the Spanish. For more than a century, it proved to be a continuous source of discord and confrontation between the conquistadores and the crown.[35] At the same time, there existed an unbridgeable gap between what the crown believed to be giving to the conqueror in trust, and the way the latter interpreted this trust. This disparity of interpretations is apparent in the royal ordinance of 1526 inaugurating the encomienda system in Yucatan:

> Moreover, we order that upon seeing the qualities, conditions or abilities of said Indians, it would seem fit to the religious and clergy that it is in God's service and for their own good, that in order for them to be separated from their vices, especially from unnatural crimes and eating human flesh. . . it is necessary that they be entrusted to the Christians so they can be used as free people. The members of the clergy can, if both sides are in agreement, place [the Indians] in trust, just as they see fit and in the manner in which they so order.[36]

The language used in the *ordenanza* reflected the attitudes and intentions of the crown, just as Isabel's original cédula had done, but at no point did this new document, promulgated almost a quarter of a century after the encomienda became official, take into consideration the expectations, desires, or even the most elementary humanity of the *encomendados*. It only considered the expectations of the encomendero and the members of the clergy, who saw this as an opening to gain further access to the hearts and souls of possible converts.

While the encomienda benefited the colonizers, it had a devastating effect on the Indian population. In addition to having to pay tribute with their labor the Indians were forcibly relocated to meet the specific needs of their new masters, as specified in the laws controlling the repartimiento. The loss of their traditional ancestral residences and their becoming virtual slaves to their new masters resulted in a multifaceted dislocation undoing any semblance of stability that had existed, even after the coming of the invaders. Although there were technical and juridical differentiation between *indios encomendados* and slaves, in practice, the difference remained academic since all natives performed the same work and were condemned to be equally consumed and destroyed by it.[37]

Servants

The accounts of the Spanish chroniclers and the members of the clergy who painstakingly collected and edited the natives' narratives of the events are responsible for capturing and shaping the history of the birth of Indoamerica as an Iberian-centered event. The intention of these early narratives varied according to the objectives of the different interest groups the chroniclers were serving at the time, and they reflected the narrators' philosophical orientation and perception of the reality they encountered in the new continent. These narratives, with the exception, of among others, Las Casas's *A Brief History of the Destruction of the Indies*, and his thoughtful and scholarly *Historia de las Indias*, rarely reflected the truly destructive nature of the enterprise of the colonizing process. As Aimé Césaire tells us, in order to understand the colonizing process, "[f]irst, we must study how colonization works to *decivilize* the colonizer, to *brutalize* him in the true sense of the word, to degrade him, to awaken him to buried instincts to covetousness, violence, race hatred and moral relativism."[38] This dehumanization of the colonizers is vividly captured in one of the most affecting passages of Las Casas's *Historia de las Indias*, when he tells the story of the cacique Hatuey's capture in 1511. After managing to escape from Española to Cuba, the Indian chieftain was captured by the troops of Diego Velázquez and, like most native leaders who resisted the invaders, was sentenced to die. The killing of Indian caciques was a common practice aimed at demoralizing their followers into surrendering, thus the leaders of the conquering expedition could distribute them "not as slaves, but to serve [their masters] in perpetuity worse than slaves." After his capture, Hatuey was tied to a stake and sentenced to be burned alive. While awaiting his execution, Hatuey was approached by a Franciscan missionary who suggested baptizing him so he could die as a Christian, but the cacique reputedly responded:

> "Why become like the Christians who are bad?" To which the friar answered: "Because those who die as Christians go to Heaven, and there they are always looking at God and enjoying themselves." Once again [Hatuey] asked if Christians went to Heaven, the friar answered that yes, those who were good went there, to which [the cacique] replied that he did not want to go there, because [Christians] went to live there. This happened at the time when they wanted to burn him, thus, they lit the firewood and burned him.[39]

Hatuey, a pagan and barbarian in the eyes of his executioners, opted not to accept an eschatological world where his tormentors would be present; instead, he chose the certainty of his own belief system to challenge the most elemental of values defended by the colonizers. He and his followers who had attempted to resist the Spanish onslaught, with their "bare bellies and few and feeble weapons, bows and arrows that were little more than children's toys," became emblematic of the process of resistance and destruction that characterized the collision of these two incommensurable and irreconcilable worlds.[40]

For the natives, the coming of the Spaniards signified the loss of freedom and traditional cultural identities. The wanton killing of Indians and their leaders not only brought about the precipitous decline in population; it created a state of collective depression from which the natives never recovered. The colonists never developed a coherent pattern of behavior toward the natives despite their contributions to the invaders' acquisition of wealth and nobility status. The lack of coherence in Spanish behavior exacerbated the endless, unresolved contradiction obtaining in America: the Spanish understood that the labor of the Indians represented an invaluable source of wealth, but they did not hesitate to exterminate them if they offered any kind of resistance.

As the native population of the Caribbean began fading into oblivion, the colonizers resorted to the costly practice of importing slaves from Africa. The prohibitive cost of doing so forced the Spaniards to venture west of their Caribbean settlements in search of more laborers and other lands to be conquered and settled. Among the direct consequences of this westward push were the conquest of Puerto Rico in 1508 and the establishment of a base of operations in the town of Daríen in Panama in 1510.[41] While the ostensible purpose had been to find slaves, the explorers also sought to "find new lands and new employment."[42] It was this westward push that led Hernández de Cordoba to explore the Yucatán, an effort that opened up the mainland and culminated with the eventual conquest of the Aztecs by Fernando Cortés in 1521, and the Inca empire by Francisco Pizarro in 1532.

As in all processes of colonial domination, the cultural conquest followed in the wake of the military conquest. Few episodes in the cultural subjugation of American natives reflect the tragedy of the destruction of a culture as utterly as the meeting that took place three years after the fall of Tenochtitlán between a group of Nahuatl wise men, *tlamatinime*, and the newly arrived Franciscan friars.[43] The tlamatinime met the missionaries in a public gathering in an attempt to explain the principles and the importance of their native belief system to the religious men who had come to carry out the spiritual conquest of the natives in the name of Christ and the mother church. As the number of their compatriots was declining, the tlamatinime realized that this was perhaps one of the last opportunities they would have to meet face to face with the newcomers to try to convey their anguish, impotence, despair, and frustration resulting from the process of forceful domination. Fully convinced that the Europeans knew nothing of their beliefs, they nevertheless wanted to impress upon them their concept of the divine and the principles they held so dear to their hearts. Although they were aware of their subordinate position as conquered people, they were neither passive nor submissive and they proceeded to present their views in the poetic manner in which they were accustomed:

> Our Lords, our very esteemed Lords:
> great hardships have you endured to reach this land.
> Here before you,
> we ignorant people contemplate you. . . .
> And now, what are we to say? . . .
> Through an interpreter we reply,
> we exhale the breath and the words
> of the Lord of the Close Vicinity . . .
> For this reason we place ourselves in danger. . . .
> But where are we to go now?
> We are ordinary people,
> we are subject to death and destruction, we are mortals;
> allow us then to die,
> let us perish now, since our gods are already dead.[44]

The Aztec wise men understood their fast-changing reality, and they were moved to speak not just out of a fatalistic sense but also as the last remaining representatives of a vanishing world. As they met, both sides were aware of the irreconcilable differences between them. The tlamatinime and the missionaries represented the two extremes of an emerging new world in which the balance of the native universe would never be restored.

When the dialogue with the missionaries took place, the tlamatinime were fully aware that the death sentence against their gods and their traditional native way of life had been decreed long before Cortés had set foot in Mexico. Thanks to their mastery of the technology of war, the newly styled Spanish conquistadores were able to defeat large armies of warriors armed with stone and wooden weapons who could not overcome the power of horses, gunpowder, the cutting edge of the Spanish swords, or the cohesiveness of their fighting forces.[45]

As native temples were razed and images of native gods came tumbling down, social, political, economic and cultural structures succumbed to the new order and the corrosive power of neglect. The Amerindians had been accustomed to war and its consequences, and they had learned to adapt to life under occupation, but nothing had prepared them for the unique characteristics of these new occupying forces. War, as Fernand Braudel indicates, is "a multiform activity, always present, even at the earliest historical level . . . In battle as in everyday life, not everyone has the same opportunities," and once the conquistadores and their allies realized their unique advantages, they seized their opportunities and conquered. The outcome of war brought about a reordering of society, because in the aftermath, groups "can be almost unerringly classified . . . into masters and subjects, proletarians and privileged, facing the possibilities, the normal opportunities of the time."[46] The possibilities and the opportunities of time had been propitious to the newcomers. As a result of their victory the invaders assumed the role of masters and the vanquished their role of servants, an incipient proletariat in an emerging neocapitalist society still redolent of semi-feudalism. The choices available to the natives were limited to working for the occupiers and perishing—or resisting, and also perishing, while struggling to retain their own way of life.

Reformers

The exploitation of the natives and the decimation of their ranks became the focal point of the debate mounting on both sides of the Atlantic. America, as the continent was now officially known, was legally divided into two republics, a *república de españoles* (republic of Spaniards), the victors, and a *república de indios* (republic of Indians), the vanquished. Although the two were diametrically different entities in their composition, they were nevertheless mutually dependent on each other. The Spanish depended on the Indians for the labor needed to reap the benefits of the resources offered by the land—agriculture and mines—and the very existence of the Indians depended entirely on the whims and dictates of the Spanish.

Only a few years after Ovando had convinced Isabel of the benefits of the encomienda, the institution came into conflict with a group of reform-minded Dominicans who had arrived in Española in 1510. For the new-comers the institution of the encomienda and the exploitation of the Indians were not only unjust but repugnant in the eyes of God. The irrepressible Las Casas would later describe it as a "deadly pestilence that consumed the [Indians]."[47] While, in the motherland, representatives of the crown, theologians, and jurists were engaged in endless discussions concerning the nature of the Indians, their juridical standing in the Spanish empire, and a workable formula for their adequate treatment, in America the Indian population was nearing extinction.[48]

Despite the crown's desire to initiate the exploitation of the land as speedily and expediently as possible, in America the unresolved contradiction still remained the question of the usufruct of the land and the preservation of its inhabitants. As we have seen, the colonizers' urgency to produce wealth as fast as possible led to the crass, irrational, and wanton exploitation of the land and the people. The Dominican reformers, at least at the beginning, had expected the colonists to behave as the beneficiaries of a gift, which Divine Providence had bestowed on Spain as a reward for its proven dedication to the service of the "True Faith." Soon they discovered otherwise when they saw the colonists despoiling and destroying their new possessions and the very people entrusted to them, almost as quickly as they were placed in their care.

Reduced to a constant struggle for everyday survival, Native Americans had little energy or opportunity to mount any kind of organized resistance against their new masters. Legally, they had been relegated to the status of minors, or, worse, they had been objectified and reduced to the status of things to be given away at will. As Las Casas wrote in his *Historia*, "these Indians so distributed were commonly called pieces, as they say: I only have so many pieces, and in order to be served [right] I need so many."[49]

Outraged by the brutality of the colonizers and the almost complete indifference of the crown, most Dominicans in America took up the defense of the Indians concerning all matters relating to their welfare. They were so convinced of the irrefutable moral validity of the argument demanding the treatment of the Indians as human beings that they began to raise their voices of protest from the pulpit. A year after their arrival in Española, the friar Antonio Montesinos, in charge of preaching a sermon on Advent Sunday of 1511, chose for his homily a theme from Ecclesiastes, "I am a voice crying in the wilderness," and he thundered his disapproval from the pulpit:

> In order to make your sins against the Indians known to you, I have come upon this pulpit, I who am a voice of Christ crying in the wilderness of this island, and therefore it behooves you to listen, not with careless attention, but with all your heart and senses, so that you may hear it; for this is going to be the strangest voice that ever you expected to hear . . . This voice says that you are in mortal sin, that you live and die in it, for the cruelty and tyranny you use in dealing with these innocent people. Tell me, by what right or justice do you keep these Indians in such cruel and horrible servitude? On what authority have you waged a detestable war against these people who dwelt quietly and peacefully in their own land?[50]

When Montesinos questioned the Spaniards' right to wage war on a peaceful people whose quiet lives had been dislocated by the intruder, he was bringing up questions of jurisdiction and sovereignty that the colonists were unprepared to answer. The colonists failed, or refused, to recognize that Montesinos was not challenging their right to receive tribute from the Indians or their right to exploit them rationally, nor was he challenging the king's sovereignty. What he was questioning was the right the Spaniards had arrogated themselves to treat the Indians as disposable instruments of labor, lesser beings unworthy of the respect that even animals deserved.

The colonists' response was elementary; outraged by the sermon, they walked out of the church and complained to the provincial of the order, Pedro de Córdoba. Instead of admonishing Montesinos, the provincial expressed his support for the sermon and the friar, who, reassured and encouraged by the support of his superior, repeated the same sermon a week later.

Montesinos's sermon had inaugurated one of the most important debates of the sixteenth century, pitting the philosophical, moral, and natural rights of the Indians to be free in their own terms against the political, economic, and juridical-theological arguments supporting Spain's claims to the jurisdiction and dominion of America. This original resistance offered by the Dominicans set the tone for a bi-continental confrontation that continued until the end of the colonial period. It also marked the beginning of the activity of a group of reformers known by the neologism "indianists."

Neither Montesinos nor his fellow reformers challenged or questioned the means or authority employed by the crown, and by extension the encomenderos, to acquire sovereignty over the land and the people.[51] This absence of questioning, almost a tacit acceptance of Spain's sovereignty in the New World, characterized the earliest work of all reformers, not excluding Las Casas's efforts on behalf of the natives. Montesinos's denunciation, of the colonists' abuses failed to alleviate in any way the Indian plight, but it won him innumerable enemies on the island and earned him an admonition from Antonio de Loaysa, the Dominican provincial in Spain, who requested that he return to Spain. This request was expressed in a letter that said, in part,

> [T]he members of the Council of the King our lord . . . determined that you should be brought back to Spain, because of certain propositions that one of you preached in detriment of our religion . . . and as a consequence of your preaching, the whole of the Indies is ready to revolt, and as a result neither you nor any other Christian will be able to remain there.[52]

In another segment of the letter, Loaysa reiterated his belief that the dominion and sovereignty of the Spanish king over the Indies was valid:

> . . . these islands have been acquired by His Highness *jure belli,* and His Holiness has made a donation of them to our lord the King,[53] . . . but even if that were not the case, even then, you should not preach or make public such doctrine without first consulting with his Highness' Council, or his government's council there . . . because one of the purposes of preaching is to win over and to have everyone's goodwill. . . therefore . . . I order all, particularly each and everyone of you, *in virtute Sancti Spiritus.* . . not to dare preach about this matter.[54]

The cleavage between the reformers and the ecclesiastical authorities, which began with Montesinos's sermon, reverberated up to the highest levels of the church-state apparatus. King Ferdinand's response to the challenge came swiftly, when in March of 1512 he added an admonition of his own to the Dominicans in America through his legal representative, Diego Colón: "I saw the sermon that you said was preached by a Dominican priest named Antonio de Montesinos [*sic*], and although he has always preached scandalously, I was greatly surprised about what he said, because he had not Theological, Canonical or Legal foundations to say what he said."[55] Ferdinand's letter, like Loaysa's, invoked the donation of Pope Alexander as the legal basis for his actions and those of his subordinates in the Indies. He invoked the legislation promulgated by Queen Isabel in favor of the Indians as another argument in favor of the dictates emanating from his office. He also expressed his disagreement with the Dominicans' refusal to grant absolution to the colonists who refused to give up their Indians, claiming that if anyone should be blamed for giving Indians away it was the king and his counselors. Masterfully, he interposed his royal persona between the reformers and the colonists. In closing, he ordered Admiral Diego to convey his wishes to the Dominicans

> I order you . . . to talk to them in the best possible manner . . . have them agree that neither [Montesinos and Pedro de Córdoba] nor any other member of their Order will talk about this matter, nor other similar ones, either from the pulpit or outside it, not even in secret, except to say that they held that opinion because they were not informed of the rights we have to these lands and to have the Indians serve not only as they now serve, but to have them serve even more; let them remain in that Island, help and favor them so they can do the best to fructify Our Faith; but if by chance they continue in their bad ways . . . send them here to their Superior in the first boat you find, so they will be punished accordingly. *This must be done with utmost diligence, because each hour they remain in that Island, holding their wretched opinions, they will do much harm to all things over there.*[56]

Ferdinand's letter left no doubt as to where he stood in the dispute. He sided with the colonists because doing otherwise would have implied going against his best economic interests and those of his councilors. To agree with the Dominicans implied giving up the 1,430 Indians that he had in encomienda. This decision would also have affected Juan Rodriguez de Fonseca, his closest advisor on matters of the Indies, who had 244, his own secretary Lope de Conchillo's 264, and the other members of his closest circle who held among them 3,312 encomendados.[57]

Imperial efforts to ameliorate the plight of the Indians resulted in the enactment of the Laws of Burgos. In the absence of divine intervention, the Dominicans deposited their faith in the viability of the juridical-theological system current in Spain at the time. To this end they sent to Spain their most eloquent advocate, Antonio Montesinos, to challenge the colonists' perspective represented by the Franciscan Alonso de Espinal.[58]

As a result of Montesinos's efforts, Ferdinand convoked a junta to study the problems of the Indians. At the junta's suggestion, he promulgated the Laws of Burgos in December of 1512. In theory, these laws were promulgated to attempt to improve the plight of the Indians. Nevertheless, and despite the reformers' good intentions, the laws amounted to little more than legalistic jargon serving the interests of the colonialists and by extension those of the crown. They made a mockery of what they purported to do: to protect the Indians against abuse. Despite their avowed aim to impede the destruction of the Indians, the laws satisfied neither the reformers nor the colonizers, for they were not even the carefully worded sophistry that Isabel's Indian legislation had been. The lack of specificity and the absence of mechanisms to enforce them rendered the laws virtually useless, further obscuring the debates surrounding the nature and rights of the indigenous inhabitants of the Americas.

The drafters' callous indifference and total ignorance of America and its inhabitants were evident in the preamble, which

> states flatly that the Indians are by nature inclined to a life of idleness and vice, and not to the learning of the Christian virtues. It further states that the greatest impediment in the way of their redemption lies in their having their dwellings removed from the Christians, for which reason they cannot learn Christian habits and doctrines, whereas if they should be gathered into villages where they might be kept from their vice of idleness and continually observe the practices of the Christians, they might be redeemed from their wickedness.[59]

Once the "deviant" status of the natives had been established, then all remedies created by the discretion of their guardians had to be accepted as prescriptive medicine for any malady affecting the new subjects of the crown. Thirty-five different articles covering all aspects of economic and social interrelations between natives and colonizers followed the preamble. Like most of the legislation affecting Amerindians, the Laws of Burgos promulgated by Ferdinand failed to affect the attitude of the colonizers toward the natives in any significant way. In addition, the laws' ambiguity left them open to individual interpretation while being subjected to the traditional practice of *"obedezcanse pero no se cumplan"* (obey but do not comply) that greeted most laws with which the colonizers disagreed. Lack of enforceability transformed the laws into a futile exercise in legislative legerdemain, such as article XX, which read in part:

> The person who has [Indians] in encomienda shall give to each of them a gold peso every year, which he shall be obliged to give them in wearing apparel, in the sight of and with the consent of our visitor, and this gold peso shall be understood to be in addition to the said hammock that we commanded above to be given to each of them. And since it is just that the said chiefs and their wives should be better dressed and better treated than the other Indians, we command that one real be deducted from the gold peso to be paid to the latter.[60]

As would be expected, the Indians never received payment in gold; in most cases they received useless trinkets in lieu of wages, yet there were no authorities to hear their cases.

Ultimately, the Laws of Burgos only served to reinforce some of the most significant demands placed upon the natives that had been evident in Isabel's Indian instructions to Ovando in 1503. Most importantly, the laws reaffirmed the need to place the Indians in *reducciones,* modern-day reservations, where their Spanish masters could control them closely.[61] The newly enacted code kept the encomienda alive while further strengthening "the intervention of the State in Spanish-Indian work relationships."[62] Nevertheless, this legislation symbolizes one of the earliest formal and legal attempts to prevent the senseless destruction of the Indians, not out of love for them, but out of the understanding of the impossibility of accomplishing the profitable exploitation of the territories without free Indian labor. This legal code, more than anything, represented, in reality, a last-ditch attempt to make the best possible use of a dwindling native labor pool.

From the perspective of the colonizers, the mere idea of having any legislation that could benefit the Indians was not only anathema but also economically and politically impractical. From the perspective of the king and his councilors there could be no viable effort to implement laws that would fundamentally challenge the encomienda as it existed, for, as we have seen, any such measures would have been detrimental to their individual interests. In the closing days of 1512, the Laws of Burgos represented the reaffirmation of the Spanish crown's unchallenged hegemony in the New World. They also signified the almost unconditional acceptance by Spaniards of the innate inferiority of the Indians and their condition of natural slavery, a belief that remained unchallenged until the debate between Sepúlveda and Las Casas in Valladolid in 1550–51.

To demonstrate its willingness to adhere to the requirements of the bulls of donation, the crown commissioned the renowned jurist Juan López Palacios Rubios to prepare a document that could be read to the Indians before any armed confrontation took place. The purpose of that document was to explain to them the source of the crown's authority to undertake a given action.[63] This most unusual document, the infamous *Requerimiento* of 1512, became one of the most salient features of the Spanish protocol of conquest.[64] The document began with an exhortation in the name of the monarchs of Spain aimed at informing the Indians of the existence of God; it continued with a brief narration of the Catholic version of the origins and history of the world and a definition of the bulls of donation. It concluded by asking the Indians to submit to the primacy of the true church and its shepherd the pope and demanded that the natives pledge allegiance to Spain or face the risk of having the most unimaginable catastrophes descend upon their infidel heads.[65] The reading of the document by an "interpreter" was invariably greeted with demonstrations of great mirth by the conquerors, who found in it a great source of hilarity, particularly when it was muttered in front of empty huts or well beyond the hearing range of those it was supposed to affect. Many Spaniards, when describing this document, have often shared the dilemma of Las Casas, who confessed on reading it that he could not decide "whether to laugh or weep."[66]

Dissatisfied with the Laws of Burgos, but undiscouraged by the original setbacks, the indianists continued their efforts to improve the lot of the Indians for the next few centuries. For the better part of the first half of the sixteenth century they did so under the leadership of the new convert to the indianist cause, the indefatigable Bartolomé de Las Casas.

While the moralists insisted on finding a moral and religious justification for Spain's presence in America, and the jurists were concerned with the legality of the act, the crown was preoccupied with keeping the ambition of its Spanish subjects in check. The colonists, who saw their interests in the

Indies threatened by the meddling of the reformers trying to influence crown policy, had only one concern: to keep the men of the cloth from altering their newly acquired status. But once again, the great absentees from the debate were those most affected by it, the natives whose existence had become a substantial point of reference for the debaters but whose material fate remained an ethereal, immaterial abstraction.

Chapter Two

Three

Conversions, Utopias, and Ecclesiastical Imperialism

And it seems that the first universal causation, which is heavenly influence, favors greatly these our Indian peoples to be intelligent, ingenious and quite able, they have thus had the good fortune of receiving from God good and noble souls.
—Bartolomé de Las Casas, *Apologética historia sumaria*

FEW PARTICIPANTS IN Spain's "enterprise of the Indies" and the genesis of Indoamerica, perhaps with the sole exceptions of Columbus and the conquerors of Mexico and Peru, have been the object of as much attention, or been the center of as much controversy, discussion, veneration, and derision, as Bartolomé de Las Casas. Rarely has a protagonist in the drama of the colonial encounter become the object of such uninhibited hagiographic adoration or condemnation by his contemporaries and future generations as the crusading Las Casas. For more than thirty years of the nearly forty-five he spent in the Americas, 1502 to 1547, Las Casas's work was dedicated to the single-minded pursuit of legislation and the adoption of measures aimed at obtaining laws to alleviate the abject situation of the Indians and their exploitation at the hands of his compatriots.

First Conversion: *"Protector de todos los Indios"*

Bartolomé de Las Casas first came to America in 1502 at the age of eighteen, accompanying his father, who was returning after an initial visit on Columbus's second voyage. In addition to the possibility of working with his father, Las Casas, who had received the tonsure, "could aspire to the position of *doctrinero*, a fairly well paid category of priests who were sent to promote the Christianization of the natives."[1]

There seems to be no doubt that the new colonist shared the dreams and expectations of others who, like him, had been lured by the promise of a better life. A better life included receiving an encomienda and establishing an agricultural enterprise in the Caribbean. Little is known about his early years, other than what he chose to say about himself in his own writings. From all indications, he did not take his final vows until 1507, in Rome, and did not celebrate his first mass in the New World until 1510.[2]

By his own admission, the priest-encomendero Las Casas was somewhat disturbed by the content of Montesinos's sermon, but he did nothing to improve the plight of his encomendados. He did not take any active steps to divest himself of them nor did he change his mind after the Dominicans refused to listen to his confession because of his unwillingness to give up his encomienda.[3]

Despite his claims to have treated his natives well (and we have only his word for this), he also admitted that he never made any effort to fulfill his commitment insofar as the religious indoctrination and spiritual care of his charges was concerned.[4] Slowly, the thought of holding natives against their will, combined with their mistreatment at the hands of the Spaniards, something he saw all around him, began to erode his belief in the righteousness of his actions. Eventually, this uncertainty led him to question his right and that of his fellow colonists to act as masters and spiritual guides to the Indians. This unrelenting questioning came to a climax while he was preparing a sermon for his congregation in the Easter season of 1514, when he stumbled on a passage from Ecclesiasticus 34, in the Apocrypha, that spoke of God's rejection of ill-gotten gifts: "Unclean is the offering sacrificed by an oppressor. [Such] mockeries of the unjust are not pleasing [to God]. The Lord is pleased only by those who keep to the way of the truth and justice. The Most High does not accept the gifts of unjust people. He does not look well upon the offerings."[5]

Like most of the events in Las Casas's life, his transformation from priest-encomendero to redeemer of the Indians was suffused with symbolism and high drama. An adroit manipulator of symbols and signs, Las Casas could not pass up the opportunity to point to the divine designs guiding his transformation. His narrative of the events invites comparisons with Paul, whose epiphanic conversion on the road to Damascus turned him from pagan into zealous Christian, in much the same manner that a converted

Las Casas became the most zealous defender of the Indians after his. As a powerful symbol, an epiphany contributes much to enhance the mythological dimension of an event, and nothing could have marked the auspicious transformation of Las Casas from sinner to savior than the occurrence in 1514.

Although the events surrounding his conversion are well known, the extent of all the factors contributing to his transformation can be only surmised from his own brief revelations. Perhaps his actions were prompted by his increasingly frustrated objections to his compatriots' behavior, or perhaps by his witnessing isolated acts of cruelty in Española and Cuba. It is also possible that the deciding event might have been the massacre of natives at Caonao, Cuba, by the troops of the hapless Pánfilo de Narváez. In Caonao, Las Casas saw hundreds, if not thousands, of Indians senselessly murdered in an unexplainable orgy of violence prompted by either panic or the blood lust of the conquistadores. It is also possible that his having witnessed the massacre only a few months before he encountered the biblical passage pushed his conscience over the edge. In his own colorful and vivid description of the horrifying event, he told how the blood of the victims formed "a stream as if they had slaughtered many heads of cattle."[6]

Regardless of the causes of his transformation, subsequent events in the cleric's life contributed to forge his image as an outstanding and unrelenting champion of Indian rights, when in actuality he was only one, albeit the most vocal, of a rather large group of clergymen-reformers. What his supporters have often ignored is that his transformation was a slowly evolving process that took twelve years from the time of his arrival on the island to his 1514 Easter epiphany. The deliberately slow manner in which he went about putting his material possessions in order after having made his decision to renounce his encomienda belies the claim of a miraculous transformation bearing instant fruits, but what became evident was that he exhibited the zealotry and dedication of any new convert to a cause.

The newly transformed reformer condemned the encomienda as "unjust and tyrannical" and found that he could not live with the double standard of preaching one thing while doing the contrary. A few months after his reading of Ecclesiasticus, he renounced his encomiendas to the governor of the island of Cuba, Diego Velázquez. Although at the time he knew that by giving up his encomendados they would revert to the crown, which would certainly redistribute them to other encomenderos, thus condemning them to a certain death, he nevertheless returned them to the authorities.[7]

A practical person, he found himself encumbered by his possessions and proceeded to liquidate the assets belonging to him and his partner, the layman Diego de Rentería. The proceedings of this sale enabled him to support himself at court for at least three years to carry on his lobbying activities.[8]

His newly found calling, as defender of the Indians, made him gravitate toward the Dominicans and their reforming efforts. By then, it had become patently clear to Las Casas that the situation of the Indians could only be altered by applying direct pressure on the crown. The Dominicans and the new convert complemented each other extraordinarily well. The first were well versed in the finer theological aspects of the struggle for justice, the newcomer was a practical man who had the dogged tenacity to dig in for a prolonged struggle. As he had demonstrated throughout his entrepreneurial career, he was not one to be easily dissuaded. To the reformers he brought "the one element they needed: the fighting man, one who had the gift of wholly accepting a doctrine with all inferences and consequences [but] Las Casas' strength and his weakness lay in his inability to change."[9]

Las Casas's transformation from encomendero to advocate of the Indians found him at loggerheads with his fellow colonists. The ensuing debate perpetuated the division of colonial society into two antithetical and inimical camps, colonists against indianists, espousing different courses of action for the incorporation of America to Spain:

> The first demanded that the incorporation of the Indian be carried out through his direct subjection to the American Spaniard—whether soldier, colonist, encomendero, *hacendado*, mine owner or merchant—in the capacity of a slave, *naboría*, or encomienda Indian. The desired incorporation of the Indian would be forcibly achieved with the Spaniard acting as his civilizer. The other trend of thought was that the Indian should be civilized gradually through a natural process of acculturation, free of all subjection by the colonist. The Indian should be placed under the tutelage of the crown and treated as a vassal of the king; the civilizing process (essentially conversion to the Catholic religion) would be assigned to missionaries; and the Indian's rights as a freeman would be upheld without detriment.[10]

The separation of the two camps along these lines found the colonists striving for a certain degree of autonomy from the crown while the reformers moved into the uncomfortable position of advocating the direct dependence of the natives on the crown rather than on the colonists. Thus, the debate became a struggle between colonialism and imperialism, with the Spaniards in America representing the former and the crown, supported by the reformers, the latter. Las Casas's efforts on behalf of the Indians were contained within the parameters implicit in the definition of the usufruct of empire as a long-range proposition rather than the rapacious and myopic immediate exploitation to which the colonists were subjecting it.

The strength of the colonists' argument came from seven propositions prepared by the Dominican Bernaldo de Mesa and approved by the junta of Burgos, essentially the same group responsible for readying the laws of 1512. These propositions justified the existence of the encomienda as a way of overcoming the Indians' "natural tendency to idleness." The responsibility of helping the Indians to overcome their negative natural inclinations fell directly to the king. Given the impossibility of having the king present in the Indies, it was the responsibility of the colonists to assume the prerogatives of the absent king.[11] Once they became legal representatives of the crown, the colonists were free to do as they saw fit with their charges, while paying cursory cosmetic obedience to royal decrees.

Las Casas, like other reformers, consistently criticized what he considered the usurpation of the rights of the king's prerogatives by the colonists. Sometimes the reformers ventured criticisms of the king's exercise of sovereignty in the Indies, but those occasions were rare. It was only during Las Casas's last years in America, at the time of his brief active tenure as bishop of Chiapa, that he began to question, in earnest, some of the basis of the king's claims to sovereignty, a criticism he reaffirmed in his later works and in his last will and testament.

The reformers, as religious men, accepted the papal donation as the ultimate dictate on the matter of sovereignty. Under these circumstances, the issue that they questioned was not so much Spain's right to the usufruct of the land and the people but the manner in which the colonists carried out this task. This is not to say that the reformers' zeal, their preoccupation with and struggle on behalf of the Indians were not genuine, because they were, but their efforts were hampered by their tacit acceptance of the monarch's dominion and jurisdiction over America and its inhabitants.

The reformers' acceptance of the fact that a requisite component of the civilizing process of the natives was their conversion to the Catholic faith, along with their religious affiliation to the church, made their aims undistinguishable from the ecclesiastical imperialism advocated by members of other religious orders. That is, their efforts only enabled the church to become "the social and intellectual catalyst of conquest in Hispanic America."[12]

The reformers' ultimate reliance on the crown to enact legislation to ameliorate the plight of the natives constituted a definite drawback, and ultimately, a futile endeavor. One of the most telling examples of this futility had been the enactment of the Laws of Burgos with its multiple promises of protecting the Indians but no provisions to enforce them. Although sympathetic to the protestations of the reformers, the king could not afford to alter the existing system for fear of incurring significant financial losses. That the reformers believed that the monarch could legislate against himself and his immediate circle, impelled by a sense of justice and fairness, suggests a naïveté from which not even the pragmatic Las Casas was exempt.

One of the original motivations for Las Casas's return of his encomienda Indians had been the conviction that one of the ways in which he could begin to right the wrongs committed against the natives was the restitution of the encomienda Indians to their original condition as free men.[13] His inability to convince the colonizers of the necessity to ask for restitution drove him to seek alternative paths of action. After long deliberation and consultation with the Dominicans, he decided to take his case to Spain. Before departing from Cuba to Española to embark on his journey across the sea, he prepared a memorial, *ad perpetuam rei memoriam*, detailing the services he had performed in Cuba, serving God and the king, pacifying Indians, preaching, baptizing, and holding services for the Spaniards. This was done "so that in case that at some time or another he chose to ask *mercedes* [grants] from the king, his services to the monarch would be taken into account."[14]

The newly transformed reformer was practical enough not to allow his years of experience in the islands to go unnoticed or to vanish because of his conversion. His detailed memorial of services could easily have meant that he hoped to be picked as the religious administrator of the islands if the monarch accepted his list of remedies.[15] In 1515, Las Casas left Española en route to Spain accompanied by none other than the fiery Antonio Montesinos and his brother. Aware that in order to influence the king he had to anticipate any move that the colonizers—already alarmed by what they considered his outrageous proposals of restitution and justice for the Indians —would make to influence the king, and to avoid unpleasant incidents, he left the island under the subterfuge of going to Paris to further his religious studies.

In December of 1515, he had his first and last interview with King Ferdinand, and he used this time to inform the king of the conditions of the natives in the Indies. The king suggested a second meeting, but it never materialized because of Ferdinand's death in January of the following year. Instead, Las Casas met with the two regents ruling the country in the absence of Prince Charles, who had not yet moved to Spain; one was a Flemish representative of the prince, Adrian, and the other, the Franciscan cardinal Ximénez de Cisneros.

He presented to the regents the memorial he had prepared for the king detailing the mistreatment of the Indians of the Antilles by the Spaniards. This represented the priest's first public written denunciation of the conditions obtaining in America. The document was little more than a detailed list of specific instances where the colonists, contravening all royal recommendations for the treatment of the Indians, ignored the good faith of the inhabitants and, unmindful of their responsibility, proceeded to exploit them in the cruelest and most irrational manner, resulting in their extermination.

Among the most significant grievances and injuries that the cleric listed was the lack of gratitude exhibited by the Spaniards toward the Indians who had treated them so well upon their arrival. He charged his compatriots with ignoring the mandates of the king to feed the natives properly while they were at work in the mines. He also accused them of not allowing the Indians to grow their own food, and, in some cases, of leaving the women and children to starve because they had drafted and removed the males, who were responsible for growing and procuring food, from the household.[16] The list of atrocities was almost endless, and it encompassed all that Las Casas had noted during his time as an encomendero in Cuba and Española. The list ended with the description of a rare manifestation of Indian resistance, which Las Casas seems to have included for the shock value it might hold for the king. A group of Indians committed mass suicide, thus depriving the invaders of the pleasure of allowing them access to their souls and converting them: "[Las Casas] says that the term Christian is so abhorrent to the Indians that they believe it is better to go to hell, in order not to have to talk to the Christians than to go to heaven where they would have to see them again."[17]

The issue of the Indians' resistance to conversion, to avoid becoming like their oppressors, remained a recurring theme in Las Casas's work. Despite his noting this phenomenon, he appears to have been unable (or perhaps he refused) to grasp all the possible implications of this form of resistance, particularly where even friendly conversion was concerned. It is as if he could only see the natives almost exclusively in terms of their worth as passive objects, instruments of production, victims without self-volition, abject beings unable to defend or speak for themselves.[18] From this rather narrow perspective, then, it follows that the Indians' sole opportunity for salvation depended on their conversion to Christianity, regardless of the worth and importance of their own value system.

During the early stage of his career as a reformer, Las Casas concentrated his attacks on the most visible agents responsible for the destruction of the Indians, the encomenderos. From his perspective, Spain's presence in America was defined by the actions of the colonists. Consequently, the campaign of the reformers had to focus on the encomenderos and "from the very start, Casas had chosen the policy of imputing the blame for the bad conditions to the King's agents rather than to the King himself."[19]

By placing the onus of the atrocities committed in the Indies on the colonists, Las Casas positioned himself squarely on the side the reformers, but at the same time he cast his fate with a crown struggling to control the aristocratic aspirations of its subjects in the colonies. His continuous denunciation of the encomenderos turned him into the lightning rod for their wrath, and his constant denunciations and fulminations made him an invaluable source of information for the crown about all aspects of its subjects' behavior. In addition, in the process of defending themselves against his accusations, the colonizers ended up providing the king with information about other aspects of their activities, information that the monarch would otherwise have never received. Thus, from the earliest time of his work on behalf of the Indians, the priest became, wittingly or unwittingly, an extremely useful tool in the imperialist designs of the monarchy.

It was also in these early years that Las Casas, rather than criticize the king, chose instead to appeal to him along purely pragmatic lines emphasizing, whenever possible, the economic loss that the mistreatment of the Indians represented. Aware of the expectations and necessities of the crown to realize a profit from its overseas empire, he lost no opportunity to point at every turn the economical potential of adopting new policies toward the Indians and the losses that the crown could suffer by doing otherwise: "[The cleric] says that more than fifty of the Lucayo islands have been depopulated, these were places where churches could be built so God and Your Royal Highness would be served and your income would be increased, because the land is rich and fruitful. If it had been adequately treated from the very beginning, Your Highness would have incalculable income from it."[20]

Las Casas's appeal to the pragmatic side of the sovereign was more than a mere tactical ploy, for he had no objection to the extraction of wealth from America, although he envisioned an idealized system of exploitation where the usufruct of the land and its inhabitants could be carried out in the best terms for all concerned. Aside from his opposition to the colonists' mistreatment of the Indians, he resented their anarchic and autarkic tendencies, but what he ended up positing was a form of systematic benevolent imperialism that ideally would result in the best of all possible worlds for all concerned: the Indians would survive, being treated kindly, and the crown would not have to relax its hold on its American possessions.

Las Casas's reputation is built on his advocacy of Indian rights, but his aspirations were often conditioned by the way in which his theoretical postulates could be implemented. In most cases what he proposed was for the crown to grant the natives partial rights subject to the whims of the economic and political needs of the motherland. This is evident in his first list of remedies for the Indians of Cuba. In this list, prepared in 1516 and presented to Cisneros as a complement to his memorial of grievances, he called for a halt in the distribution of encomiendas but only until new legislation safeguarding the Indians could be enacted, as is evident in his leading remedy:

First remedy: That while Your Highness orders an investigation and determines what must be done in those islands . . . it should be ordered that all Indians from all islands should cease working and serving in all capacities. First, because in accordance with the pernicious habit of the Spaniards to make use of the Indians, they will kill or cause them to die in a short time. . . especially knowing of the King's death. . . Second . . . because the little idle time *they have will serve [the Indians] to recover their strength, to have some leisure time and to have the chance to put on some weight or become stronger, so when they return to work, they will be able to bear it.*[21]

This first remedy, followed by a list of thirteen other remedies, constituted a detailed plan for the exploitation of the islands with the full cooperation and utilization of the Indians. In essence, the "Memorial de remedios" was little more than a primer for the acculturation and successful exploitation of the Indians,[22] but some *lascasistas*, of the stature of Hanke and

Giménez Fernández, have called this form of enlightened exploitation a "new and autochthonous attitude of the Spanish Renaissance."[23]

In the earlier years of his practice as reformer, the liberty that Father Las Casas envisioned for the natives was little more than a liberty predicated on their ability to maximize their productive capacity through less violent means than those used by the ordinary conquistador. Although, later in life, Las Casas's condemnations of the encomienda became more vociferous, these manifestations came well after the whole continent had been militarily conquered and the establishment of almost irreversible exploitative practices had been validated and enforced, if not by law, by force of habit.

As one of Las Casas's earliest proposals, the "Memorial" is most revealing insofar as it demonstrates that the best alternative that Las Casas saw for the salvation of the Indians was tied to a scheme to make the natives as Spanish as possible. From his perspective, the Indians could be saved if they abandoned their traditional way of life and accepted the new one through a process of conversion and assimilation.

The impact of this memorial was felt beyond the confines of the colonies and of Spain itself. In addition to its influence on the bishop of Michoacán, Vasco de Quiroga, it is assumed to have also influenced Thomas More's *Utopia*.[24]

After requesting a temporary cessation of Indian labor in the first remedy, at least until a new king could be crowned, in the second remedy Las Casas recommended that no Indians should be assigned to individual Spaniards, but that the king should order the Indians placed in a communal pool within each village and Spanish town.[25]

The call for relocating the Indians in centers close to the Spaniards implied removal from their residences and the abandonment of their traditional way of life, but these implications were not considered in the proposal. This specific *remedio* was essentially a variation of the first article of the Laws of Burgos calling for the placement of Indians in gatherings, nameless at the time but later identified as reducciones. Fifty years later, Viceroy Francisco Toledo would use the same principle of reducciones to effectively accomplish the bureaucratic and political conquest of Peru.[26]

In addition to all its other requisites, the remedio also made provisions for the king to obtain his royal *quinto* and for the majordomos in charge of supervising the communities to allocate money to feed and take care of the Indians' every necessity. Resolving the problem of the residence and sustenance of the natives would make it possible to instruct them in matters of the Christian faith so they might save their souls. Putting this specific proposal into practice was aimed at preventing the premature death of the Indians. It also assured the king a guaranteed income and having "[his] lands populated and filled with vassals: taking into account how the people of this land multiply so marvelously, thus everyday their help and their usefulness will increase to the great utility and permanence of the kingdom."[27]

Despite its good intention, the document did not take into consideration the cultural, social, and political dislocation that further contributed to the natives' increasing depression and death, which further reflects the absence of dialogue between indianists and the subjects of their concern. The only possible justification for such an approach was that, in fulfillment of the indianists' charitable Christian duty, it was intended only to transform the condition of the Indians from one akin to slavery into a more benign form of exploitation under the supervision of the state, rather than to bring about any significant structural changes.

A third remedy introduced one of the cleric's favorite concepts, that of the peaceful colonization and settlement of the New World with Spanish farmers.[28] He suggested to the king that he send to each village and city in the occupied territory of the islands forty farmers with their wives and children and have five Indians assigned to each farmer. The colonists would then teach the Indians, by example, the best way to farm and to make the land productive. This type of arrangement was intended to serve the dual purpose of transforming the Indians into farmers while providing the colonists with a productive stake in the settlement of the islands. The cleric also expected this original arrangement to result in a demographic increase through miscegenation of Spaniards and Indians, something that, from his perspective, would bring about a productive and peaceful society. This particular remedy, more than any other, provides evidence of the naïveté and myopia about the nature of colonization that characterized Las Casas's efforts, at least in his early years as a reformer.

The memorial includes other remedios covering a wide range of proposals for improving the lot of the natives. Among other things, Las Casas suggested that the new reforms should be announced to the Indians of all islands in their own language, so they would have no doubt that the old conditions of servitude had been abolished. To enforce the proposals, he suggested the appointment of an ecclesiastical representative to administer the affairs of the natives and to administer justice, including the punishment of any Spaniard denounced by an indigenous person and accused of mistreatment. He also suggested that the Indians should have direct access to these authorities and bypass their Spanish supervisors. Another proposal stipulated that no person who had been to the Indies or had any relation to the administration of its affairs should participate in any aspect of this plan.

Other provisions of the plan suggested that laws detrimental to the Indians should be abrogated and those aimed at protecting them should be kept. Traditionally, it had been more profitable for the colonists to disobey the laws than to observe them; Las Casas's plan, not surprisingly, called for the adequate enforcement of the law. The proposal suggested that the punishment applied to the Indians should not be the same as that applied to the Spaniards, in an effort to remedy the absence of punishment in the case of crimes committed by Spaniards against Indians. The former could act with impunity and never be punished for crimes against the natives, but the latter were severely punished or killed for insignificant offenses.

Of all the remedies espoused by Las Casas at this time, the eleventh, proposing to replace Indian workers with black African slaves, has been at the center of some of the greatest controversy swirling around the reformer. The proposal recommended that the king not allow his own encomienda Indians to be part of the communities suggested by the scheme. As the cleric saw it, there existed the potential for demanding greater productivity for the king if the Indian subjects were gently treated. He suggested that the sovereign should replace the natives with "twenty blacks or other slaves in the mines. . . because they will gather more gold than having twice the number of Indians," but he never explained the origins of his calculations.[29] In his addendum to the memorial, he suggested the possibility that the encomenderos, and not just the king, could receive either black or white slaves to compensate them for the loss of their Indians.[30] Ultimately, this would have resulted in the granting of licenses for the importation of slaves with the corresponding profits for the crown. Although the king never approved the plan, it sheds useful light on this early phase of the Dominican's career as a reformer and the extraordinary lengths he was willing to go to attain his objectives.

The remaining remedies were requests for the king to appoint a minimum of two priests per island, provisions forbidding taking the Indians outside their islands, and a suggestion for the king to study the proposals of Palacios Rubios and Matías de Paz concerning the governance of the Indies.

To the original list of remedies, Las Casas appended an additional wish list of provisions for the other islands and the rest of the Indies in general. He suggested sending a team of one Franciscan and one Dominican with the expeditions to the Lucayo islands for the purpose of supervising the procurement and treatment of the Indians to be brought back to Cuba.[31] Another provision involved the founding of a hospital in each community to take care of sick and injured Indians. The plan included a detailed description of how these hospitals should be built so that the patients could attend mass without moving from their beds. Las Casas also called for establishing an office of the Holy Inquisition in the islands, for he considered it a high priority to fight the possibility of someone sowing the "appalling corrupting vice of heresy."[32]

Another remedy worth noting is his call for the Indians to be provided with clothing and to be taught to eat sitting at the table instead of on the "ground like dogs." To illustrate the feasibility of his proposals, Las Casas enclosed a budget detailing the expenses of implementing his plan. The list of expenses made allowances for an administrator appointed to oversee the successful implementation of the overall scheme, with a compensation of 400 *castellanos*. It is possible that Las Casas had expected to be named to such a post, hence the preparation of his *información de servicios* before leaving for Spain in 1515.[33] As Hanke and Giménez Fernandez write, "Although this noble and utopian plan never received the approval of the king or the court, it constitutes an extraordinary revelation, not only of what Las Casas and his Dominican companions sought while they toiled in Spain in their quest to save the Indians, but also of the existence of a powerful current of *humanitarian and paternalistic thought that, in the Spanish character, ran parallel to the dominant imperialistic attitude*."[34]

The Dominicans and Las Casas were thus on separate but parallel paths to the "dominant imperialistic attitude" prevailing in the mother country at the time. This coincidence makes it difficult to separate and differentiate the aspirations and expectations of Las Casas and his fellow reformers from those of their king or their "lettered" compatriots who had never been to America. Although often the position of the Spanish crown is characterized by proponents of the Golden Legend as displaying an apparent genuine preoccupation with the Indian question, more so under Charles V than under Philip II, it rarely allowed humanitarian concerns to override pragmatic considerations. Unsurprisingly, Las Casas's role in this imperialist scheme is not so much defined by his insistence on the need to preserve the integrity of the indigenous way of life as by his insistence on the profitability of the colonizing venture. Consequently, we see him opposed less to the principle of conquest than the manner in which it was conducted.

In his early proposals, Las Casas showed almost a total disregard for the cultural integrity of those he was supposed to protect. In these early memorials, he seemed indifferent to the way in which converting them to Christianity, moving them into reducciones, or making them subjects of Spain might have affected their traditional way of life. Often his work seemed intent not so much on protecting the natives as on recreating them as extensions of Spain. Despite identifying these "humanitarian paternalistic" tendencies in Las Casas and the reformers, Giménez and Hanke seem to accept them unquestioningly. They ignore the fact that his paternalistic policies toward the Indians made Las Casas a benevolent but pragmatic agent of imperialism acting in sharp contrast to the mindless, cruel, and myopic colonists, one incapable of breaking through the invisible wall of alterity separating the natives from the Europeans.

Las Casas's religious and political paternalistic benevolence provided the humanistic and humanitarian element absent among ordinary colonists, and this is what has contributed to the creation of the myth of love and abnegation that has surrounded his image through the centuries. Wittingly or unwittingly, he served the role of an imperial agent at the service of a king who not only tolerated his particular form of dissent but encouraged it because it benefited his august interests in the struggle between the centralized empire and the aristocratic aspirations of his Spanish subjects. The kind viewed with alarm the semi-feudal attributions adopted by the encomenderos, who, in their private authority over the Indians, were "inevitably repugnant both to a centralised monarchy and to autocratic missionary orders."[35]

The cleric's early proposals often give the impression of a person willingly assuming the role of caretaker of the "goose with the golden eggs," whose function was to keep it alive and producing, to avoid having it killed by the colonizers in the vain hope of getting to the eggs faster.[36]

As a reformed encomendero, Las Casas was familiar with the expectations and demands of his former allies and could effectively interact with them on equal terms whenever necessary. At the same time, keeping with his utopian perception of the "salvific" role of Christianity, he saw the church as the ideal head and administrator of the conquered territories. His belief in the beneficent role of the church and the creation of a quasi-theocratic government, as well as his advocacy of the implementation of the far-reaching reforms contained in the "Memoriales" he had presented to Cardinal Ximénez de Cisneros, influenced the regent's decision to assign a religious body to administer Española. After requesting a description of the qualifications from Las Casas, the cardinal apparently decided in favor of a triumvirate of Jeronymite monks, to avoid friction between Franciscans and Dominicans in Spain and the islands.[37] According to his own version, Las Casas was asked by Cisneros to participate in the selection of the Jeronymite representatives to be sent to the Indies.[38] Once selected, the friars received detailed instructions from the cardinal concerning a proposal for a government closely adjusting to Las Casas's original remedies.

Among other things, they were instructed to take away the encomiendas held by all royal officials and were expected to hold hearings about specific Indian grievances and problems with the encomenderos. They were also expected to supervise the orderly relocation of Indians into the protected communities whose creation had been suggested by Las Casas. The instructions followed almost literally some of the cleric's proposals for miscegenation and teaching the Spanish language to the natives and also stipulated that at any given time one third of the indigenous men between the ages of twenty-five and fifty were to be engaged in the mining of gold in two-month shifts. Provisions were established for compensating the Spaniards forced to give up their encomiendas, allowing them preference in the sale of their land and the possibility of becoming public employees.[39]

After the selection of the friars, there remained the matter of the appointment of a *juez visitador extraordinario* to oversee the officials charged with taking the *residencias* of all judges and public officials in the Indies. The juez visitador was also expected to act as an advocate for the indigenous people "incapable of demanding justice for themselves."[40] The naming of the jurist Alonso de Zuazo, a man with a well-earned reputation for probity and juridical acumen, marked the first instance in which the Spanish government appointed an official for the exclusive purpose of investigating Indian grievances. Nevertheless, this powerful juez visitador was placed under the jurisdiction of the Jeronymites, who by the time they left Spain were predisposed against Las Casas by the representatives of the colonists in the islands. The final chapter of the rupture between the friars and the cleric, a process begun long before the mission had even started,[41] came with Cisneros's appointment of Las Casas as advisor to the friars and as "procurador o protector universal de todos los indios de las Indias" (procurator or universal protector of all the Indians of the Indies).[42]

Las Casas's official title and the actual scope of power of the religious junta has occasioned considerable controversy, but it is almost certain that the Jeronymites' power was comparable to that of royal governors. On the other hand, Las Casas's official title as *defensor de los indios* remained vague insofar as it did not specify the authority, prerogatives, or the jurisdiction that accompanied the position despite the hundred gold pesos a year in salary assigned to him.[43] Unable to influence the Jeronymites to carry out their instructions in the manner he thought adequate, Las Casas returned to Spain to file a grievance against the triumvirate while attempting to regain Cisneros's sympathy.

The pattern of returning to the seat of power to attempt to influence the central authorities whenever things did not go according to the way he had envisioned events characterized most of his endeavors in America. This action often had the unintended effect of forcing him to abandon the scene of a proposed project, usually at the beginning, during the most important phase of the project's inception. As a result, the project inevitably ended up unfinished or unsatisfactorily implemented, nullifying any salutary effect it might have had for the natives.

By the time Las Casas arrived in Spain to speak to Ximénez de Cisneros, the cardinal had already been predisposed against him, and his delicate health prevented him from granting the priest more than a cursory hearing. In America, the Jeronymites had set out to fulfill their instructions, but they met with the resistance of the colonists, who were loath to give up a way of life to which they had become accustomed. Faced with the near extinction of the native population, the Jeronymites, like Las Casas before them, suggested an increase in the number of African slaves brought to the Antilles. They also experimented with trying to relocate the Indians into thirty *comunidades* they had built, but by that time the indigenous population of Española had been so decimated by an epidemic of smallpox that any orderly relocation was impossible.

Despite doing little or nothing to affect the lot of the encomenderos, the triumvirate of priests managed to earn their opposition and enmity, eliminating any possibility of productive, effective work. The three also managed to earn the animosity of the reformers for not doing enough. They were further hampered by an irresolvable dilemma: they could not get rid of the encomienda, for fear that the Spaniards would abandon the islands, but at the same time, they could not continue to tolerate it, for that meant certain death for the Indians.[44] In a world where choices were dictated by the overpowering need to recover investments and to pay debts, neither the Jeronymites nor the reformers had the option of consulting the natives, nor could they do anything to alter their powerlessness in the equation. Thus the few remaining natives learned a first-hand lesson in primitive capitalism where the objective conditions requiring the existence of the encomienda had sentenced them to a premature death to fulfill the aspirations of a handful of invaders unwilling to compromise:

> All ameliorative legislation (which, to be sure, was unrealistic and impracticable) met with the unyielding opposition of the Spaniards, an opposition that cannot be disposed of merely by calling it wicked . . . [The men of the conquest] were proud, ignorant, credulous, unstable, callous to suffering, ambitious of rank, scornful of demeaning labor, and almost invariably hard up . . . But when they had come to the Indies these adventurers were caught in the net of their own incompetence and brought down with them the whole of the native population. The island people, in their turn, perished because their primitive economy could not support the burden of the harsh and wasteful parasite class which had been imposed upon them.[45]

Meanwhile, the "protector of all the Indians" was away from America, ruminating about his failure to implement a viable alternative for the governance of the Caribbean islands. After Cisneros's refusal to hear him out, Las Casas found himself at loose ends, but he soon encountered a new project to occupy his full attention for nearly three years. This plan was born out of a request by Pedro de Córdoba, the Dominican prior in Española, to obtain a strip of land in *Tierra Firme* (the mainland) where the missionaries could catechize the Indians free from the meddling of Spanish colonists. Las Casas saw this as an opportunity to demonstrate in practice what he had postulated in his memorial, that is, to create an outpost where the Indians could be protected while being converted to Christianity at the same time that their labor could be used in a meaningful way that would not spell their destruction.

The experience he had gained after the Jeronymite debacle had begun to transform him from naïve colonist cum reformer into a skilllful courtier ready to embark on the arduous project of demonstrating his entrepreneurial capacity and the validity of his postulates for the peaceful usufruct of the New World, while protecting the natives from extinction.

Utopia in Tierra Firme

The Dominican reformers had turned their eyes to the mainland, seeking refuge in an attempt to stop, or even slow down, the extermination of natives in the islands. As early as 1513, Pedro de Córdoba and the Dominicans had viewed with increasing interest the possibilities of transferring their missionary labor to the Tierra Firme region, which despite its potential riches boasted a largely untouched Indian population.[46] The Dominican prior had originally obtained from King Ferdinand the license to begin his missionary labor on the coast of Paria (present-day Venezuela). One of the stipulations of the license forbade other Spaniards from going to the area assigned to the missionaries. The unusually ambitious and wide-ranging project of conversion and colonization had all the characteristics of a grand utopian scheme conceived by Pedro de Córdoba, who was "the first among the missionaries in the Indies to nurture the ideal of an exclusively Indian society converted to Catholicism with a minimum of Spanish colonization, under the nominal sovereignty of the King of Spain and paternalistically administered by the mendicant missionaries, provided, for that purpose, of ample and extraordinary prerogatives granted by the Pontiff."[47]

After the original concession made by Ferdinand, the missionaries experienced great difficulty in restraining Spanish adventurers from carrying out their acts of pillage and slave hunting in the area specified by the king's royal cédula. While he was in Spain—awaiting an audience with the newly anointed king, Charles I[48]—Las Casas received a letter from the Dominican prior informing him of the latest raids off the coast of Trinidad and the slaughter of a large number of Indians. In the same letter Fray Pedro asked the cleric to request from the king an additional one hundred leagues of mainland territory, including Chiribichí and Cumaná, where the Dominicans and Franciscans, respectively, had set up their missions on the mainland. If that were not possible, the Dominican prior suggested that he would be satisfied with only ten leagues, and if that was not possible, then he asked to see if they could get the Alonso islets, located ten to twenty leagues offshore. The land or the islets would serve as a sanctuary for natives escaping from the persecution of raiders and the mistreatment of the encomenderos in the Caribbean. If none of this were possible, the letter continued, Fray Pedro was ready to remove all missionaries from the mainland altogether and retreat to Española. The possibility of abandoning the Indians of the mainland without the spiritual succor of the Catholic missionaries disturbed Las Casas immensely and he hastened to comply with Córdoba's request.[49]

The cleric, who by this time had become acquainted with the Flemish counselors of the king, in particular the chancellor Jean le Sauvage, whose sympathy he enjoyed, dutifully presented his request to have one hundred leagues of mainland assigned to the missionaries. Despite the increasing support at court, he met with the stubborn, and not insignificant, resistance of Bishop Rodríguez de Fonseca, who reputedly advised the king not to give up the hundred leagues to the missionaries. He claimed that the men of the cloth did not intend to make a profitable use of them and would deprive the king of the earning potential that such an amount of land represented.[50]

Las Casas, who was not easily dissuaded, submitted another proposal containing even more ambitious suggestions than the original request of one hundred leagues. Although his original petition for the land request in Tierra Firme was rejected and his influence at court was severely diminished with the sudden death of Jean de Sauvage, he nevertheless gained a measure of success with a suggestion for the peaceful colonization of the mainland with Castilian farmers.[51] In his petition, he claimed that the farmers would provide a counterbalance to the encomenderos by working the land without resorting to the use of forced native labor. His plan for recruiting three thousands farmers to colonize the Indies peacefully was approved in September of 1518. As part of the plan, he was granted a salary to implement the project and the opportunity to hire assistants to help him with the recruitment of future colonizers.[52]

As part of the design to create a sanctuary for the Indians—as suggested by Córdoba—Las Casas requested one thousand leagues of land. This proposal, like his previous list of remedies, emphasized the economic advantages to the crown if it were to implement the plan in accordance with his suggestions.[53] It also called for building fortresses every hundred miles to be populated by Christians under the command of a captain.[54] This specific proposal was not much different from the one suggested by John Major, the Scottish Dominican who had neither a practical nor a personal interest in the Indies but had nevertheless emerged in the early sixteenth century as one of the most vocal defenders of Spanish imperialism.[55]

Like Las Casas's previous project of theocratic rule in Santo Domingo, the plan for peasant colonization also met with failure despite the support he received from the king and his Flemish advisors. Accosted at every turn by the plotting of Rodríguez de Fonseca and Francisco de los Cobos, as well as the resistance of the Spanish grandees whose peasants he was trying to recruit, Las Casas was unable to implement the most important utopian provision of his plan,

> the enterprise of taking to the Indies, instead of rough military men, avaricious miners or incorrigible merchants—who would kill, work to death or sell the Indians—peaceful peasants who would civilize them teaching them to live in the context of that rural economy—today known as petite bourgeois—of which Casas was so fond, represented for him a tremendous failure, even greater, but not as spectacular as his enterprise of mixed colonization in Cumaná.[56]

Las Casas's efforts were further hampered by the fact that the assistants recommended and assigned to him by Rodríguez de Fonseca and Cobos, then running the *Casa de Contratación* (House of Trade), seriously undermined his efforts.[57] By the time they disembarked in Santo Domingo, the prospective peaceful colonizers were in such straits that upon his arrival in February of 1521, the cleric was forced to ask the crown for wine and flour to help them survive. By the time the provisions arrived, the aspiring colonists had scattered to pursue their own designs, pillaging and enslaving Indians, while others left for unknown destinations in search of chimerical visions of the promised land.[58]

Undaunted by the difficulties he encountered, La Casas left Santo Domingo for Tierra Firme on July 30, 1521. In Cumaná, Franciscan missionaries from the French region of Picardy received him warmly, but the soldiers who were supposed to be placed under his orders greeted him with hostility. Soon after his arrival, some of the soldiers left him to go to the island of Cubaguá, off the coast of Paria, where they continued conducting slave-hunting raids in the region of Cumaná, creating a hostile environment among the natives. Faced with a mounting crisis and a rapidly deteriorating situation, Las Casas decided to travel to Española to file his grievances. After his ship was blown off course, he arrived there early the next year, 1522, only to find out that in his absence the settlement at Cumaná had been attacked and destroyed. The abuses of the slave hunters had outraged the natives, who burned the settlement and killed six people, among them the cleric's second-in-command, a Franciscan, a soldier, and their Indian interpreter.[59] In a few short days, Las Casas's project for Tierra Firme, which had taken the better part of the last three years of his life to build, had been thoroughly demolished and another of his utopian dreams had crumbled.

The failure of Las Casas's Cumaná project could have been predicted almost from the time of its formulation. At first there had been the opposition of influential figures at court who sabotaged the project from the very beginning. Another significant factor was the distraction of the Spanish government with the rebellion of the *comuneros* in Spain and the inability of the Casa de Contratación to produce the money necessary for the venture precisely because of the comunero conflict. Conscious of the difficulty of obtaining money from the crown, Las Casas had devised a complex fund-raising plan which called for establishing a society formed by fifty partners, each contributing as his monetary share the not inconsiderable amount of two hundred ducats. If it had materialized, this would have provided the enterprise with enough money to buy the food and the beads and trinkets necessary to attract the Indians.[60]

The economic plan prepared by the enterprising priest specified that the partners, among other things, would participate in the pacification of the Indian population and the colonization of the coast of Paria, which the cleric had secured from the crown.[61] It also guaranteed the king the payment of rent, in appreciation for the *capitulación* granting them the land, the founding of Christian towns, the discovery of new territory, and the conversion of the natives who would, then, become tribute-paying subjects.[62]

In exchange for the demands placed on the participants in the venture, their privileges included the running of the fortresses erected to protect their colonizing endeavors. They were guaranteed the exclusive prerogative of occupying the positions of *regidores, alguaciles, procuradores,* and *alcaldes* in the colonized territories. Furthermore, they were granted the right to establish their residences in the cities founded, giving their factors the privilege of residing there in the absence of the titular holder. They were also granted the privilege of discovering and populating any undiscovered territories in the Atlantic or Pacific oceans for a period of ten years from the date of the signing of the capitulación.[63]

Another privilege, not to be overlooked, was the incorporation of each of the partners into a religious-lay brotherhood, modeled after the traditional orders of Santiago and Calatrava, granting each member knighthood in the order of the Golden Spur, a hereditary distinction which could be passed on to their progeny.[64] The Cumaná project also included innumerable other privileges for the colonists, but given the circumstances under which the colonizing project got underway, the possibilities of success diminished almost daily as the time to implement them drew near, and anyone less stubborn and with something less to prove than Las Casas would have renounced the undertaking.

In addition to the opposition of the royal counselors to his projects of peaceful colonization, there were obstacles almost impossible to overcome, among them the complexity of managing the enterprise as a business venture. Even if the cleric's business experience before his conversion in 1514 is taken into consideration, the task that he was committed to undertake in Cumaná posed incalculable risks, which he was unable to predict or manage at the time.[65]

Las Casas's final plan was, essentially, a capitalist primer for the exploitation of Tierra Firme with little consideration given to the Indians as complementary participants in the venture. Despite his constant denunciation of Spanish enslaving practices and abuses, the friar himself had agreed to allow the enslaving of mainland Indians by order of the members of the *consulta* of Santo Domingo in exchange for obtaining their support to make his way to Paria.[66] Manuel Giménez Fernández, a most fervent admirer and biographer, captured the contradiction between these two aspects of Las Casas, the Spanish entrepreneur struggling with the cleric-reformer, when he focused on the process of self-criticism in which Las Casas engaged after the debacle at Cumaná:

> Although he absolved himself of responsibility for the death of the men who fell at Cumaná; he reproached himself harshly because in his desire to prove to his adversaries (Fonseca, Cobos, Oviedo) that he was right, he had committed the grave imprudence of persisting in his enterprise after its serious initial failures and, above all, had compromised himself by accepting the slave-hunting expedition designs of his associates, the oligarchs of Española.[67]

The enterprise like so many of his earlier undertakings had been predicated on the possibilities of material gain, a purely profitable venture for the crown and the other participants. The added benefit, for the natives, was that this time the conquest of the territory and its inhabitants would be carried out in a very different, almost gentle, manner from the one to which the colonists had been accustomed. In a contract signed with Diego Columbus, to obtain his support to build the military fortresses required, Las Casas included a plan to attract the Indians with "conversations, contracts and friendship," and while no Indian would be subject to being placed in encomiendas, the majority, if not all, of the Indians would still have to pay tribute.[68] It is worth mentioning that a great deal of Las Casas's plan for peaceful colonization implied the uneven exchange of beads, *rescates,* and other Castilian trinkets to obtain the loyalty of the Indians and to

> trade for gold and silver and pearls and precious stones, [and in each fortress have a few members of the religious orders that would be in charge of preaching the Gospel] this way it would be possible to obtain as much gold and things of value as the Indians have [and] to earn their love and friendship, having earned their goodwill, in due time build fortresses inland making it possible to uncover their secrets and with the industry and diligence of the missionaries the people could be progressively converted and begin confirming the truth of the Spaniards' friendship and in turn teach them about the kindness and the justice of the king so they could be easily won over and of their own free will become his subjects granting him, with full awareness of it, their obedience.[69]

In proposing this plan, Las Casas was not only emulating Major but he was adding uniquely refined modifications to a plan for the peaceful but exploitative conversion of the natives. The difference resided in the form but not in the essence of the nature of an invasive act that implied a total disregard for the cultural and territorial integrity of the natives.

Henry Wagner has suggested that "anyone reading [Las Casas's proposal] without a knowledge of his character might imagine he was putting up a money making scheme to the King; apparently after the rejection of the Dominican request he had learned that something of the sort was necessary."[70] Although there seems to be some validity to the argument that many aspects of the cleric's plan answered to strategic and tactical needs, the fact remains that the Indians were ultimately left unprotected, and that the proposal was little more than a "money making scheme" to ingratiate Las Casas with the powerful emperor.

In the process of implementing his plan for the peaceful colonization of the coast of Paria, Las Casas relied on a select list of statutes, largely drawn from his memorial to Cisneros, to protect the Indians. But as had been the case with the Laws of Burgos and other earlier reformist efforts obtained through the juridico-political system of Spain, he was unable to put in place a mechanism to implement the statutes that he had formulated once the king had agreed. After his efforts at Paria met with failure, he once again was forced to face the daunting task of reevaluating his approach to the question of the peaceful colonization of the Americas.

Second Conversion: Imperial Faith and the "Only Way"

The failure of the Cumaná project had a most profound impact on Las Casas. It plunged him into depression and a deep spiritual crisis, much like the one he had suffered at the time of his conversion from cleric-encomendero to reformer and protector of the Indians eight years earlier. He questioned his own moral integrity and wondered if perhaps the catastrophic events at Cumaná were God's punishment for compromising his principles. Las Casas himself provides the details of the magnitude of his agonizing despair after the events of Cumaná, his conversion, and his subsequent approximation to the Dominicans. Like his first conversion, the second one is also rich in dramatic and religious significance. As he tells the story, on his way to Santo Domingo he fell asleep and when he awakened overheard a conversation between two travelers about how "the Indians of the Pearl Coast had killed the cleric Bartolomé de Las Casas and his whole family."[71] While his companions argued that that was not the case,

> the cleric awoke as if from an abyss and having understood the news, he did not know whether to believe it, nor what to say . . . he began to believe and to fear that all he had worked for he had lost, and later, when he knew more of these things, he believed that it had been a Divine judgment aimed at punishing and afflicting him for joining in partnership with those he knew would not help him, neither out of dedication, nor love of God, to save the souls that were perishing in that province, but only out of avarice to become rich. It seemed that he had offended God by soiling the purity of that most spiritual end, only intended for God, which was for him to go to help the religious and with them illuminate those people with the preaching of the Christian Faith and Doctrine; [he had soiled it] with the garbage and impurity of such earthly human, and even inhuman means used, which were so antithetical to those used by Christ.[72]

Unsure of himself, and lacking a clear course of action, he retreated to the Dominican monastery in Santo Domingo. This represented no great effort, since he had been traditionally close to the Dominicans, in particular to the Montesinos brothers and the late prior Pedro de Córdoba. They had provided him with the connections to gain access at court and they had supported him in word and deed from the time of his first conversion and his early battles for reforms in Española to his proposal for the peaceful colonization of Tierra Firme.[73] Thus, it was almost natural for him to seek refuge among his only friends at a time of acute spiritual crisis.

Joining the Dominican order, like his first "conversion," was not a hurried affair. Las Casas carefully weighed the advantages and disadvantages of such a move. He considered the restrictions on his freedom of movement. As a member of the secular clergy in Española, he had no immediate superior to whom he had to answer, but this was not the case in the order. On the other hand, the Dominicans could lend the weight and the influence associated with an established religious order to his claims in favor of reforms for the New World.

After Cumaná, he felt vulnerable and alone. He had written the king and had received no answer, but the Dominicans had been there to offer their support. Ironically, it was the controversial derider of Indians, Fray Domingo de Betanzos, who in 1534 had written "a shocking defamation of the Indians, declaring them incapable of receiving the faith . . . and saying that God had condemned the Indians to extinction for their bestial sins—and all laws to protect them were pointless and all efforts to convert them were useless!" who argued eloquently with the cleric and convinced him to join the order.[74] In attempting to convince Las Casas, Betanzos argued that if God had wanted the successful completion of Las Casas's scheme for Tierra Firme, the venture would have been a success, but it had failed, indicating God's lack of support for such an enterprise. When Las Casas argued that he was expecting an answer from the king, Betanzos countered: "Tell me dear Father, if you die in the meantime, who will receive the king's orders or his letters?"[75] The conversation, according to Las Casas's account, moved him so deeply that he considered himself dead to the world and joined the order by the end of 1522.[76]

Becoming a member of the Order of Preachers marked the beginning of a new process for Las Casas, who in a few short years had transformed from colonist and reformer into a theologian-jurist-activist.[77] The sophistication in academic, legal, and political matters that he obtained through experience and the rigorous academic discipline of the order provided him with the tools to develop a solid theoretical base to confront and influence the authorities in the motherland about the need to protect the Indians. This opportunity, paired with his direct exposure to some of the most brilliant juridical minds of his time, Palacios Rubios, in Madrid and Valladolid in 1516 and 1517, the royal preachers in Barcelona in 1518, and later his contact with the faculty of Salamanca in 1542, lent greater authority and weight to his voice, despite the controversy concerning the extent of his formal education.[78]

His early years as a Dominican were outwardly uneventful; he spent his time as a novice and his early years as a friar in much the same manner as other new members of the order. The importance of that apprenticeship resides in the fact that, as a new recruit, he was forced to dedicate inordinate amounts of time to the study of the different subjects to be learned by all initiates.[79] His incorporation into the Order of Preachers afforded Las Casas a unique opportunity to become acquainted with the finer aspects of theology and scholastic philosophy, which had been absent in his education. In 1527, he was commissioned to help build a convent at La Plata, on the northern coast of Española, and to serve as prior. Although Las Casas had withdrawn from the world temporarily, he remained aware of the events taking place outside the convent. He knew of the publication in Toledo of *Sumario de la general y natural historia de las Indias*, by his old adversary Gonzalo Fernández de Oviedo. It was the publication of this treatise, with Oviedo's depiction of the Indians as less than human beings, which prompted Las Casas to begin writing his *Historia de las Indias* as a refutation of his compatriot's work. The *Historia* is an ethnographic and natural history of the newly encountered continent, from the period before the arrival of the Europeans to its emergence as a "New World," a colonized dependency in the aftermath of the Spanish conquest. In the words of Lewis Hanke, who is familiar with almost the entirety of Las Casas's literary output, this "detailed narration of the discovery, exploration and colonization of the New World by Spain until 1520 was the most lasting intellectual effort made by Las Casas during his whole life."[80]

During the time Las Casas spent in seclusion, his name often came up in the conversations of the New World's most influential religious personages. Julián Garcés and Juan de Zumárraga, bishops of Tlaxcala and Mexico respectively, wrote to one of the king's counselors in 1529 requesting ecclesiastical reformers for New Spain; Las Casas's name appeared as one of the friars they most recommended, alongside the likes of Antonio Montesinos and Tomás de Berlanga.[81] Although Las Casas was temporarily gone, he was not forgotten, nor did he seem to have forgotten his title as *protector de los indios*, which caused him to break his self-imposed silence with a letter to the Council of the Indies in 1531 to protest the abandonment of the Indians by the crown and their mistreatment by the colonists.

The long, rambling letter began by asking for divine illumination for the souls of those in charge of the affairs of the Indies. It then went on to challenge the crown's neglect of its overseas possessions. This neglect of Indians in the New World was, the letter asserted, an affront to the Christian community the world over, but it could be easily remedied if Christian charity became the norm and the crown fulfilled its duty to Christianize the natives.[82] The letter was a clear reiteration of Las Casas's deep-seated belief in the principle of assimilation by conversion. Echoing his earlier writings, such as the memorials of grievances presented to Cisneros years earlier, Las Casas was convinced of the messianic role of the Spanish religious working in the New World. Although he consistently insisted on the peaceful conversion of the natives, not once did he question the fact that the natives, in exchange for having their physical integrity respected, were forced to renounce their gods and religious practices in favor of the more "benevolent" and acceptable Christian deity. Underlying Las Casas's writings is an inescapable design for the unlimited expansion of an imperial Christian church voraciously swallowing and assimilating all other cultures in its own terms.

Typical of the time, his call for the conversion of the natives was largely supported by provisions from the Alexandrian bulls pertaining to Spain's role in the evangelization of the natives, which, in a show of newly found erudition, he quoted extensively. The letter to the council represented only one aspect of the transformation of Las Casas. His style had become more baroque and pedantic than before, hence reading his letter was almost a difficult chore, more so than with many of his other writings. The letter also inaugurated a new period in his mode of argumentation; from this time forward, his arguments were invariably backed by documentary evidence and his denunciations acquired a more apocalyptic tone, as if becoming a member of a religious order had conferred on him a higher level of righteousness. As Marcel Bataillon writes, "Las Casas never felt so efficacious, so supported by God, as when he made kings and their ministers hear the truth about the Indies."[83]

The letter to the council also reached new heights in Las Casas's denunciation of Spanish atrocities in the New World. Alongside the figures of speech and metaphors, there were statistical ciphers, or what seemed to pass for statistics, to make his arguments more forceful:

It had been enough for these miserable people to go to hell with their lack of belief [in Christianity], alone with the little they had, without having to have their saviors, our Christians, driven solely by cupidity, take them out of this world in a span of a few days, and send them into darkness and endless lamentations where the presence of their miserable companions will not alleviate their suffering; because burning together will not make the burning less atrocious . . . testimony of this [are the] two million dead souls from the surrounding area (a million and one hundred thousand in this island alone) burned alive, torn by fierce dogs, knifed, sparing neither the old nor the young, neither pregnant [women] nor women who had just given birth, sometimes choosing the fat ones to kill them and use the fat (because it is said that it is good to heal the sores of the killers). . . . The outcries of so much spilled human blood rise to Heaven. The earth can no longer suffer to be soaked with the blood of men. The angels of peace, and even God himself, I believe, are crying.[84]

The tone and the text of the letter became the foundation upon which the friar built his treatise *Brevísima relación de la destruición de las Indias*, which he prepared for the king almost a decade later.[85] To his damning of the Spanish colonists, Las Casas added his criticism of the court for granting the German bankers of the house of Welser license to exploit a region of Tierra Firme.[86] In the letter, in a clear show of nationalist pride, he implied that the Germans were even more likely to steal from the land and the king and to decimate the native population than the Spanish. As he had done previously, Las Casas posed a remedy for the grievous situation that he described, albeit one not much different from his plan for Cumaná. He called for the erection of fortified towns throughout the territory. To lure the king and his officers into accepting his proposal, he referred to the millions of Indians who could pay tribute to the king after their peaceful colonization and catechization: "Truly, gentlemen, I can feel and see, as if it had already taken place, such plentiful weights of gold going to His Majesty, every year, like the barrels of sugar or cane . . . we are used to seeing on the ships; and I believe it is very clear, considering the infinite number of these people and their certain conversion, and the plenitude of precious things in this land."[87]

Unlike his earlier proposal, where the income of the king depended on the success of the Spanish colonists, this time he dangled in front of the king the possibility of even greater rewards than before in the form of Indian tribute. In this case, there was the certainty that the tribute from the natives would be sure to go to the king because it was obtained by religious men rather than the traditional tax collectors who were guilty of stealing from the crown and were distrusted by the Indians. The settlements would have large representations of members of the orders of Santo Domingo or San Francisco commanded and administered by a bishop chosen from one of the orders. The proposal was only slightly different from the one Las Casas had prepared for Española, prompting Cisneros to send the Jeronymite fathers. Henry Wagner, in his biography of Las Casas, suggests that, as in the case of Española, the friar left open the possibility of having himself appointed to the job of administrator.[88]

Despite his profession of faith with the Dominicans, Las Casas had not abandoned his desire to demonstrate the feasibility of his materialist schemes in association with his plans for peaceful colonization. The fact that the 1531 scheme called for the building of fortresses, a proposal repeated in his memorial of remedies in 1542, as a solution to his grievances, clearly indicates the presence of an unresolved contradiction in Las Casas's psyche. This was the inability to resolve the clash between his simultaneous desire to foment the profitable exploration and exploitation of the American possessions against the preservation of the natives from the depredations of the explorers and colonists. It was only after his return to Spain in 1547, and after his stormy tour of duty as bishop of Chiapa, that he abandoned his insistence on this type of capitalist scheme. According to Marcel Bataillon: "[N]ever again did he advance ingenious constructions in which temporal and spiritual interests supported each other; he now understood the fragility of such a house of cards."[89]

Immediately after his reinsertion into the Spanish court orbit, following his letter to the council, Las Casas began work on a primer for the peaceful conversion of the Indians. This first full-length book of Las Casas, originally written in Latin, *De unico vocationis modo omnium gentium ad veram religionem*, was appropriately called in Spanish *Del único modo de atraer a todos los pueblos a la verdadera religión* (The Only Way to Draw All People to a Living Faith).[90] Despite the author's display of erudition, the primer is stylistically more reminiscent of his earlier tracts than the letter addressed to the Council of the Indies, but its abundance of references to biblical, patristic, and ancient philosophical sources makes it a rather difficult work for the average member of the clergy to read, understand, or implement.

It is also difficult to establish precisely when it was written, a task further complicated by the fact that only chapters 5, 6, and 7 of the original book survive.[91] The book, which together with *Historia de las Indias* and the

Apologética historia is considered one of Las Casas's three major works, was another denunciation of the cruel and tyrannical wars waged against the Indians. It called on the faithful to wipe out the iniquity of unlawful conversion and expropriation of the natives by demanding the restitution of their gold, silver, and the lands taken away from them. At the same time, it was an unapologetic reaffirmation that salvation, and ultimately assimilation, was only possible through the purifying grace of Christianity. As the title indicates, from Las Casas's perspective there was only one way to spread the Gospel and the "true" faith:

> *One way, One way only, of teaching a living faith, to everyone, everywhere, always, was set by Divine Providence:* the way that wins the mind with reasons, that wins the will with gentleness, with invitation. It has to fit all people on earth, no distinction made for sect, for error, even for evil.[92]

The infallibility of Christianity as the only viable and friendly way to lure the unconverted to the true faith is reiterated throughout the thirty-six sections of chapter 5.[93] Once he establishes that the only way of bringing the faith to the natives is through conversion, Las Casas proceeds to illustrate what constitutes a violation of the most elementary principles of evangelization, the unleashing of war:

> No Christian pagan in his right mind, especially a pagan prince would surrender to political control by a Christian people or a Christian prince.
>
> There would have to be war. . .
>
> War like a tornado, like a tidal wave of evils, runs amok destroying everything, whole cities, whole regions. War paves the way for atrocities, it causes bitter hatreds, it makes people boldly vicious . . . People lose their souls in war, they lose their lives and their livelihood.[94]

By applying universal moral principles, drawn from his European perspective, to the specific case of America and condemning all those who advocated forceful conversion, Las Casas managed to indict all Spanish practices of conquest. He concluded his work by reaffirming the belief that war was contrary to human and divine law and that any conversions made by means other than friendly persuasion were invalid.

Del único modo was the result of a growing spirituality Las Casas had been experiencing over a long period, from the moment of his early failures with Cisneros to his acceptance into the Dominican order. His withdrawal from the world, his "buried" time, had contributed to hone his verbal skills to express his opposition to the armed conquest of the New World and his advocacy of the peaceful activity of religious missionaries.[95]

Despite his vehemence in denouncing his fellow Spanish colonizers, Las Casas, as on previous occasions, seemed unable to comprehend that his goodwill and wishful thinking notwithstanding, the crown was not about to desist from its imperialist designs for America. While the Dominican was able to comprehend, through personal experience and observation, the harmful effects of forceful conquest on the inhabitants and the land, he remained incapable of grasping the contradictions implicit in the ecclesiastical imperialism responsible for the spiritual conquest of the natives. This is not surprising given his messianic belief in being one of the chosen singled out by God to carry out his providential work.[96] At the same time, his own "providentialism" did not allow him to understand how the imposition of an alien faith was contributing to the cultural genocide of the very people he claimed to be trying to protect from physical extinction.

In addition to writing innumerable memorials, his *Historia de las Indias*, and his primer for conversion, the decade of the 1530s was a time of unusual activity for the friar. During this period, by his own account and that of his sworn enemy Fernández de Oviedo, he acted as a mediator for negotiating a peace with the rebellious cacique Enrique (Enriquillo) in Española.[97]

His intervention in the pacification of Enriquillo reveals a great deal about Las Casas's worldview, his self-absorption concerning his role as a historical protagonist, and his ambivalently complex relationship with the American natives and their aspirations. Chief Enriquillo had been brought up and educated in the Franciscan monastery of Verapaz in Española, where he learned to speak, read, and write Spanish. On reaching the proper age, he returned to his native province, Baoruco, married, and settled there. At this point, the Spanish encomendero for whom he worked abused the cacique's wife sexually and stole the cacique's mare. Unable to gain satisfaction from the audiencia, which kept shuffling him back and forth between unsympathetic officials, Enriquillo sought refuge in the mountains with a few followers and refused to rejoin his Spanish master. Incensed by the Indians' attitude, the encomendero journeyed to the Enriquillo's refuge to demand his surrender, and in the confrontation the Indians killed two Spaniards and routed the rest.[98]

Enriquillo's actions prompted instant reprisals by the Spanish authorities and increased resistance by the rebels, who by that time numbered nearly three hundred people, including runaway African slaves and other natives. For more than thirteen years, the Indian chieftain and his irregular army waged a guerrilla war that not only kept the Spanish authorities in check but also caused them to spend considerable sums of money trying to repress the cacique and his followers. Even the Council of the Indies was forced to intervene to quell the unrest by sending a detachment of two hundred men to capture Enriquillo.[99] Despite the inability of the Spanish troops to operate in hostile terrain and under the duress of an irregular war, Enriquillo seems to have succumbed to the exhaustion of all those years of struggle, finally agreeing to sign a peace treaty with Captain Francisco de Barrionuevo in August of 1533. The peace accord extended a full pardon to the rebel as well as the title of *don*, which he used from then until his death a year later.

From all indications, Las Casas contacted Don Enrique at about the time of the signing of the peace accord with Barrionuevo.[100] According to his own testimony, provided in a letter to the council, he ventured into the cacique's stronghold to convince him of the importance of coming into town to be greeted by the Spanish residents:

> I went—with only the grace of God and a companion friar, provided to me by the Order—to Baoruco, and reassured Don Enrique and confirmed him in the service of the Emperor our lord. I was with him a month, and confessed him and his wife and all his captains, and relieved them all of their very just fears. I would not leave from there, until I took him with me to the town of Azúa, where he was embraced by the citizenry who made merry [with] them. . . And in truth, noble sirs, had the Dominican Order not sent me, to serve God and his Majesty, and had I not gone there, it might be a hundred years before Don Enrique would have been seen outside the impregnable peaks and highlands where he was born and possesses his patrimony.[101]

Fray Bartolomé's high level of satisfaction with his role was unmistakable, especially since Don Enrique seemed to have adhered fully to the terms of the peace treaty. Nevertheless, the chronicler's portrait of the rebel sanitizes the cacique's image and turns him into an idealized model of goodness and Christian kindness. Even at the most crucial points of the struggle, the rebel leader, according to Las Casas, instructed his forces not to kill the Spaniards but to take their weapons and treat them gently.[102] This attitude flies in the face of reality and can only be explained by Las Casas's belief in the Indians' childlike docility. Insisting on his role of peacemaker, the Dominican claimed that if he had been given the opportunity earlier, the island would have been pacified for many years and "would have been safe through my own doing, and Don Enrique would have been at peace with the other inhabitants."[103]

Las Casas's letter to the council was written in the wake of charges that he had refused last rites to a Santo Domingo encomendero unless he agreed to renounce his encomienda and to distribute his wealth among the Indians. From this perspective the friar's participation in the pacification of Enriquillo was not entirely the result of altruistic motives but a serendipitous and opportune event that served to enhance the preacher's accomplishments at a time when his activities were being severely questioned by the authorities.

The Dominican friar and his numerous admirers have only taken into account the most romantically alluring and superficial aspects of the historical events surrounding Enriquillo's uprising. Las Casas, like his biographers and hagiographers, seems to pay little attention to Don Enrique's death only a year after the meeting in Azúa. They fail to mention that the chieftain had died like a caged bird deprived of freedom. After thirteen years of struggle, the tangible gains made by the rebels did not extend beyond the honorific title for the cacique and the symbolic distribution of bread among the Indians of the island, revealing the futility of the peace treaty signed by Don Enrique, particularly since the rebellion gained little more than lip service about the authorities' willingness to respect the rights of the natives and slaves. From the perspective of Las Casas and his followers, Enriquillo became more useful as a symbol after his death than he had been during his life as rebel leader. The Dominican and his admirers celebrated him as a demonstrable example of the application of the friar's theories about the value of peaceful catechization. At the same time, the friar's detractors, particularly Oviedo, attempted to diminish the significance of Las Casas's actions. They accused him of serving only his own ends and not those of the rebel leader. In one his most recent attacks against the friar, the Spanish academician Ramón Menéndez Pidal not only denies the validity of any of Las Casas's claims in the affair but anoints Enriquillo as an earlier-day Inca Garcilaso de la Vega acting as a bridge between two colliding worlds:

With all the moderation and generosity possible in a war, [Enriquillo] fights a powerful state for thirteen years and wins, having his individual rights recognized; his is an splendid triumph, seeing himself recognized and invited to make peace by the great Emperor Charles V. He has no inclination for the wild life. He does not hate the society in whose midst the injustices that injured him were committed; he admires the powerful state's organization and professes that State's divine religion. Having vindicated his individual honor, he does not feel a partial Indian nationalism, but like the Inca Garcilaso, he foresees that the two races must form a historical unity, and accepts with stoic or resigned conformity the consequences of the cultural inferiority of the Indians, thus responding to his Franciscan education, supports the encomienda and he feels satisfied cooperating in the preservation of this institution.[104]

Menéndez Pidal, like Las Casas before him, draws his own conclusions about Enriquillo's actions to serve his own ends while attacking the credibility of the Dominican, exalting the virtues of the Spanish conquest, and reaffirming Spain's cultural ascendancy over the Indians. Although the friar had a unique opportunity to use Enriquillo's uprising to advance indigenous claims, he failed to do so. He was overcome by his preoccupation with his own role as protagonist in the event, trying to validate his own conversion theories and exalting his own accomplishments. Thus, instead of using this event to advance indigenous causes, he turned it into an act of self-promotion.

Las Casas objectified Enriquillo, just as he did other indigenous people. The chief emerged as a noble savage forced by circumstances to kill Spaniards, a valiant but desperate individual who regretfully must take up arms out of a sense of self-preservation. The Dominican, like his compatriots, did not deviate from the prevailing generalizations about the nature of the natives, a view that made all natives essentially interchangeable. From this perspective, Enriquillo was no different from Tamayo or Ciguayo or any of the other native rebels. Since Las Casas played no part in their pacification, it was as if the others had not existed, and their resistance became anecdotal, for they were only relevant as long as they could be linked to Enriquillo and by extension to Las Casas.[105] In the friar's narrative, Enriquillo's heroic challenge to Spanish authority is secondary to his own accomplishments, for Las Casas seemed more concerned with capturing his own heroic deeds and the effect that his actions could have in his relationship with the crown than he was with presenting Enriquillo's action as a viable form of resistive action against the atrocities that he so decried and that he allegedly was working so hard to correct.

This tendency of Las Casas to emphasize and highlight his own role as main protagonist, not just in the pacification of Enriquillo but also in a multitude of other significant events of the colonization of the Antilles and the mainland, is reminiscent of the claims of some of his contemporaries. His narration of events brings to mind Bernal Diaz's chronicle of the conquest of New Spain, where the author figures so prominently in all significant events in the conquering march. This ubiquity so exasperated H. R. Wagner that it led him to proclaim that in the case of Díaz "it was always I, I. One cannot imagine how Cortés could have conquered [Mexico] without Díaz by his side to advise him and to fight for him."[106] By extension, it is difficult to imagine that there would have been any natives left in America if it had not been for Las Casas's ubiquitous intervention. His exaltation of himself as protagonist and his constant self-promotion amply support Anthony Pagden's claim that "no historian of America is so tirelessly self-referential [as Las Casas]."[107]

One of the greatest ironies concerning Las Casas's reputation is that it is largely built around his work on behalf of the Indians, but during his long cumulative stay in America, roughly forty years, he rarely had direct contact with them. From all available information, the most prolonged contact he might have had with natives was when he participated in the conquest of Cuba as chaplain for Pánfilo de Narváez's invading army in 1513. A second occasion was when he joined the Order of Preachers and as part of his duties was expected to preach to the Indians, after meals on Sundays and religious holidays.[108] Outside of these two instances, the third most prolonged contact he had with the natives took place in Central America, precisely in Nicaragua and in Tuzulutlán, in the years 1536–38. It appears that one of the difficulties of establishing an ongoing dialogical relationship with the Indians was Las Casas's ignorance of native languages and the natives' ignorance of Spanish. This forced Las Casas to rely almost exclusively on the services of interpreters to communicate with the indigenous people.[109] Nevertheless, despite this shortcoming, he accomplished some measure of success in his indoctrinating labors in Central America, as, for example, when he converted a group of native Nicaraguans in a relatively short period of time: "The fruit of [our proselytizing] labor has been so great, in the course of the two months we have been here, that the residents of this town of Granada, where we are preaching at present, are amazed. This causes great confusion among those who so unjustly maintain that these nations want nothing to do with God's teachings."[110]

Despite basking in the success of the catechization of natives in Nicaragua, and despite, or perhaps because of, his perceived success in the Enriquillo affair in Española, Bartolomé de Las Casas never hid his desire to be at the center of power in the motherland, the familiar surroundings of the Spanish court, instead of being in America. In several of his letters in the 1530s he expressed his profound longing to be in court to plead the cause of the Indians as he had done before. However, his wish was not fulfilled until 1540, when after a stormy stay in Central America he finally left for Spain. His return to the European continent took place after a short but relatively successful stint in the area of Tuzulutlán, where he demonstrated the viability of some of his tenets for the peaceful catechization of the natives.

His stay in Nicaragua had come about quite by accident after the ship in which he was sailing to Peru was becalmed for two and a half months, an eternity, before he was finally able to reach Nicaragua in a barge with three other monks in mid-1535.[111] Once ashore, he proceeded to denounce from the pulpit the colonizing expeditions organized by Governor Rodrigo de Contreras. As part of his campaign against the abuses of the colonists, Las Casas threatened to deny absolution to any of the participants in what amounted to enslaving expeditions.[112] In the *información* (report) prepared by the governor against Las Casas, he claimed that it had never been his intention to carry out enslaving expeditions. He stated that all along he had intended to "peacefully, attract the naturals of the province they were about to explore, and to make sure they were not hurt or harmed." The governor also explained that he had asked Las Casas to accompany the expedition, but the Dominican had demanded to go with fifty men and without a captain to carry out the peaceful settlement of the natives. After his request was denied, Las Casas launched into a public attack on the colonizers and "our Lord God and His Majesty, which was enough to unhinge the people," setting them against the friar.[113]

In less than a year in Nicaragua, Las Casas had become persona non grata among the authorities and the colonizers, and because of the información, he was forced to leave the territory. Before leaving, he informed the king of the events taking place, and as a result, "on July 7, 1536, the King ordered a two-year suspension of the Contreras expedition to allow Las Casas an opportunity to achieve his mission by peaceful means."[114] Nevertheless, as was often the case with the tasks he started, Las Casas did not return to

Nicaragua to complete his work. Instead, he began a tour of duty in Guatemala after his return from the episcopal conference in Oaxaca, Mexico, where he had been summoned by bishops Juan de Zumárraga of New Spain and Julián de Garcés of Tlaxcala. The most significant outcome of this conference was a set of petitions to the papacy with suggestions for the proper evangelizing of the Indians drawn up at the urging of Las Casas.[115] The Dominican Bernardino de Minaya was commissioned to present these petitions to Pope Paul III in Rome. It is widely assumed that the pope promulgated the bull *Sublimis Deus* of 1537 because of said petitions. This document remains one of the most important proclamations in favor of the struggle for the protection of the Indians. The bull proclaimed, in open opposition to pervasive opinion, that Amerindians were rational beings equal to all other men, hence they were capable of receiving and practicing the Christian faith. The document was unambiguous in its call for equality and the most elementary human rights for natives:

> We are the unworthy Vice-regent of the Lord on earth. We try with all our might to lead into the flock of Christ committed to our care, those who are outside the sheepfold, we are aware through what we have been told that those Indians, *as true human beings* have not only the capacity for Christian faith, but the willingness to flock to it. The Indians we speak of, and all other peoples who later come to the knowledge of Christians, outside the faith though they be, *are not to be deprived of their liberty or their right to their property*. They are to have, to hold, and to enjoy both liberty and dominion, freely, lawfully. They must not be enslaved. Should anything different be done, it is void, invalid of no force, no worth. *And those Indians and other peoples are to be invited into the faith of Christ by the preaching of God's word and the example of a good life.*[116]

Although the Spanish authorities revoked the other two documents issued by the pope, *Altitudo divino consilii* and *Pastoralle officium*, Las Casas had obtained at last theoretical validation emanating from the highest religious Catholic authority supporting his claims in favor of the equality of the Indians. Strengthened by the support he had received from the bishops of New Spain, Las Casas went back to Guatemala, ready to face the colonists and to implement his theory of peaceful colonization.

It was in Guatemala that Las Casas became the protagonist of the historical events of Tuzulutlán, which together with the responsibility for the issuance of *Sublimis Deus* remains one of his most significant practical accomplishments.[117] According to the Dominican Antonio de Remesal, one of his earliest biographers, Las Casas and his concepts of peaceful conversion became an object of scorn and the laughingstock of the colonizers in Guatemala. As a result of their attitude against him and tempted by the colonists' offer that if he succeeded in the peaceful conversion of the Indians of the region of Tuzulutlán, the "land of war," they would renounce their slaves and the fruit of their conquests, the Dominican agreed to embark on an expedition to convert the natives.[118] The colonists saw his acceptance of this mission, as if of a dare, as the most expeditious way of ridding themselves of the meddlesome friar, for they were certain that he would either be killed in his attempt or be so shamed by his failure that he would have to leave Guatemala altogether.[119] Early in 1537, Las Casas obtained permission from the acting governor, Maldonado, ruling in the absence of the *adelantado* Pedro de Alvarado, to go into the province of Tuzulutlán to convert the natives and to carry out his designs for conversion.[120] To avoid possible conflicts with the Spanish colonizers, the terms of the agreement, which called for the penetration of the area only by members of the religious orders while banning the distribution of encomiendas and the presence of lay colonists, were kept in the most absolute secrecy.[121] The viceroy of Mexico, Antonio de Mendoza, later ratified the agreement in February of 1539; King Charles did the same in June of that year; and finally the Council of the Indies did so in November of the following year.[122]

Las Casas and his fellow missionaries were allowed a period of five years to carry out their plans. They began work by sending their ambassadors, converted Indian merchants, into the area. Their representatives visited the warring natives, carrying colorful trinkets and chanting songs in Quiché especially composed by the missionaries for the occasion. The missionaries meanwhile began to operate from surrounding friendly Indian settlements ruled by sympathetic caciques. This painstaking process took the better part of the first year, and some of the caciques of the targeted area, impelled by their curiosity, began to approach the preachers staying in the areas already pacified.[123] Slowly the men of the cloth began to get a foothold in the area of Zacapulas, where they built a church and the local chief was converted and baptized with the name of Juan. In time, Chief Juan became an invaluable asset for Las Casas and his associates, bringing other caciques to converse and receive trinkets and exchange ideas with the missionaries. The preachers were using their power of persuasion to the fullest, as Bataillon tells us:

The conquest of America, whenever it was constructive and not destructive, was a clamorous triumph for the Spanish *"don de gente"* that great human sense that makes them recognize in people so different from them, powerful allies and supporters, and gives them at the same time a certain ascendancy over others. The monks discovered and used the caciques, keeping the right proportions, like Cortés discovering Doña Marina and the Tlaxcalan supporters.[124]

After his initial success in Tuzulutlán, Las Casas was recalled to Santiago de los Caballeros by Bishop Francisco de Marroquín. As might be expected, Las Casas's preaching against the encomienda revived the enmity of the colonizers, and shortly thereafter he returned to Indian territory to continue his work. After a brief stay in the area, he left to attend the provincial chapter of the Dominicans held in the capital of New Spain. He remained there from August 1538 until February 1539. From all indications, his journey seems to have been extremely successful in obtaining three important concessions affecting him and the work he was performing. First, he was commissioned to return to Spain to recruit missionaries to come to America—for the first time in nearly twenty years, he would be returning to the mother country. The second concession was that the Dominican chapter would assign six additional friars to Guatemala. And last, he obtained from the viceroy of New Spain, Antonio de Mendoza, the ratification of the treaty signed with Maldonado for the pacification of Tuzulutlán a few years earlier.[125]

In all likelihood, given his manifest wish to return to Spain, it is very possible that he himself had suggested the possibility of returning to recruit missionaries. This desire, so often repeated in his letters, conveyed little doubt that it was in the milieu of the labyrinths of power that Las Casas could be most effective:

> When Las Casas was at court, it can be said that he found his center. It was there where he could openly and productively give way to the most dominant passion of his life, his soul's only thought. To present claims incessantly in favor of his Indians, to be the protector of that helpless flock, to be ready to pounce on anyone who wanted to abuse or injure their rights.[126]

Before leaving for Spain, Las Casas once again returned to Santiago de los Caballeros, where he denounced the armed expedition being planned against the Lacandón Indians of Chiapa by Governor Maldonado and Bishop Marroquín. This event might very well have set the stage for the unending animosity between Las Casas and the other two. Las Casas departed for Spain in early 1540, carrying letters of recommendation from Pedro de Alvarado, Bishop Marroquín, and one of his most "constant and profound friends," Bishop Juan de Zumárraga, among many others.[127] In Spain, where he remained for the next five years, the friar renewed, once again, his struggle to obtain new legislation to modify the behavior of the conquistadores in the New World. Although it had been nearly two decades since the failure at Paria and his entry into the Dominican order, Fray Bartolomé de Las Casas's vociferous denunciation of the abuses committed by his compatriots against the native inhabitants of the New World had lost none of its vigor. To make up for lost time he once again threw himself into the grinding task with all his considerable energy.

The Preacher and the King

Las Casas's earlier failures in America and at court had taught him the need to change his approach toward those whose decision-making powers could either bring about the desired changes or derail his requests permanently. Since his last sojourn at court, his formidable enemy Rodríguez de Fonseca had died, and the affairs of the Indies were being handled by a different generation of officials in the Council of the Indies; at the time of his arrival the council was headed by Las Casas's fellow Dominican García de Loaysa. From his previous experience in court in 1517–20, Las Casas had become convinced that King Charles was someone he could trust. Like other Spaniards, "he held firm to the Spanish perception that the people like their leader the King were good, and all moral, social, juridical and even economic evils were the responsibility of bad ministers interposed between the two."[128]

Las Casas had hoped to meet with the king on arriving in Spain, but Charles had left for Ghent and did not return for more than a year, somewhat humbled after his failure in Algiers.[129] Almost simultaneously with Las Casas's departure for Spain, the Council of Santiago de los Caballeros in Guatemala had learned of the cédula issued by the king in June of 1539 in support of the Dominicans' venture in Tuzulutlán, and it also discovered the secret agreement between Maldonado and the Order of Preachers. The colonists reacted bitterly, denouncing Las Casas in yet another letter to the king. They accused the friar of being merely a figurehead for the operation, charging that he had spent most of the time traveling to Nicaragua and Mexico, when he should have been with the natives. They also charged him with spending more time agitating than converting the Indians. The letter concluded with a plea to the king to send religious men who "would be more concerned with converting indigenous people instead of writing about outlandish goings on."[130]

While awaiting the monarch's return from Ghent, Las Casas busied himself recruiting missionaries, this being the ostensible purpose for which he had been sent to Spain. He also spent a great deal of energy trying to obtain as many legal sanctions as possible for Tuzulutlán. On October 17, 1540, the Council of the Indies issued a cédula prohibiting Spaniards from entering the area. The cédula also left open to friars Las Casas and Pedro de Angulo the option of assessing a tribute to the Indians if they saw fit. At the same time letters of gratitude from the emperor were sent to the governor of Guatemala and to the caciques who had collaborated with the Dominicans.[131] As a way to publicize the cédulas for all those who might be interested, Las Casas had them proclaimed from the steps of the cathedral in Seville before the departure of six Franciscan missionaries for Guatemala.[132]

Despite his involvement in the conversion process in Tuzulutlán, Las Casas had written a letter to the emperor in December of 1540 requesting Charles to order him to remain in Spain until the two had an opportunity to meet. Like many of his previous projects, Tuzulutlán was relegated to a secondary plane so he could have the opportunity to speak with the king about more pressing matters. As he expressed in his letter:

His Majesty ordered that myself, with other religious members of my order of Santo Domingo should continue with the pacification of the many provinces that are at war, bringing them into the service . . . of His Majesty which had begun so auspiciously . . . but because more important things and far greater services and utility to His Majesty's Royal estate in that place concerning the universality of that New World [emerged] . . . it was necessary to suspend such negotiation ordered by His Majesty, for it would not suffer too much of a risk to postpone it some . . . In order for me to obey my superiors of the order, and in accordance with the vow of obedience I took. . . His Highness must send royal instructions ordering me to wait, and asking the provincial of Castile to order me to wait, and I know for a fact that His Majesty will consider himself well served by myself and by the Order of Santo Domingo, if not, I will return to the Indies and will believe that before God and his majesty, I will have fulfilled my duty.[133]

Las Casas was granted his wish almost immediately; the king answered his petition the following month, and he was able to assume, once again, a leading role at court in his defense of the Indians. Despite his protestations to the contrary, Las Casas had temporarily sacrificed sending Dominican missionaries to Guatemala while he presented his projects to the king. Clearly, then, he viewed his conversation with the king as being more important, in terms of its impact for the empire and its colonies, than the experiment being implemented in the small Central American settlement where the Indians were, at last, being peacefully converted to Christianity.

The years "buried" in the Dominican convents in America were beginning to pay off. The Las Casas who had returned to court was a more patient person than the one who had left, and it is entirely possible that his avowed intention to come to Spain to engage in the recruitment of missionaries for Tuzulutlán might have been only an excuse to gain access to the king. By then it had become increasingly clear that he saw his stay in Spain as taking priority over his going to America to face the hostility of the colonists.

Just as had happened twenty-six years earlier, in his meeting with Cisneros, Las Casas found in Charles in 1542 a king predisposed to listen to what he had to say. Charles's opinion of Las Casas seemed to have been positively influenced by the French Franciscan Jacobo de Testera, whom Las Casas had used as an intermediary to deliver the letter. At almost the same time the Cortes meeting in Valladolid requested of the king "to remedy the cruelties that were being committed in the Americas against the Indians."[134] The following month Charles began a *visita* of the Council of the Indies while ordering the creation of an extraordinary junta to examine the problems of the New World.[135] One of the consequences of this visita was the permanent removal of two members of the council, Diego de Beltrán and Juan Suárez de Carvajal, and the president, García de Loaysa, was replaced by a person with ample experience in matters of the Indies, Sebastián Ramírez de Fuenleal.[136] It was at that point that Las Casas's activities in favor of the Indians intensified and reached a zenith of sorts. He had the king's ear, and he intended to make the best use of that fact.

Four

Theory and Praxis

For he is a slave by nature who is capable of belonging to another—
which is also why he belongs to another—and who participates in
reason only to the extent of perceiving it, but does not have it.
—Aristotle, *The Politics*

A PERSON OF UNERRING political instincts, Las Casas was aware of Charles's dissatisfaction with the challenges to his absolute power in the Americas. He understood the king's displeasure with the attitude of the conquistadores, who used the measure of safety provided by distance to ignore royal directives from home. In the conquest of New Spain, Cortés had ignored the orders of the king's representative, the governor of Cuba, about the limitations put on his journey; in Peru Pizarro had committed regicide; and conquistadores everywhere in the new territory were establishing their claims of possession. In the presence of such favorable conditions and the clamoring for reform in the Indies, Las Casas, either by coincidence or by design, launched one of his most vehement and concerted attacks against the conquistador-colonists.

A Brief History

During his stay courtside, he wrote a long letter to the king denouncing the atrocities committed by Spaniards against Indians. This long letter became the treatise known as the *Brevísima relación de la destruición de las Indias* (often translated into English as *A Short Account of the Destruction of the Indies*). The tract, consisting of less than a hundred pages, was dedicated to Crown Prince Philip and was designed to shock and impress on the reader the horrors perpetrated on the vanquished by the victorious Spaniards.

From his early days as a reformer, Las Casas had written an endless number of memorials, and an equal number of quasi-legal tracts, exclusively concerned with presenting the grievances of the religious reformers against the encomenderos in the Antilles. His desire to inform, to illustrate, and to denounce was shaped by his early participation in the conquest of Cuba with Diego de Velázquez and Pánfilo de Narváez. The horror of the destruction carried out by his compatriots remained imbedded in his psyche, and the images from this period often appeared in his writings supporting his arguments against the practices of the conquistadores.

A person not easily dissuaded, Las Casas never ceased in his efforts to impress upon the king the colonizers' profound disregard for the lives and well-being of the Indians. To illustrate this point, as he often did, he drew from his autoptic experience in the New World. As he explained, the Indians in Cuba had fed and opened their houses to the newcomers, but when they came under attack, they had responded and killed, in justifiable self-defense, around fifteen or twenty Spaniards. The colonists, on the other hand, had killed at least one hundred thousand natives through starvation resulting from preventing the natives from planting and harvesting their own crops so they could work in the mines for the benefit of the colonists.[1] As with his other memorials, Las Casas was attempting to document for the crown and for posterity the dire consequences of an unregulated exploitation of the natural resources and the human riches that had so serendipitously come into the possession of Spain.

Ironically, but not unsurprisingly, it was this slim, virulent, and apocalyptic portrait of conquest and its consequences, one of the briefest of the more than three hundred works he produced in his eighty-two years of life, that has most clearly defined his historical legacy and persona.[2] Rarely has a publication shaped public opinion about any European country's colonial exploits as conclusively as the catalogue of horrors depicted in this slim *relación*.[3] Finished in 1542, the memorial is credited by most admirers of Las Casas with having provided the inspiration for the proclamation of one of his final utopian projects, the much-publicized New Laws of 1542 aimed at curbing the ambitions of the conquistadores and ending all abuses against the natives.

After the *Brevísima* was first published, together with seven other tracts, in 1552, without official permission, it became one of the most widely circulated documents of its time.[4] In 1578, the tract was translated into Flemish and a year later into French, and before the century ended it had been published in English, Latin, and Italian.[5] Its widespread popularity in Spain, and, more significantly, among Spain's European enemies, earned Las Casas the dubious distinction of being identified as the progenitor of the "Black Legend" of the Spanish conquest (although, as Benjamin Keen indicates, the Black Legend "has a history much older than the term itself," going back to its use by fourteenth-century Italians to express their unfavorable opinion of Spaniards).[6]

Like all of Las Casas's other writings, *La Brevísima* had multilayered and multifaceted purposes: to inform, to invite reflection about what he conveyed as the reality of the Amerindians, and to request the implementation of sets of "remedies" to correct the seismic faults threatening the integrity of the colonial edifice. This multiplicity of objectives, and the need for a response, helps us understand the apocalyptic nature of the *Brevísima*, some of his other treatises, and his last will and testament. The more grievous and dire the situation in the Americas, the more appropriate, beneficial, and healing the remedies he proposed. Bartolomé de Las Casas was aware not only of the historical reality he was witnessing and recording but also of the way that history would judge him and his ability to affect the course of events. The *Brevísima*, more than any other of his works, has been integrated into the historical reality of the individual. As Michel Foucault points out, the function of the document "is no longer for history an inert material through which it tries to reconstitute what men have done or said, the events of which only the trace remains; history is now trying to define within the documentary material itself unities, totalities, series, relations. History must be detached from the image that satisfied it for so long."[7] In the case of Las Casas, the document, the text, became synonymous with its author, demanding a break from the status quo that "satisfied it for so long" while becoming part of a totality unifying Las Casas and the cause of the natives.

The authorship of such a document placed Las Casas at the heart of a multi-tiered conflict pitting the centralized aspirations of the crown against the semi-feudal aspirations of the colonists. Las Casas's indictment of the genocide committed by his compatriots against the indigenous American population was akin to Hamlet's play being the thing wherein he intended to catch the conscience of the king. Absent the play, and firm in his conviction that all a monarch needed to do to right wrongs in his kingdom was to be informed, the friar assumed the responsibility of informing the king, for he seemed to believe that the king's inaction owed to ignorance rather than to a conscious effort on his part to ignore the state of affairs in his colonies. The friar seems to have been working under the assumption that all it would take to move the king to action was to inform him. As he stated in the tract, "it follows that the simple knowledge that something is wrong in his kingdom is quite sufficient to ensure that [the king] will see that it is corrected, for he will not tolerate any such evil for a moment longer than it takes him to right it."[8] This almost naïve belief bore out his conviction that writing the tract was his moral duty and the only adequate response to the prodding of his conscience:

> I therefore concluded that it would constitute a criminal neglect of my duty to remain silent about the enormous loss of life as well as the infinite number of souls despatched to Hell in the course of such "conquests," and so resolved to publish an account of a few such outrages (as they can only be few out of the countless number of such incidents that I could relate) in order to make that account the more accessible to Your Highness.[9]

By making his accusations public, Las Casas cast his fate with the crown in the confrontation between the crown's absolutism and the encomenderos' aristocratic aspirations, believing the alternative offered by the absolute imperial rule of king and church to be the most authentic sources of authority and justice. One of the main differences from his contemporaries in Spain and America is the fact that he undertook as his life mission to transform the relationship between the center of power and the peripheral forces represented by Spain's possessions in the New World, while the rest of the colonists struggled for autonomy from the crown in their quest for wealth and power.

Aside from the memorial's reputed influence in the enactment of the New Laws, the text more than any of his other works was responsible for generating bitter polemics at the time of its publication in 1552—polemics which, far from abating, have continued well into our own time. As noted above, the enemies of Spain wasted little time in deploying the document as a battering ram to demolish Spain's reputation in the world, giving birth, in the process, to a revived Black Legend to tarnish the much-hated and envied Spanish empire.

Las Casas was fully conscious of the emotional impact that an eyewitness narrative of the horrors of the conquest would have in helping to dispel the ignorance of the people in Spain and in exerting influence in a move to adopt new policies toward the indigenous subjects of the crown. As he explained in his own synopsis of the memorial:

Brother Bartolomé de Las Casas, or Casaus, came to the Spanish court after he entered the Order, to give our Lord, the Emperor, an eye-witness account of these enormities, not a whisper of which had at that time reached the ears of the people here. He also related these same events to several people he met during his visit and they were deeply shocked by what he had to say and listened open-mouthed to his every word; they later begged him and pressed him to set down in writing a short account of some of them, and this he did.[10]

It is highly unlikely that in 1542, a full half-century after Columbus first arrived on American soil, anyone in Spain could have been ignorant of the exploits and excesses of their compatriots in America, from the founding of Española to the conquests of Mexico and Peru and the creation of a New World. What Las Casas seems to have attempted to confront at the time was the relative indifference with which the king and his advisors regarded the native inhabitants of their overseas possessions; this "brief history" was the best available tool he found to prod them into action.

The *Brevísima* is little more than a synoptic version of his *Historia de las Indias* augmented by texts from some of the letters to the council from bishops and other members of the cloth in America. However, unlike the *Historia*, the shorter treatise worked like a dazzling display of fireworks to try to catalyze its readers into reacting with alacrity and taking action to deal with the plight of the Indians. Curiously enough, despite the calculated intent to shock the audience, the tract avoids identifying by name any of the perpetrators of the heinous deeds that Las Casas imputes to them. The accusations were left to dangle anonymously for the readers to fill in the names. This is an apparent contradiction of Las Casas's reputed modus operandi and his avowal to inform the monarch. Despite his willingness to denounce his compatriots publicly, he did so in such a manner as to avoid carrying the confrontation to its furthest possible consequences. Although in his *Historia* he identifies the perpetrators by name, it is noteworthy that he requested that his fellow Dominicans not publish that work for at least forty years after 1559. If after "those forty years, they saw that it would benefit the Indians, and Spain," then it should be published.[11]

The *Brevísima* is more than coincidentally reminiscent of a letter sent by the Dominicans of Española to Gillaume de Croy, Sieur de Chièvres, de-nouncing the atrocities committed by the Spaniards on the island between 1492 and 1516.[12] The letter to Monsieur de Chièvres describes in rich and graphic details the one-sided conflict between Spaniards and Indians from the time of the first arrival of the conquerors to the atrocities being committed at the time of the writing. According to the friars, the natives assumed that the newcomers were angels: "Certainly the Indians thought [the Spaniards] were angels from heaven, and they thought that the ship's sails were the wings which they had used to descend."[13] In the tradition of Columbus, expressed in his letter to the monarchs, the friars felt free to "attach" their perceptions onto the natives. The Dominican letter also told of how the natives had extended their hospitality, but instead of repaying with kindness, the Spaniards took their houses and their women for their own use and pleasure. The letter went on as a catalogue of horror and atrocities, something that Las Casas would recapture in his famous tract twenty-six years later.

By the time the *Brevísima* was written Cortés had already conquered Mexico and the cost in native lives had been incalculable in Cholula and Tenochtitlán. In Peru, Pizarro had executed the last Inca, decapitated the empire, and the Indian population was dwindling geometrically. The intensity of the genocide and the urgent need to stop it might help to explain, at least in part, the apocalyptic tone of the treatise.

When Las Casas wrote his tract, the idea of the ultimate destruction of the Indies was but another manifestation of a prevailing theme at the time: the concept of a war between believers and infidels, taking place in Europe and transferred to the reality of Spain in America.

In this context, according to Alain Milhou, everything is interpreted from the perspective of a destruction-restoration dichotomy.[14] Milhou examines this dichotomy carefully and explains it in terms of the medieval worldview influencing many of the Spanish reformers of the sixteenth century, who compared the Arab invasion and occupation of Spain to the Spanish occupation and "destruction" of the Indies. In both cases the traditional order had been altered and "destroyed" but in the mother country, thanks to the Reconquista, there had been a national rebirth. Las Casas could only express himself in terms with which he was familiar, thus he approached the subject of the Indies from a medievalist's perspective:

> Bartolomé de Las Casas, in his most famous work [whose content is] evident in its title—*Brevísima relación de la destruición de las Indias*—makes a comparison between the conquerors "destroyers" of the Indies and the *moros* (Moors) "destroyers" of the sinful Spain of king Rodrigo; one could fear, according to Las Casas, that God might provoke through the intervention of the Turks or other calamities, a

new *destruición de España* for the purpose of punishing the sins of the conqueror, the colonizers and all those who directly or indirectly, through action or omission, in America or Spain, had been accomplices in the "destruction of the Indies."[15]

No one reading the tract could harbor any doubt about the friar's intention: this work was an indictment of the whole Spanish enterprise in the New World. It listed one heinous crime after another and the conquistadores, the perpetrators, emerged as one-dimensional individuals devoid of any redeeming social or moral value, depicted as little more than unreasoning, bloodthirsty beasts of prey:

> [The Spaniards] forced their ways into native settlements slaughtering everyone they found there, including small children, old men, pregnant women and even women who had just given birth. They hacked them to pieces, slicing open their bellies with their swords as though they were so many sheep herded into a pen. They even laid wagers on whether they could manage to slice a man in two at a stroke, or cut an individual's head from his body, or disembowel him with a single blow of their axes.[16]

To capture the horror of the conquest Las Casas drew from his forty years of listening to the tales told in the Indies about the exploits of the conquerors. Some of these events he himself had witnessed, particularly in Cuba and Española. Although he saw himself as the self-appointed conscience of Spain in the New World, he was not alone in his denunciation of the cruelties perpetrated against the natives. His was one of the many voices of religious and laymen alike who protested the mistreatment of the indigenous people. Men of the cloth such as Fray Toribio de Motolinía, a sworn enemy of Las Casas, protested the killing of natives in the mines of Oaxaca. Pedro Cieza de León produced an indictment of the cruelty of the conquistadores in the Antilles and the South American mainland. In Mesoamerica, the visitador Tello de Sandoval's final report on the visita of Viceroy Antonio Mendoza and the atrocities committed during the Mixtón war added to the numerous and conscientious denunciations of Spanish excesses.[17] Las Casas stood out from the others by the sheer volume and vehemence of his work and because the issue of destruction was the focal point of his discourse. To magnify the importance of his own proposals for restoration and give them a more urgent character, he had to bring to the forefront at every available opportunity the question of destruction. From his perspective, the only way in which the Indies could be restored was through a reliance on the effectiveness of the law to reconstruct them. Traditional Visigoth tradition, so influential in the creation of the legal and moral wellspring of Spanish society, maintained that "the law existed as a manifestation of justice, but did not itself create justice. As violations of justice became evident, a ruler created new laws; justice itself remained eternal and external."[18] As Las Casas saw it, in the Indies, justice was being violated and the only solution was the enactment of more laws in order to halt this transgression.

Las Casas's fixation on the process of destruction left little alternative but to approve additional laws necessary to stop the accelerated decomposition of the continent and its inhabitants. Confronted with the state of affairs in America, the king found himself in the position of having to avoid the charge of abandoning the Indies into the hands of the irresponsible encomenderos. The *Brevísima* stood apart from the works of other reformers in both content and style. Sometimes it appears Las Casas opted to play out his role as the conscience of Spain to an extreme extent. This was particularly evident when he seemed to abandon all restraints while painting extremely graphic pictures of mayhem and destruction, which he often exaggerated to the point of surreal fantasy. Although the 1516 letter of the Dominicans and his own letter of 1531 served as precedents, his position at court in 1542, a time when even the king was questioning his own role in determining the fate of the Indies, augured a good reception. Ultimately, as surprising as it might appear, aside from the incendiary language, the brief treatise presented nothing radically different from his earlier proposals. However, the timing of the tract, its indictment of official policy, and its attempt to present the "truth" about Spain's presence in the Americas demonstrated Las Casas's unique skills as a political manipulator of opinion:

> Las Casas' ability to draw up new schemes and modify old ones to take advantage of the perceived preference of high officials made things difficult for his opponents. Moreover, acquiring information on the actual state of affairs in the Indies proved difficult in the early period. Each side sought to discredit the other as well as influence the nature of official reports.[19]

In view of the difficulties of obtaining valid information in the mother country, the *Brevísima*, despite its statistical inaccuracies, was the most effective vehicle to inform the crown and the public at large, while forcing the former to adopt measures to avoid any perception of indifference to the wanton destruction of the colonies. Once he set himself an objective, Las Casas rarely deviated from it, and if exaggerating and inflating his figures would accomplish his ends, he did not shy from resorting to those measures. In fairness to Las Casas, this proclivity to exaggeration was no different from that practiced by his contemporaries Oviedo, Díaz, and López de Gómara, among the better-known chroniclers of the time.[20] Although this tendency to exaggerate tended to weaken his validity as a serious writer in the eyes of some of his contemporaries and future detractors, his use of the pen as a propagandistic weapon was more than amply rewarded by the swell of public opinion condemning the actions of the conquistadores.

The controversy generated by the *Brevísima* revolves around its perceived aim of informing the crown of prevailing conditions so it could ameliorate the plight of Amerindians. Nevertheless, the tract's perpetrator-victim dichotomy objectified the Indians, robbing them of volition and casting them as helpless victims without the capacity for self-defense, much less self-determination. Despite Las Casas's claims of having had firsthand experience with the natives of Santo Domingo, Cuba, and Central America, he fails to represent the Indians as the equals of the Europeans and thus capable of social organization, adaptation, or rebellion. His is a myopic vision that did not look far into the historical background of some highly civilized cultures nor could he envision a future where ethnic and racial lines could be erased in an amalgamated society emerging from the main streams conforming Indoamerica. It is as if he imagined only an irreversible present, needing a few cosmetic changes, which he would bring about. The Dominican, carried away by his own momentum as the *protector universal de los indios*, did not see the contradiction implicit in maintaining that the Indians should be freed while remaining vassals of the king of Spain. As he was inclined to do, Las Casas equated the subjection of the natives to the king with being not only free but also better off than they had been before the coming of the Spaniards.[21] In this respect, he was one of the forerunners of the modern dependency school that views native Indoamericans as helpless beings unable to break away from the servitude of underdevelopment without the aid of the benevolent but superior colonizer.

The role of the *Brevísima* in the enactment of the New Laws seems unlikely given that the tract was concluded after the New Laws were promulgated. However, it is very possible that Las Casas had been at work on the letter for several months, perhaps since his arrival in Spain if not earlier.

Thus, it is possible to surmise that the king was familiar with the contents of the document long before it was concluded, and it was this knowledge that influenced him to sign the New Laws as soon as they were drafted.[22]

Undoubtedly Las Casas and the body of written work he had produced up to that time influenced the content of the New Laws of 1542, but it is difficult to evaluate the extent of his participation. The signing of the laws came at a crucial time for the crown. In the face of the flagrant violations being committed by Spaniards against the physical integrity of the American natives, it became imperative for the crown to formulate some form of legislative plan, as had been recommended by the Cortes at Valladolid, if not for humanitarian reasons, at least for fiduciary ones. The New Laws seemed undoubtedly the most appropriate course of action, if only from the practical perspective of preventing the total depopulation of Spain's possessions and the subsequent loss of profits and revenue that such a demographic disaster implied.

The New Laws consisted of fifty-four articles, of which twenty-three were directly concerned with the status and treatment of the Indians.[23] These regulations, reflecting Las Casas's dearest utopian expectations for the natives, were "so sweeping and so strongly in favor of the Indians that Las Casas himself might well have drafted them."[24] Ostensibly, the laws spelled the doom of the institution of the encomienda as the colonizers had known it up until that point. They severely curtailed their power by prohibiting the employment of Indians in personal service and abolishing enslavement resulting from "just wars" while decreeing that any slaves obtained in that manner had to be freed thenceforth.

As in the case of all laws previously enacted by the crown, the New Laws would have necessitated a legion of bureaucrats backed by a military army to enforce all of their provisions. The New Laws exemplified the belief that law was a reflection of justice rather than the fountainhead of justice.[25] This is evident in article 27:

> Since we have ordered that henceforth in no wise shall Indians be made slaves . . . we order and command that the audiencias, having summoned both parties, shall summarily and briefly without quibbling, the truth only having been ascertained, set them at liberty if the persons who hold them as slaves do not show title of legitimate possession; and in order that, because of failure to petition . . . the Indians do not remain slaves, we order the audiencias to place persons to plead these suits for the Indians, and let them be paid out of the court fines, and let them be men of confidence and diligence.[26]

Although the intentions were commendable, the execution of the laws depended on too many variables: the audiencias' willingness to hear the suits, the appointment of special prosecutors, and the question of their pay, among many others.

Article 30, one of the most controversial clauses of the New Laws, abolished the perpetuity of individual encomiendas beyond the death of the original encomendero.[27] According to this provision, after the death of the original holder the encomienda was supposed to revert to the crown. This one provision, if it could be implemented, intended to get rid of the encomienda as an inheritable institution, by making it disappear through the natural process of attrition of the first colonizers. Aside from responding to the humane changes recommended by the missionaries, the king saw the New Laws as a unique opportunity to attempt to curb the quasi-feudal power of the encomenderos, which increasingly threatened the king's absolute power.[28] However, in the colonies, the authorities found themselves in the difficult position of having to obey the crown in enforcing a set of laws the colonists rejected as being most inimical to their interests.

In previous instances, the colonists had viewed the advent of new laws with an attitude of *obedezcanse pero no se cumplan* (obey but do not comply). This time they went into open rebellion. In Peru, the rebels under the leadership of Gonzalo Pizarro had the first viceroy sent by the crown to implement the New Laws, Blasco Nuñez Vela, executed. In New Spain, a rebellion of major proportions was averted only by the intervention of the *visitador* Tello de Sandoval, who abolished on the spot some of the strictest requirements of the laws.

Contrary to what the reformers might have expected, the New Laws met with universal criticism in the New World, not only from the colonists directly affected but also from respected members of the clergy. Bishops Zumárraga and Marroquín and Toribio Benavente and Motolinía reacted swiftly to express their discontent with them. Like all previous pieces of legislation, the New Laws were reactive in nature and targeted specific problems—the working of the Council of the Indies, slavery, and the encomienda, among others.[29] They covered so many different legal areas, and in such fastidious detail, that their enforcement was impossible.

Because of their ambitious scope, taking on the formidable task of abolishing the encomienda, the New Laws appeared doomed to failure from their inception. Juan Friede goes to the heart of the problem:

From the moment the Crown allowed, or permitted, the conquest and occupation of America through the private initiative of discoverers, conquerors and colonists, it was utopian to believe that thanks to laws and ordinances they would cede to the Crown, rights acquired *de facto*, *"Por su cuenta y misión,"* as they said then. From the division [*reparto*] of Indians among the conquerors—which Columbus was obligated to carry out to put down Roldán's uprising—and the subsequent official support to establish in America a social structure based on the exploitation of the Indians, no law could be capable of changing the situation, unless through more or less violent imposition, which the Crown was not ready to undertake.[30]

Despite their stringent character, the New Laws did not go as far as Las Casas would have liked. They did not abolish the encomienda outright and did not place an interdiction on the future conquest of undiscovered American territory.[31] Decisive action on the part of the monarch might have made the abolition of the encomienda possible, but the king was either unable or unwilling to run the risk of another rebellion like the one led by Gonzalo Pizarro.

Meanwhile, Las Casas focused all his attention on having the Council of Indies enforce the New Laws. With the passage of time, he became aware that although the New Laws were necessary, and he had enthusiastically welcomed their enactment, in practice they were unenforceable because the crown had neither the economic nor the human resources to create an efficient apparatus to execute them. Nevertheless, he did not cease in his efforts to obtain new cédulas and provisions to implement them while his faith in the efficacy of the Spanish politico-juridical system was unshaken. He also blamed the partial failure of the laws on his traditional enemies, the encomenderos, and their untrammeled ambition, along with the corrupt officials in the overseas possessions.[32]

Meanwhile in the colonies, the Indians, unaware of the debate concerning their status, continued to suffer the same indignities they had experienced before the enactment of the New Laws. Moreover, the colonizers unanimously turned their mounting anger on Las Casas, who, in 1544, in his role as bishop of Chiapa, had the opportunity to experience it firsthand.

The Bishop and the Colonizers

At about the same time of the signing of the New Laws, Charles V—probably at the suggestion of his secretary Francisco de los Cobos and Cardinal García de Loaisa, prior of the Dominicans—offered Fray Bartolomé de Las Casas the richest bishopric of the New World, the bishopric of Cusco, Perú, which Las Casas refused.[33] Three months after declining the nomination to the Peruvian see, for reasons that have never been clearly established,[34] he was offered the impoverished bishopric of Chiapa, which he finally accepted at the urging of his Dominican superiors.[35]

The nomination came at a time when Las Casas found himself at "the peak of his influence" with Charles V, as a result of his continued presence at court as an advisor on matters pertaining to the Indies and his presumed collaboration with the king in the proclamation of the New Laws.[36] However, some advisors to the king, most likely under the leadership of Francisco de los Cobos, did not see Las Casas's ascendancy at court very favorably. As a result, they began an active campaign for his removal, culminating with the Dominican's nomination and acceptance of a bishopric in the Indies, which, according to Helen Rand-Parish, was not so much a prize but a hardship.[37]

A mature Las Casas must have weighed the options open to him in accepting the nomination to the Chiapa bishopric, although many of his brethren would have considered it an honor and would have accepted it without hesitation. The Dominican was no longer the starry-eyed reformer who had come before the court in 1516; experience and knowledge had transformed him into a calculating politician. In this light, his acceptance of the nomination must have reflected a multitude of personal and political reasons. It is quite possible that Las Casas saw the nomination as another opportunity to put into practice the proposals for peaceful colonization and the protection of the Indians that he had been advocating so vehemently since 1514. He might have also seen the bishopric as an opportunity to vindicate himself, given that most of his earlier plans and projects had failed. The sole exception to this pattern had been the relatively successful beginning of the pacification of Tuzulutlán, a project that in typical fashion he had abandoned in favor of traveling to court to pursue his role as protector of the Indians.

Upon accepting the nomination, Las Casas wrote a thirty-point petition requesting a multitude of prerogatives from the crown; the contents of this memorial shed important light on his tenure as bishop of the Mexican state. The first point of the petition was a request for a geographic delineation of the boundaries of his bishopric. He then asked for the territories of Tuzu-lutlán, Lacandón, and Yucatán to be included within the boundaries of his new diocese. The crown's sanctioning of this second point, Las Casas claimed, was one of the main reasons for his acceptance of the appointment.[38] The fact that Las Casas's petition aimed at tangible concessions for the effective governance of his future diocese seems to cast some doubt on the argument that he had been forced to accept the nomination, as opposed to accepting it willingly. In view of the available documentary evidence, even the claim of one of his most fervent detractors, Menéndez Pidal, that the Dominican's acceptance of the miter was not a reluctant decision into which he was forced but a deliberate act whereby he could create for himself an exemplary diocese in the area surrounding Tuzulutlán, seems perfectly valid.[39]

Another segment of Las Casas's petition asked that the juridical and political authorities support the bishop in everything pertaining to the ecclesiastical jurisdiction of the province. There were also requests for maintaining the inviolability of religious immunity and the meting out of severe punishment to those who violated it. Other provisions called for the extension and strengthening of the prerogatives of the ecclesiastical authority (the bishop) to hold administrators fiscally and politically accountable and to choose religious representatives. Likewise, Las Casas requested authority to inquire about the mistreatment of the Indians anywhere within the confines of his diocese; this item and others like it were intended to validate the functions traditionally reserved for the *protector de Indios*, a title which was nowhere in evidence in the petition but was nevertheless defined by the functions that he had listed. In closing, Las Casas asked for economic support from the crown for the venture, as well as an interdiction against further expeditions of lay Spanish colonizers and the removal of the conquistador Francisco de Montejo as governor of Yucatán.[40] The broad spectrum of prerogatives demanded, as well as his request for the outright removal of Montejo, left little doubt as to the causes of the tense political and emotional climate that awaited him on his arrival in his new diocese.

The main difficulty Las Casas faced as bishop was not so much getting his proposal accepted as the absence of effective means to implement it, as had been the case with the New Laws. By the time he left Spain en route to the Indies, he had only a hastily assembled collection of royal cédulas and dispatches spelling out his duties and the limits of his jurisdiction, while still lacking the official dispatches from the papacy.[41] As on other occasions, his impatience and his desire to implement his specific ideas about the governance of the Indies had prompted him to act before completing the cumbersome bureaucratic requirements demanded of public officials.

Even before Las Casas literally set sail for America in July of 1544, his journey to Chiapa was besieged by numerous obstacles. The first was his lack of the official documents from the papacy attesting to his nomination; when he left, he was operating under a mere grant of power to act pro tempore until he could receive the official bulls.[42] Second, although he had recruited the largest contingent of missionaries ever to travel to America in one journey, forty-six friars, the Casa de Contratación, which was supposed to provide him with 250 ducats, could not find the money to support his journey.[43] Only at the last minute was a loan arranged with a banker to pay for the trip.[44] To complicate matters, a group of nineteen missionaries took nearly six months to journey from Salamanca to San Lúcar de Barrameda.[45] To add to their travails, sailing to America was further delayed for another two months because of heavy flooding of the Guadalquivir River, which also prevented the exhumation of Columbus's remains, which his daughter-in-law, Diego Columbus's widow, had been commissioned to take to Santo Domingo. Furthermore, the ship carrying the bishop and his entourage was in such poor condition that it almost sank; it had to be dry-docked in Gomera in the Canary Islands for extensive repairs. Finally, to cap an inglorious, humiliating, and difficult journey, the vessel barely avoided a collision when the fleet reached Santo Domingo.[46]

The bishop's reception by the colonists of Española, who placed on him the blame for the New Laws, was overtly hostile and foreshadowed the one he would receive in his own bishopric. In Santo Domingo, where Las Casas and his entourage were stranded for three months, the colonists tried to starve them off. By refusing to give alms to the convent of Santo Domingo to punish the preachers, the colonizers expected to break down the will of the group. In view of the damage inflicted on his fellow Dominicans, Las Casas suggested moving to the Franciscan monastery, but they managed to remain where they were and survive through the intervention of one of the richest widows in the city, who made sure they received the needed support. Further exacerbating the situation, some of the missionaries who had accompanied Las Casas from Spain deserted him. He faced additional difficulties in attempting to secure the money necessary to charter a vessel to Yucatán to avoid passage through New Spain, where the bishop feared that an attempt would be made on his life.

In Yucatán, he also encountered difficulties in securing overland passage to Chiapa.[47] The relatively warm welcome extended to him by the people of Campeche soon vanished in the heat of the dispute over whether Yucatán fell under the jurisdiction of Chiapa. Meanwhile, Montejo, whose removal as governor of Yucatán Las Casas had advocated, refused to recognize him as bishop of his province. Unable to find money anywhere, Las Casas requested and received assistance from some of his future parishioners in Ciudad Real, the seat of his see. With the money, he hired a small barge to carry some of his friars and their baggage. The overloaded barge was caught in a storm and sank off the coast of Tabasco; thirty-two persons drowned, including nine friars and twenty-three lay Spaniards.[48] Despite the calamities befalling him, Las Casas, undaunted, continued on his way to Ciudad Real and his new office.

At the time of his arrival in Yucatán, an anonymous document, addressed to an equally anonymous "your highness," was making the rounds, and it reflected the depth of the anger and the unfavorable sentiment felt by the colonizers against the bishop. The document charged Las Casas with claiming that he was bishop of half of New Spain and not just of Chiapa.[49] The letter also expressed the colonists' chagrin that Las Casas had not been on the barge where the other friars had drowned. Finally, it accused the Dominican of putting on royal airs and acting pretentiously.[50]

Las Casas finally arrived in Ciudad Real on March 12, 1545, nine months after leaving Spain. Hostility toward him had been evident from the time of his arrival in the New World, but nothing could have prepared him for the reception he encountered in Chiapa. The citizens of the province had been whipped into a frenzy by news traveling ahead of the bishop blaming him for the New Laws, specifically for the clauses ending the perpetuity of the encomiendas and abolishing slavery. They "were literally seething with enmity towards their new prelate."[51] Shortly after reaching his destination, and despite the vicissitudes of the exhausting voyage and the hostility he encountered, he issued his first pastoral letter.

As expected, his first directives were aimed at implementing some of the main dispositions contained in the New Laws. Since his only advantage in carrying out his mission consisted of the powers vested in him by virtue of his episcopal chair, he authorized only two priests, Dean Gil Quintana and Canon Juan Perera, in addition to himself, to hear confessions and grant absolution; they could do so in all cases except those involving violations committed against the Indians, when the bishop himself had to be consulted.[52] As a safeguard against reprisals by the colonists, he also resorted to using the weapons of excommunication and interdiction whenever he deemed that a grievous offense against the Indians or the New Laws had been committed.[53]

La Casas prepared and circulated his *Avisos y reglas para los confesores*, better known as the *Confesionario*, a manual of instructions for priests in charge of hearing confessions. The manual instructed them to refuse absolution to "all conquerors, encomenderos and merchants, even on their deathbed, until they signed a formal act of restitution, returning to the Indians all the goods and property they had unjustly acquired since their arrival in the New World."[54] The *Confesionario* also spelled out in minute detail the requirements that the colonizers had to meet in order to receive confession and absolution.

The first section, subdivided into six subsections, set the tone for the document by establishing the prerequisites for confession *in extremis* for three different types of penitents: conquistadores, *vecinos* who had encomienda Indians, and merchants who sold weapons or supplies to those who fought against the Indians:

> The first thing he must have taken down in his deposition and say, as a loyal Christian who wants to leave this world without offense to God and with a free conscience, is that he elects for a confessor so and so, cleric priest, or religious from such and such an order, to whom he grants power of execution (insofar as he is capable of, under the prescriptions of divine and human laws in order for him to discharge his conscience) for everything which he deemed necessary for his salvation. And if it seemed to the confessor that it was necessary to give back [to its original owners] the whole estate in the manner that he [the confessor] deemed necessary without leaving anything to the heirs, he is free to do so, just as the sick man or penitent could do of his own free will, depending on what is convenient for the safety of his soul. In this case he submits his whole estate to the judgment and opinion [of the confessor] without any objections.
>
> Second, to declare to the notary, in what conquests or wars against the Indians he participated in these Indies, what he did and how he helped to steal, to perpetrate violence, harm and killings and captures of Indians, and the destruction of towns resulting from the conquests.[55]

The first rule had an additional four points running along the same lines as the two listed above. The second rule stated that having fulfilled the requisites demanded by the first one and having signed a power of attorney for the confessor, the penitent was allowed to confess and after recanting all the abominations he had committed could then be absolved. The fifth article called for very specific procedures in the case of living penitents not threatened with immediate demise. The rules for the living were similar to those for dying parishioners. The last rule required the penitents to promise never to engage in wars of conquest against the Indians, nor go to Peru as long as those "tyrants continued up in arms against the king, and even if they repented and came back to obedience, as long as they continued to destroy and harm those people, contrary to the precepts of our holy faith."[56]

The procedures for confession outlined by Las Casas were akin to turning the sacrament into a judicial procedure where the ecclesiastical authorities became judges and enforcers. Faced with the absence of legal mechanisms to implement the New Laws designed to protect the Indians, Las Casas depended entirely on the weapons afforded him by his religious investiture. Unlike his earlier proposal of 1514, in which he had suggested the institution of a theocratic government to deal with the problems of the Indians, this time he invested ecclesiastical laws with juridical value.

Under Las Casas, the church in Chiapa had the opportunity, just as it had in Santo Domingo in the 1520s, to become an active force in the process of social change in the New World. However, Las Casas's inflexibility turned the whole of Spanish colonial society against himself, the church, and everything that he represented, in this case the laws for which he had fought in order to protect the natives. Las Casas, despite his hard and fast proclamation of his love for the Indians, had been blinded by what can be perceived as his inflexible loyalty to the absolutism of imperial laws, an imperial crown, and an imperial church. The bishop of Chiapa once again demonstrated that he was unable to adapt to the reality of a changing, dynamic, emerging society that was developing in the New World. His theoretical perspective, grounded in a rigid scholastic tradition, had imprisoned him in an ideological straitjacket that he could not escape.

As might be expected, the response of the colonists and some of the secular members of the clergy was one of outrage. The honorable "God-fearing" citizens of Chiapa, prevented from performing their sacramental and religious duties, faced the danger of eternal damnation, and this was intolerable and unacceptable. To resolve the situation, they sought the help of Dean Gil Quintana, a rebellious young secular cleric who, sword in hand, defied the bishop's authority to deny absolution to those guilty of exploiting the Indians.[57] In addition to the rebellion of his secular dean, Las Casas was denounced to the Audiencia de los Confines, to the archbishop of Mexico, the pope, the kind, and the Council of the Indies as a troublemaker, a "disturber of the peace and a protector of Indian dogs."[58]

In an effort to find relief from the inordinate pressure to which the colonists were subjecting him, and in partial fulfillment of his episcopal duties, the bishop left Ciudad Real to tour the Indian villages that formed part of his diocese. Still ignorant of native languages, Las Casas had to rely largely on either native translators or his religious brethren who, as part of their missionary effort, had found it indispensable to learn Indian languages and dialects. To his credit it must be said that despite the hostility he encountered, he made an effort to visit the native members of his diocese to reassure them with his presence. The purpose of Las Casas's visits to native settlements, in addition to witnessing the actual conditions of the Indians, was to demonstrate to the new missionaries the need to recruit even more missionaries from among their brethren in Spain to satisfy the demands to convert the natives to the new faith. Years later, Antonio de Remesal delightedly recalled the bishop's triumphant entrance into the Indian villages where his path was strewn with flowers and the prelate had to make his way under flowery arches. In the villages, Las Casas listened to the Indians' complaints and demands and promised to try to find remedies for them, specifically those concerning the abuses of their encomenderos.[59]

While the discontent of the colonists continued to simmer, Las Casas ventured out of the capital city once again, this time to journey to Honduras and to visit the settlement of Tuzulutlán (land of war) in Guatemala, which he had helped to pacify so successfully in 1537 and which, as a result, had been renamed Verapaz (True Peace). Faced with Spanish encroachment of the territory that the crown had granted the Indians, Las Casas once again directed a petition to the king demanding royal cédulas to prolong the exclusion of Spaniards from the lands of Verapaz for another five years. Unfortunately for Las Casas and the Indians, the royal cédulas did not arrive until well after he had left Chiapa never to return.[60]

His last few months in Chiapa only served to further exacerbate the contradictions and animosity between himself and the colonists. While the bishop exhausted all legal and ecclesiastical recourses at his disposal to enforce the reforms embodied in the New Laws, he became the target of insults, slander, and threats both by lay authorities and other men of the cloth. Ironically, despite the bishop's struggle against the practitioners of what Bataillon has called the "homicidal system of the encomienda," it was Las Casas, "one of the most hated men who had ever been in the Indies," who ended up succumbing to the pressure and leaving the New World.[61] The encomenderos, in a rare show of colonial unity, had aligned themselves against him in a united front whose actions ended up expediting his departure. More significantly, the president of the Audiencia de los Confines, Alonso de Maldonado, and the bishop of Guatemala, Francisco de Marroquín, both of them former friends and supporters, became his active enemies. Both attacked the bishop on several occasions, privately at first and then publicly, and what had started as a jurisdictional conflict soon became a vitriolic war of words and charges and countercharges presented to the imperial government.

Maldonado publicly called the bishop a "scoundrel, a bad man, a bad friar, shameless and worthy of punishment."[62] Realizing that an insult of this nature to a prelate of the church signified automatic excommunication, Maldonado recanted and issued a weak and belated apology. Marroquín for his part launched his public attacks from the pulpit while privately writing letters to the king complaining about Las Casas's abuse of authority in enforcing the New Laws. In the meantime, forced by the increased pressure from the colonists and their ambassadors, Charles V had no choice but to sign the Cédulas de Malines revoking article 30 of the New Laws and returning the encomienda to its previous status of inheritability for the period of two lives.[63]

The seething resentment of the colonists and their representatives could only lead to one final confrontation with the bishop. As he became more isolated, the colonists grew bolder, and finally, on December 15, 1545, the citizens' council agreed to suspend the payment of tithes and to withdraw recognition of Las Casas's office. They based this rejection on the technicality that he had never officially presented the bulls and cédulas confirming his nomination as bishop. Unwilling to heed the warnings of his religious brethren, Las Casas interrupted his visits to the surrounding area and returned to Ciudad Real, where he faced a mob demanding his expulsion. Unable to prevail on his opponents, he withdrew to the Mercedarian convent,[64] where once again the rioters massed and attacked the bishop's servants, and one of the rioters even took aim and fired a harquebus at him.[65] Finally, convinced of his inability to bring about any positive changes to the colonists of Chiapa, Bishop Bartolomé de Las Casas heeded the advice of his brethren and the few authority figures that had remained loyal to him and left for the city of México on January 12, 1546.[66] His physical presence in Chiapa had proved totally counterproductive in contributing to the actual application of the New Laws. The realization that he was leaving his diocese never to return must have dawned on him as he made his way to the episcopal conference in the capital of New Spain.

Despite his professed affection for the Indians, and the show of support he had received from them in his visits to their settlements, Las Casas, as usual, seemed more concerned with the behavior of his fellow Spaniards than with becoming closer to his native parishioners or with attempting to bridge the chasm between colonized and colonizers. As he was the representative of an imperial church and an imperial economic power, his participation on behalf of the Indians, at the legal level, could not resolve the essential problems of their exploitation. Las Casas essentially preached to and worked with Spaniards, while the natives stood invisibly in the background. The Dominican tried and failed to effect drastic changes from the top down, while remaining ignorant of the process of resistance and adaptation in which the Indians were actively participating. After decades of subjugation, the natives had discovered the advantages of reaching a modicum of understanding with the colonizers, not because they unquestioningly accepted the superiority of the invaders but because, after their military defeat, they had realized that they could retain far more of their traditional prerogatives if they collaborated or appeared to collaborate with their oppressors.

The bishop of Chiapa could only draw resources and the value of experience from an anachronistic perspective learned under a very different set of circumstances in the Antilles. Despite his good intentions, his actions only furthered the dependency of the Indians on the benevolence of their Spanish masters or their representatives, in this case the members of the religious orders and himself, as the banner carriers of Christian love and justice in America. Moreover, by abandoning his diocese without the authorization of the political and religious authorities, Las Casas further exposed the natives to the rage of the colonists, a rage that his provocations had aggravated. He had disturbed a wasp nest and the Indians were left there to pay the consequences.

Las Casas came to his diocese hoping to influence his parishioners through what he believed was the moral authority granted to him by the crown, the pope, and the New Laws. This authority was sometimes expressed as a form of moral superiority, a patrimony of the self-righteous, evident in his writings and actions, particularly where religion and legality intersected. From his perspective, his actions were justified in terms of his desire to help the Indians, but this motivation, more than a genuine sharing with the Indians and a partaking of their reality, arose out of a conviction of the moral, religious, political, and military superiority of his world. Insufficiently informed about the society or the individuals he intended to help, his Samaritan tendencies required his intervention as a member of the dominant group dispensing out favors to the members of the oppressed. This is not to say that other missionaries working with the natives did so from a perspective of equality, but Las Casas, more so than the others, could not help but act from a paternalistic perspective augmented by his episcopal status and his vaguely defined title as protector of the Indians. The conflict between Las Casas and the colonists of Chiapa was little more than another act in the unfinished drama of the encounter between two incommensurable worlds: an internal, eternal, and endless struggle between two aspects of empire, the centralized authoritarianism of the king pitted against the semi-feudal aspirations of a vested colonial aristocracy trying to recreate a world in its own terms; an ongoing tragedy with no clear winners among the dominant factions and once again only the natives as losers.

Encounter in Valladolid: Two Views of Empire

Las Casas returned to Spain by way of Mexico where he participated in the episcopal conference of 1546 to which he had been providentially invited by the visitador Tello de Sandoval.[67] At the conference he proposed a successful resolution calling for a modified application of the doctrine of restitution to the Indians by the encomenderos who had unlawfully dispossessed them. Although all the attending bishops, including Marroquín, signed the resolution, no effort was made by the political authorities to implement it in New Spain for fear of reprisals by the colonizers.[68] After the conclusion of the episcopal conference, Las Casas left for Spain, where he arrived in March of the following year.

In Spain Las Casas busied himself working against the enforcement of the Cédulas de Malines of 1545, which had wiped out some of the most significant legal gains of 1542. It was also at this time that the humanist priest Juan Ginés de Sepúlveda, at the urging of Fernando de Valdés, archbishop of Seville and inquisitor general of Spain, applied for permission to publish his book *Democrates Alter*, a work that has been characterized by Anthony Pagden as "the most virulent and uncompromising argument for the inferiority of the American Indian ever written."[69] Finished in 1544, it had allegedly been written under the auspices of the president of the Council of Indies, the same Fernando de Valdés.[70] Permission to publish it in Spain had been denied because of negative opinions of the work by members of the faculty in the universities of Alcalá and Salamanca, as Las Casas pointed out in one of his *tratados:*

> It was agreed by the gentlemen of the Royal Council of Castile, in their just wisdom, because the subject matter was mostly theological, to send it to the Universities of Salamanca and Alcalá, recommending that they examine it and sign it if it were to be printed. [The universities] after prolonged discussions determined that it should not be printed, it being unsound doctrine.[71]

The approval of Sepúlveda's petition to publish his book would have been tantamount to legitimizing his views, and by extension those of the colonizers.[72] Also, it would have signified official acceptance of the theory in favor of using force to convert the Indians to Christianity as well as accepting that the American Indians were natural slaves and therefore subject to being enslaved by the Spanish.[73] If Sepúlveda were allowed to publish his book, his success would have also signified the abrogation of important legal provisions, gained by missionaries like Las Casas and other reformers, guaranteeing the rights of the Indians to be treated as subjects of the Spanish king rather than as slaves.

Fresh from his bitter experience in Chiapa, Las Casas led the fight against Sepúlveda's renewed attempts to publish his book from his arrival in 1547 to their final encounter in Valladolid in 1550–51. His nearly fifty years of experience in the Indies, the majority of which, as he claimed, had been spent defending the Indians, constituted his main qualification. What was at stake was not so much the question of whether the book should be published as the question of whether the wars of conquest being waged against the Indians could be justified.[74] The lines were clearly drawn: Sepúlveda represented the interests of the colonists and the call for justifying the use of force in conquering the new continent; Las Casas, the *protector de los indios,* argued for an end to conquest of the Indians and the imperative to convert them to Christianity by peaceful means.

The confrontation at Valladolid afforded Las Casas with a unique opportunity to settle accounts with Sepúlveda, who, in 1548, had denounced him to the royal council of Castile, accusing him of questioning the jurisdictional right of the Spanish crown to the Indies. Sepúlveda's accusation referred to the Dominican's writing of *Avisos y reglas para los confesores*, which he had distributed among his brethren. In response, the council reprimanded the bishop and prohibited the circulation of the *Avisos* indefinitely.[75]

A furious controversy, between moralists and theologians on one side and conquistadores and entrepreneurs on the other, had been raging from the time of the promulgation of the New Laws in 1542, and by 1550 it had become a war of words and deeds. The first group considered it their Christian duty to protect the Indians from inhuman exploitation and extermination. The second, more preoccupied with maintaining their newly acquired privileges, profits, and political position, saw its interests in the Indies threatened by the meddling of the missionaries. The discrepancies between the two worldviews assumed a level of virulence that continuously disrupted the successful exploitation of the New World. This forced Charles V, at the suggestion of the Council of the Indies (April 16, 1550), to call for a moratorium on the discoveries and conquests being carried out at the time and to convoke a junta of theologians and jurists to meet in Valladolid to attempt to reach a conclusion about the debate.[76] It was also agreed that sometime in the course of the year there should be a meeting between Sepúlveda and Las Casas.

The confrontation between the two factions, aside from the personal enmity of the two protagonists, pitted Sepúlveda's unequivocal defense of the naked exploitation of the natives of the New World by semi-feudal entrepreneurs against the more benevolent form of imperialism regulated by laws and run by ecclesiastical elements proposed by the protector de indios. The two opponents represented "two divergent, yet complimentary tendencies of the imperialist theory of their time," yet both agreed on the mandate to convert the New World native inhabitants to Christianity.[77]

In August of 1550, the opponents met in Valladolid. The scheme of Sepúlveda's book could be reduced to three basic points: first, Indians were culturally inferior to Spaniards. Second, the Indians' unnatural crimes deprived them of their rights of *dominium*; and finally, the bulls of donation represented a valid charter for the Spanish Conquest.[78] In a very real sense Sepúlveda had become the main disseminator of the harsh image of American natives put forth by Las Casas's long-time enemy Gonzalo Fernández de Oviedo in his *Historia general y natural de las Indias*.

Sepúlveda spoke for three hours to outline the tenets of his case. He presented four arguments emulating the principles laid down by Thomas

Aquinas to support the existence of just wars and by extension attempting to justify war against the American natives as one such case. Sepúlveda's four arguments can be summarized as follows:

1. The Indians can be reduced and placed under the dominion of the Christians "because [they] are, or at least were, before falling under Christian *dominium*, barbarians in their habits and customs, and the majority of them are unlettered and without prudence and contaminated by various barbaric vices."

2. "These barbarians are guilty of grievous sins against natural law." War can be waged against these people to extirpate idolatry [because] there is pontifical and legal authority to do so.

3. "All men are obligated by natural law to prevent that innocent men be put to death, if it is possible without great harm to themselves." War is also justifiable to prevent cannibalism. The validity of this reason, from his perspective, was unquestionable.

4. "It is required by natural and divine law to prevent men from continuing their march to perdition and to bring them to salvation, even against their own will." This can be accomplished either by having missionaries preaching by themselves, or preaching accompanied by force to prevent any impediments presented against such exhortation.[79]

Las Casas countered each one of Sepúlveda's arguments by reading from a prepared apología, written in Latin, for five consecutive days. It appears that he droned on until he either concluded, or was asked to stop by the members of the illustrious jury.

He first undertook the task of defining what constituted a barbarian and came up with four categories, of which the third refers to the Aristotelian classification of "slaves by nature." However, Las Casas argued that the number of these barbarians, people without recourse to powers of reason, was extremely small in the whole world, and that the American Indians did not naturally fall under this category, but even if they did, the approach to them should be as good Christians through peaceful persuasion rather than forceful conquest. To lend force to his argument, he expostulated in typical Lascasian fashion: "Let us send Aristotle packing, because in Christ, who is the eternal truth, we have the following command 'Love thy neighbor as thine own self.' "[80] He further argued that no person "no matter how civilized could force a barbarian to be subject to him if the 'barbarian' had not injured him beforehand."[81]

Against his opponent's second argument, Las Casas developed an extremely complex counterargument concerning the question of punishment being directly linked to the issue of jurisdiction. In the first place he established that the American infidels did not fall under the jurisdiction of the church; consequently, they could not be punished. Since the Indians had not known of the existence of Christ, unlike the Moors and Jews, they could not be held accountable for their beliefs since they came from omission rather than commission.[82]

Sepúlveda, who unlike Vitoria did not recognize the existence of even a rudimentary international law,[83] relied nonetheless on the principles of natural law to intervene and to justify aggression against a group of people perpetrating crimes against another group of innocent people. Las Casas argued that the only authority the church and the Christian princes had been granted by papal donation had been the obligation of preaching the Gospel. However, preaching to the infidels had to meet very specific criteria concerning methods and conditions under which conversion could be carried out. He also argued that in the case of protecting a few victims, it was necessary to weigh the conditions of any intervention so that the corrective measure did not result in the wholesale slaughter of those who were sacrificing the innocent. In the case of the American Indians, it was better to forgive them, in view of the fact that the offenses were "so rare" and only occurred as part of the Indians' religious rites.[84]

Las Casas countered the fourth and final of Sepúlveda's arguments, concerning the use of force to spread the Gospel, by establishing a difference between heretics and pagans. While heretics were errant members of the church and could consequently be punished for their deviance, the pagans, who were ignorant of the existence of the church, fell outside its scope. Thus, the work that had to be done with them was similar to that at the dawn of Christianity when people had to be shown slowly the true way. According to Las Casas, this and only this was the only acceptable way of dealing with the American infidels.[85]

In sum, Las Casas maintained that despite the cultural differences between Spaniards and American natives, the same social and moral imperatives existed in all cultures made up of rational beings. Naturally, for him, the Indians were no exception. Concerning violence, he argued against justifying its use by either Indians or Spaniards. He also argued that the ultimate judge was God and that human beings were ultimately responsible to God and not to other human beings who deemed themselves superior.

The most important element in all of Las Casas's arguments was his insistence on the theme of liberty, liberty for all human beings from all forms of oppression.[86] On a different tack, Las Casas also attacked the orthodoxy of Sepúlveda's work by pointing out that the Council of Trent had refused to take a closer look at *Democrates II*; had the council done so, it "would undoubtedly have forbidden its publication and imposed silence on its author."[87] The argument concerning orthodoxy brought up an interesting contradiction. While Las Casas reiterated his approval of the Inquisition as an agent to enforce the true teachings of the church in the New World,[88] Sepúlveda had been encouraged to pursue the publication of his book by none other than the inquisitor general of Spain, Fernando de Valdés, the man responsible for the ultimate guarantee of orthodoxy in the empire: "Valdés reinforced with all the weight of his authority Sepúlveda's thesis, by telling him that it would be better if all those doctors would make sure that his book should be printed in very large letters and its contents preached from their pulpits."[89]

At stake in Valladolid was much more than the mere permission to print a book. Beneath the surface, numerous philosophical and political issues were in contention. First, there was the question of waging war against the Indians, although at the time of the debate the most active fronts of conquest in the Americas were Chile and the La Plata regions, remote confines of South America removed from the central consciousness of the empire. Another issue at stake was the question of jurisdiction, which Las Casas had questioned in his *Confesionario*, or so Sepúlveda had argued in his charges to the Council of Castile. Third, and indirectly, there was the question of natural servitude, although the issue of the encomienda had been officially almost laid to rest in 1545 with the abrogation of Article 30. To accept Sepúlveda's views would have implied the ultimate official sanction of the institution. There were also the questions of political and professional rivalries, the enmities between Sepúlveda and Melchor Cano, and between Inquisitor Valdés and Bishop Bartolomé Carranza, who served with Cano in the Valladolid jury and was eventually imprisoned by the Inquisition on charges of heterodoxy.[90] It is precisely the prevalence of all these undercurrents in Valladolid that prevented a clear verdict as an outcome of the debate.

The junta of Valladolid did not grant Sepúlveda permission to publish his *Democrates Secundum*, and many of Las Casas's followers saw this, and continue to do so, as an unqualified victory for Las Casas. However, this claim must be tempered with a closer examination of the multitude of factors implicit in the outcome. Sepúlveda was not refused permission to publish his book because Las Casas had disproved the validity of the ideas expressed in it or because the Dominican had demonstrated a greater moral and philosophical superiority. He was denied permission because, among other reasons, the judges found his theory inhumane, and because his theory in support of paternalistic enslavement and exploitation of Indian serfs could set the stage for the creation of a powerful nobility with vested economic rights interposed between the king and his Indian subjects. He also did not receive permission because the encomienda, which represented "a form of private authority over the Indians, was inevitably repugnant to a centralised monarchy and to autocratic missionary orders."[91]

The judges at Valladolid, who came from the school of Salamanca, had reached by induction the same point of view that Las Casas had reached empirically, and this earned him their respect.[92] The academic world in Spain "continued to frown upon the system which Sepúlveda had supported." Unofficially Las Casas had won a qualified technical victory in the debates, in addition to denying Sepúlveda permission to publish his book; all available copies published in Italy were withdrawn from circulation in October of 1550.[93] Yet, at the same time, Las Casas had suffered a practical defeat in terms of not obtaining the permanent abolition of the encomienda. Although it was established that the Indians were not "slaves by nature," their condition as encomendados and their mistreatment at the hands of the Spaniards remained unchanged. The encomienda continued in force throughout the remainder of the century, and although it was formally abolished in the eighteenth century, it lingered, in different incarnations, well into the wars of independence of the nineteenth century.

The debate at Valladolid is often cited as a reflection of the much-vaunted sixteenth-century Spanish spirit of tolerance that allowed for a considerable degree of free expression and open discussion that extended to the American domains, as Lewis Hanke stated so unequivocally in his famous book about Spanish justice: "The historian today would know much less about the struggle for justice, if the Spaniards had not discussed their American problems so freely and so frankly ... What makes the freedom of speech enjoyed in sixteenth-century America so notable is that the Spanish rulers not only permitted, but encouraged it."[94]

The idea of a free and open discourse about the New World had been reinforced throughout the years thanks to the royal convocation of juntas whose function had been to reinforce the impression that the sovereigns of Spain were concerned about the plight of people in their domains. In actuality, the opinion of the juntas had served to augment the size of the imperial archives or had resulted in the enactment of unenforceable laws. The patina of legitimacy and the "Spanish Struggle for Justice" is little more than an artificial construct to gild over this stormy period of Spanish history and does not stand up to any kind of conscientious scrutiny. In Valladolid, the two currents of thought that met were both essentially Christian and humanistic and both sought the conversion of the same group of people, but through different means and for different ends.[95]

Ultimately, Valladolid was little more than a confrontation between two faces of the same empire. One belonged to the colonists and was represented by Sepúlveda; it demanded a free hand in the exploitation of Spanish territories and its people as the colonists saw fit. The other was represented by Las Casas, who advocated a more benevolent and systematic imperial exploitation while positing the crown as the overriding regulator of the exploitation of the colonies and their people in a rational and productive manner. Las Casas had served to attack Sepúlveda and the threat presented by the semi-feudal ambitions of the conquistadores in the New World, and although Giménez Fernández and Hanke considered the outcome at Valladolid a tie,[96]

[in] reality, the Crown, free to pick and choose arguments to suit its needs, won. Sepúlveda's position because of its harshness, had limited utility, except in the negative sense of supplying the foil for the positive justification supplied by Las Casas. The official meeting in Valladolid proved to be the last significant debate involving the legitimacy of Spanish rule. Philosophically, the monarchy had met the challenge and turned it to its own advantage. In the end, Las Casas served to legitimize colonial authority.[97]

By the time he debated Sepúlveda at Valladolid, Las Casas had formally resigned his post as bishop of Chiapa, citing his age and poor health as a reason. Slowly and systematically he began the process of resettling in Spain permanently. At long last he found himself in a milieu where he no longer had to fear for his life, a position where he could become significantly more effective in the day-to-day workings of the imperial government and its policy-making process for the Indies. Finally he found himself close to the center of power where he had always wanted to be. Thanks to his royal stipend as retired bishop, Las Casas set up residence in the Dominican Colegio de San Gregorio in Valladolid, where he established his base of operations with his faithful companion Rodrigo de Ladrada.[98] Having established residence at the monastery, he devoted himself to playing out his role as *procurador universal de todos los indios* (universal procurator for all the Indians). And he continued to pursue the goals to which he had dedicated his life: first, to organize missions "staffed by learned and saintly religious who would convert, baptize and educate the Indians,"[99] and second, to defend the Indians' equality and dignity against all those who advocated their enslavement and mistreatment. The last task he set for himself was to write and publish his doctrines and conclusions, further advancing the claims made in the *Historia general* and the *Apologética*, and focusing on legal concerns such as the right of conquest, the right of restitution, slavery, the encomienda, and personal and political freedom. The three tasks allowed him to continue his work on behalf of the natives well into his productive final years.

Five

Toward a Restoration of the Indies

It is holiest, truly Christian and suited to the diffusion and the
exaltation of Christ's glory, to invite pagans to the faith through the
word of God and evangelical behavior.

—Bartolomé de Las Casas,
Apología o declaración universal de los
derechos del hombre y de los pueblos

IN SPAIN, IN THE PROXIMITY of the court, Las Casas found the security
he lacked in American territory. Far from the threats against his life and
other dangers faced by the reformers, such as the one who had claimed the
life of his friend Bishop Antonio de Valdivieso in Nicaragua, he felt capable
of defending his political and philosophical positions even more forcefully
than before.

Universal Procurator for All the Indians

Immediately after his return from Mexico, Las Casas was confronted with
the interdiction of his *Aviso para confesores*. By November 1548 all manuscript copies of the book circulating in New Spain had been requisitioned by
royal order on the pretext of a lack of approval by the Council of the Indies.[1]
To answer the charges of *lesae majestas* that accompanied the prohibition
of his confessors' manual, he wrote his *Treinta proposiciones muy jurídicas*
(Thirty Very Juridical Propositions), followed shortly thereafter by another
treatise along the same lines, his *Tratado comprobatorio del imperio soberano*
(Treatise Verifying the Sovereign Empire).[2]

Using the two treatises as support, he attempted to demonstrate to the
king that the charges of lese majesty were unfounded, and that his intention

had been to question the morality and legality of the conquests and the actions of the participants who had directly benefited from them, not the jurisdiction of the monarchs. He began the argument by focusing on the pope's spiritual authority and power over "all the men of the world, whether they were believers or infidels, whenever he deemed it necessary to guide men on the correct path to eternal life," granted to the pontiff by Christ himself.[3] The pope, he argued in propositions 6, 7, and 8, could entrust a temporal prince, or princes, with the task of carrying out a Christianizing mission as agent of the church. Aside from requiring the sovereign to act as a caretaker of the Indies—for that was the true Christian mission implied in the original donation of Alexander VI to the Catholic Monarchs—he reiterated in propositions 17 through 19 the sovereignty of the monarch of Castile and León over the American territories and their inhabitants. The next to last proposition stands out as one of his most severe admonitions against the encomienda, an institution he continued to condemn in the strongest terms, depicting it as the fountainhead of all the tragedies suffered by the Indians:

> [E]ncomiendas and *repartimientos* of men, distributed like animals, from their tyrannical beginnings, were never ordered by the kings of Castile nor did they ever think of it. Because such iniquitous, tyrannical, and genocidal governance of such immense kingdoms, which places everyone in permanent, harsh, horrendous and deadly servitude, is incompatible with the righteousness and justice of anyone who is a Christian Catholic, or even gentile infidels, possessing royal reason.[4]

In the last proposition he straddled a fine line to avoid offending the king, maintaining that everything that had been done in the name of Spain in the New World was null and void because the conquest of the Indies had been carried out by tyrants, without just cause and without the authorization of the monarch. Returning to the familiar position of exonerating the crown and separating it from the actions of the colonists, he argued that the manner in which the conquest and colonization had been carried out had contradicted the best wishes and beliefs of the king.[5]

These thirty propositions are indicative of a profound transformation in Las Casas's general line of argumentation. Unlike previous arguments, in which he had sought to ingratiate himself with the crown at all costs, this time he appeared less afraid of challenging at least some aspects of what until then had been the untouchable subject of the jurisdiction of the Spanish monarchs in the New World. However, he carefully avoided charging the sovereign directly and blamed instead the private entrepreneurs in a move designed to force the king to react against the colonists who, in their condition as autonomous semi-feudal lords in the isolation of the colonies, were attempting to challenge the king's authority.

Aware that the shift in the responsibility for administering and granting encomiendas from Charles to Philip in the 1550s demanded a new strategy, Las Casas changed accordingly. Philip, unlike his father, was willing to avoid the extremes represented by opposing parties in a debate and find a juridical middle in most disputes. Since the crown increasingly supported the practice of the *repartimiento*, Las Casas was forced to resort to Thomistic principles of natural law to substantiate his views suggesting that the king could not justify through the passage of law something which by natural right was clearly unjust.[6]

As an advisor of the Council of the Indies, Las Casas participated in many of its deliberations and was instrumental in the passage of an unusual amount of legislation favorable to the Indians.[7] Largely as a result of his efforts, the crown approved, in 1549, a law calling for the review of the titles of Spanish colonists in the New World, to determine whether they possessed just titles or not.[8] The former bishop of Chiapa spent the better part of 1551 and 1552 "personally recruiting and dispatching friars to the New World" and traveling through Spain for this purpose. He also obtained funds from the emperor to buy different commodities for the convents and churches of the Dominican order in Chiapa.[9]

In 1552, Bartolomé de Las Casas published in Seville a collection of nine treatises, written over a ten-year period and containing some of his most polemical writings. The first was the widely publicized attack against the encomienda, *Brevísima relación de la destruición de las India*. The others ranged from a reproduction of fragments of a letter describing the horror of the conquest by one of its participants to a reproduction of his *Confesionario* and his *Thirty Propositions*, culminating with a treatise entitled *Principia Quaedam* (Some Principles). This last treatise is a collection of four principles examining the question of dominion exercised by stronger beings over weaker ones and exploring, once again, the issues of liberty, sovereignty, and the obligation that a ruler has to exercise his government for the good of society.[10]

The timing of the publication of his treatises, and the fact that these were printed without license, seemed to reflect a carefully prepared plan to familiarize the king and the crown prince with the ideological foundation on which he hoped to erect his case in favor of restoring the Indies, which, from his perspective, had been destroyed by a concerted attack which was "far worse than the assault mounted by the Turk in his attempt to destroy Christendom."[11]

The publication of his treatises, while placing him at risk, demonstrated Las Casas's ability as a propagandist aware of the value of the printed word and its effects on his contemporaries. It also revealed an uncanny ability to grasp the intellectual and social climate of his time.[12] This particular quality led Angel Losada to proclaim admiringly that Las Casas was "the first writer in the world to perceive *the value of the written press as a tool for propagandizing an ideal* [el valor de la prensa escrita como medio de propaganda de un ideal] and the first one to put the idea into practice; in this *manner he could be considered the precursor of modern day journalism*."[13] Despite the exaggeration about Las Casas's contribution to modern-day journalism, Losada's statement contains a significant element of truth in recognizing the Dominican's ability to maximize the usefulness of the written word in his campaign to "restore" the Indies.

As would be expected, the first consequence of the publication of the treatises resulted in the denunciation of Las Casas to the Inquisition.[14] Henry R. Wagner unearthed information about the charges brought against Las Casas from an entry in Juan Antonio Llorente's book on the Inquisition, published in the early nineteenth century. In the book, the former inquisitor indicated that charges were brought against Las Casas because the material he had written was, allegedly, contrary to the "doctrine of Saint Peter and Saint Paul concerning the subjection of serfs and vassals to their lords and kings."[15] Wagner also infers, based on documentary evidence provided by Antonio María Fabié, that it was Sepúlveda who, once again, turned Las Casas's name over to the Inquisition after the encounter at Valladolid.[16]

By printing his tracts without authorization, Las Casas demonstrated yet again his readiness and ability to use any means necessary to accomplish his objectives, even if these were the same means used by his opponents. The publication of the tracts without permission was no different from what Sepúlveda had done in printing the infamous *Democrates Secundum*, although the humanist's book had been printed abroad and Las Casas's treatises had been printed in Seville. The printing represented a double act of defiance, for the *Confesionario* had previously been banned and Las Casas was clearly contravening a directive that he was more than willing to see enforced against others. If his intention had been to gain the attention of the king, he had the option of circulating a few manuscripts among the members of the court, but the printing of the tracts points to a desire to reach a much broader audience. This concern seems to have overridden the fear of having the editions of his book sequestered for lack of a license, something that eventually occurred in 1566 when all books pertaining to matters related to the Indies printed without the license of the Council of the Indies were pulled from circulation.[17]

Aside from his efforts to recruit missionaries and his publishing activities, Fray Bartolomé was in constant motion, acting as either consultant or active member of the various juntas called by the king to resolve problems dealing with the conditions arising from the relationship between encomenderos and Indians. During his final years in Spain, the friar participated in the arguments surrounding one of the most heated points of contention between colonists, natives, and crown, the issue of the perpetuity of encomiendas.

The argument first gained notoriety when, in 1550, the priest Pedro La Gasca, relatively fresh from defeating and executing the rebellious Gonzalo Pizarro in Peru, came to court precisely to discuss the issue of perpetuity. There, he joined representatives from New Spain, including Bernal Díaz del Castillo, and participated in a junta with various other experts including Las Casas and Ladrada. The junta questioned La Gasca's right to grant titles to various Spaniards in Peru as a reward for fighting Pizarro, a practice for which he was severely criticized by many of the participants. It was at this time that Díaz del Castillo suggested that too many members of the junta— Las Casas, Ladrada, La Gasca, the Dominican Tomás de San Martín, and two of the *oidores*, among others—were opposed to granting perpetuity to the encomenderos. In response to Díaz's intervention the issue was postponed until a more propitious occasion.[18]

The question of perpetuity was then revived in 1554 when the Peruvian encomenderos once again sent an envoy, the *licenciado* Antonio de Ribera, to court with a tempting offer for the economically strapped sovereign. At this time Charles was in Brussels and Prince Philip was residing in England with his wife, Mary Tudor. Ribera promised to pay the crown millions of ducats as compensation for the perpetuity of the Peruvian encomienda.[19] A previous junta, convened in Spain in 1553, had been unable to reach a decision in favor of perpetuity, just like the one in 1550. This time, Philip convened the meeting of yet another junta in London. The junta recommended approving the petition of the Peruvian envoy by a vote of ten to two, despite the vociferous opposition to the proposal by Philip's confessor and future archbishop of Toledo, Bartolomé de Carranza y Miranda, who in the heat of the moment came to blows with the president of the junta, Pedro de Castro.[20]

The sentiment of those voting in the majority was reflected by the favorable *parecer* (opinion) written by Fray Alonso de Castro. In arguing against the main tenets espoused by Las Casas and maintaining that the abolition of the encomienda would create disturbances grave enough to endanger the sovereignty of the king over his American dominions, Castro concluded that it was mandatory to have at least some repartimientos. He further argued that the king should give these repartimientos freely, without charge, but in case of economic duress, he could sell them as if they were public offices.[21] Encouraged by the support of his father and the outcome of the junta, Philip felt free to ask his sister Princess Juana to present the case to the Council of the Indies for final approval in February of the next year. However, the council, meeting in May of 1555, still refused to grant outright approval. The council did not categorically deny its approval, but it claimed not to be able to come to the best possible decision concerning the issue at that particular time. Instead, it asked the crown to wait for matters to be settled in Peruvian territory before reaching a decision.[22]

Informed of the events taking place in London, Las Casas sent a long letter to his friend Bartolomé de Carranza, emphasizing, once again, the arguments against the encomienda in general and perpetuity in particular. The letter, known as the *Carta grande*, was intended for Carranza, but Las Casas requested that it be shown to the king, although it contained some of the most provocative challenges that Las Casas had ever presented to the Spanish occupation of the Indies.

The Carta grande, like his *De regia potestate*, ranks as perhaps one of the most defiant tracts that Las Casas ever composed, and for that reason it bears close scrutiny. Given the climate in favor of accepting perpetuity, Las Casas went to dangerous extremes to chip away at the proposal and incurred the danger of again being charged with lese-majesty for writing the letter. He began by pointing out the importance of the matter and asking, indirectly through his fellow Dominican, that the prince and the emperor refrain from reaching a hasty decision before they returned to Spain to meet with a suitable group of advisers and experts. As the letter evolved, its accusatory tone mounted in intensity:

It has already been sixty-one years since those innocent people [in the Indies] have been robbed, tyrannized and devastated, and forty years since the Emperor of Castile has been ruling, and he has never put a remedy to it, except for small repairs . . . and now the Kings of Castile, holed up in England or Flanders want to deal so hurriedly with such a red hot and fictitious proposal! I believe that even if it was carried out, it would be considered by humanity a grave error loathed and punished by God . . . .

Father, what obligation do the oppressed, the hapless, tyrannized, pauper-ized, annihilated inhabitants of the Indies, who never before found themselves so lacking in possessions or roots in this whole universe, have to get the Castilian crown out of hock and to help it fulfill its necessities?[23]

It is apparent that much of the text had borrowed heavily from the *Brevísima*, particularly the parts describing the atrocities committed by the conquerors, which were being reenacted by the encomenderos in the act of "perverting the natural order of things decreed by God." In the letter to Carranza he also made reference to a new and more sophisticated mode of oppression and exploitation. Since the outright sale of slaves was illegal, the *hacendados* were resorting to selling their *haciendas* for a higher value than the ongoing market value of the land, but in reality what was being sold was not so much the land but the Indians in the hacienda. When this was not the case, an encomendero could sell a shirt being worn by an Indian for an unusually high price, but what was being sold in reality was the Indian wearing the shirt, and the sale of the garment was only an excuse to justify the transfer of individual slaves.[24]

To get rid of these exploitative practices, Las Casas called for the freeing of Indians from all encomiendas and for the restoration of traditional native rulers to the positions of authority in their traditional communities.[25] He also suggested that in order to maintain the kingdom as part of the empire and to ensure the orderly behavior of the king's subjects, military garrisons manned by a few soldiers in the king's payroll should be maintained.[26] As he had done in previous proposals to the crown, the Dominican emphasized that the peaceful usufruct of the land would benefit all future colonizers and soldiers coming to America. In addition to the benefits to be gained by the colonists, all the Indians who had been freed would provide the king with a handsome return in the form of tribute.

Las Casas's petition failed to sway Philip, and a year later, the newly anointed king wrote the Council of the Indies from Ghent on September 5, 1556. The monarch maintained that after having examined the question innumerable times and considering that the province of Peru could not support itself without grants of perpetuity to the encomenderos, he had "resolved to grant [perpetuity] and wanted it to be put into practice without any further delay."[27] However, the granting of perpetuity to the Peruvian encomenderos was a complex process which, in order to be implemented in a manner beneficial to the crown, required the creation of a structural mechanism capable of implementing the change. To accomplish that end, Philip ordered the Council of the Indies to name a commission to leave for the New World in early 1557. The naming of the commission presented some difficulty, and after inordinate delays, its members finally arrived in Lima in April of 1561.[28]

At the same time that the king was choosing the commissioners and the period when the commission actually began its process of deliberation, the *kurakas* of Peru also met in San Juan de los Reyes and decided to make a counteroffer to the one presented by the encomenderos. They chose as their official representatives the Dominicans Fray Domingo de Santo Tomás, Alonso Méndez, and Bartolomé de Las Casas. In July of 1559, in the presence of a notary, the caciques granted the three Dominicans absolute legal power to become their official procurators before the pope and the king.[29] Armed with the official power to represent the Indians, Las Casas and Santo Tomás presented a memorial to the king and the Council of the Indies as a counterproposal to Ribera's offer. The memorial attempted to illustrate the harm that would come to the king and his possessions in the New World if perpetuity were approved. The proposal emphasized the possibility of the crown losing vassals and revenue, and the possibility that the encomenderos, emboldened by their new status as semi-feudal lords, would be tempted to revolt. In its conclusion the memorial reminded the sovereign that granting perpetuity would prevent him from administering justice and helping the natives and "giving orders to the effect that they be converted and become Christians, because then, truly there would not be any Christianity."[30]

The Dominicans, arguing that they only wanted the crown to benefit, made an ambitious and attractive proposal to the king by offering, in the name of the Indian caciques they represented, one hundred thousand ducats above and beyond any bona fide offer of the colonists. If there were no set amount offered by the Spaniards, then they promised the king two million ducats payable in four years. The attractive offer was tempered by a set of demands that the representatives of the natives expected the king to meet. The Indian caciques committed themselves to serve as faithful vassals as long as the king agreed to protect them and to guarantee that protection forever, giving them for this purpose all the authority, documents, and titles necessary to fill their offices.

To ensure that their requests would be met, the representatives further asked the king to meet other specific conditions. They required that once their encomenderos died, the Indians of Peru were not to be given in encomienda. They also demanded that the encomenderos, their families, and their African servants should be forbidden from entering Indian towns. Another demand called for a reassessment of tribute under extraordinary circumstances of demographic decline. The provisions also called for a partial restoration of indigenous hierarchies. As the encomiendas were vacated, lesser caciques would be placed under the leadership of the more important ones, according to the policy under Inca rule. Their last demand was that neither water nor land should be taken from either the community or individuals, and what had been forcefully taken up to that point should be restored to their lawful owners.[31]

This was, undoubtedly, one of the most daring and ambitious proposals ever presented by Las Casas, and the reformers, to the crown. It is possible that it was the huge sums of money promised by the caciques that allowed Las Casas to feel "freer" to impose "radical" conditions. Unlike the letter to Carranza, where he still seemed to have some faith in the impartiality and good judgment of the reigning sovereign, in this case he felt he could make more demands based not so much on matters of faith or piety but on practical considerations. Prompted by his desire to tilt the balance of power in the colonies in favor of the Indians, Las Casas contributed to help the Indians challenge and weaken the power of the encomenderos in favor of the king. However, Las Casas's inability to understand the complexity of class differentiations among the natives lent support to the creation of a dominant native class willing to continue exploiting other natives in the same way the Spaniards had been doing up to that time. Once again, in his attempt to abolish the hold of the encomenderos on the Amerindians, he ended up helping to strengthen the centralist imperial designs of the crown.

The commissioners sent to Peru, first by the king and later by the Council of the Indies, came up with a set of very cautious recommendations. They feared the danger resulting from the excessive autonomy that the colonists would obtain after receiving their encomiendas in perpetuity. The first recommendation of the commissioners suggested a compromise calling for a division of the encomiendas into three categories. The first category limited the number of encomiendas that could be given to the original conquerors, or their descendants, perpetually as a reward for their services. A second category called for some encomiendas to be granted to an encomendero for a lifetime, reverting to the crown upon his death. The third category called for all the encomiendas that had been vacated, up to that time, to revert permanently to the control of the crown.[32]

Neither the council nor the king could reach an official decision on these recommendations, and in 1565 Fray Alonso de la Vera Cruz read a memorial to the Council of Indies from Las Casas, who was unable to attend the session because of sickness, requesting a decision and continuing his line of argument against perpetuity.[33] Three years later some members of the council warned about the potential dangers inherent in the semi-independent status of the colonizers and the threat they posed to the crown if they decided to rebel trying to become autonomous. These arguments were met with passionate arguments in favor of perpetuity. Unable to reach a consensus, the council referred the matter back to King Philip for a decision, but the issue remained dormant until it came up for discussion again in 1578, twelve years after Las Casas's death.[34]

The battle against perpetuity was one of the last significant battles fought by the Dominican. In the nineteen years between his return from the Indies in 1547 and his death in 1566, he saw a significant transformation take place in court: a shift from the benevolent and humanitarian preoccupations of Charles V for his American subjects to the more meticulous and pragmatic approach of Philip II, whose main concerns about the Indies were based more on economical practicality for the empire rather than on subjective or moral considerations. Despite his professed respect for the authority of the crown, Las Casas demonstrated that in the environment of the court, where he was in his natural element, he could be a formidable contender who could produce impressive arguments to support his positions.

The bishop's effectiveness was never greater than when he acted as part of the official apparatus in Spain. It was there, as defender of the interests of Native Americans and consultant to the crown, where he seemed to accomplish more, at least in the theoretical realm of lobbying for, and enacting, legislation pertaining to the Indies—more than he ever could as a direct participant in the conflicted, and conflictive, New World, a realm where the dialogical possibilities between himself and his fellow Spaniards were nil.

Although he had been unable to convince the king to decide against perpetuity, his actions had the effect of first delaying the execution of the sovereign's decree and finally of having the matter shelved indefinitely.

The last years of his life in Spain were characteristically filled with the drama and controversy that had always accompanied him in his long journey. Removed from the immediacy of the contradictions inherent in the New World, he found the time to expound and develop his political theories while producing lengthy histories and political treatises. It is this period that his admirers and hagiographers hold up as the best example of his work.

From the fateful moment in 1514 when he realized his calling as a protector of the Indians, Las Casas actively argued against the different manifestations and incarnations of the encomienda and its practitioners. After the failure of the New Laws and the reversal at Malines, the question of perpetuity became his foremost preoccupation and he could not consider his struggle completed until some resolution could be reached.

Aside from the Carta grande to Carranza, which in essence was a long well-articulated tract against the encomienda, there were memorials to the king and the Council of the Indies, and a letter to his Dominican brethren in Chiapa and Guatemala questioning their conformity in accepting the encomienda. Perhaps anticipating the proximity of his death and reflecting his exhaustion, the letter to the Dominicans shows evidence of the disillusionment generated by the passivity of his brethren of the cloth. In the letter to his fellow preachers, he recalled, with undisguised pride and a touch of nostalgia, the intervention of Bartolomé Carranza de Miranda and his determined stand against perpetuity in the junta of London, where he had led the opposition against Pedro de Castro's opinion in favor of the encomenderos.[35] He also used the opportunity to defend his friend and to deny the charges brought against Carranza, then bishop of Toledo, persecuted by the Inquisition as a heretic.[36] Throughout the letter, he urged his fellow preachers not to forget the years of work spent in the struggle against the encomienda.[37]

His last significant written contributions during this period were his will and testament, prepared in 1564, and Los tesoros del Perú and the brief treatise Tratado de las doce dudas, both written in 1563 and presented to the king at the beginning of 1565. There was also the posthumously published De regia potestate, which appeared in Germany in 1571. These last four works represent the culmination of the evolutionary process of the friar's legal and political thought over some fifty-two years. Essentially, they were a summing up of his theoretical and political positions concerning the Spanish possessions in the New World. Although he chose the specific theme of Peru as the main focus of *Los tesoros* and the *Tratado de las doce dudas*, it is clear that centering on a specific region was just a means for him of finding a vehicle to summarize his opinions and position on all matters concerning the Indies.

Los tesoros was aimed at answering the question of whether or not the treasures found in the *Huacas* of Peru, where the ancient pre-Columbian cultures buried their dead, belonged to the finders or to the Spanish king to give away or to keep. Las Casas began by putting forth three different propositions examining the motivation and the cultural and political significance that being buried with their own treasures had for the individuals of a given group. He asserted that even if the people were dead, they still had dominion and rights over the treasures accompanying them in their tombs. Having settled the question of proprietorship, he concluded that to take these treasures was akin to thievery and rapacity. Furthermore, he claimed that not even the king of Spain could give those treasures away or alienate them, unless he received them from the Inca king or his rightful heirs. This treatise went beyond the mere question of dominion and rightful possession of buried treasures and touched on the important theme of the validity of the Spanish occupation of the Indies. This had been evident in his dispute with Sepúlveda, where the friar had vehemently opposed the interpretation of Alexander's donation and the legality of forceful conquests. Las Casas maintained that, because of the donation, the Spaniards had a right to be in the Indies, but they could not exercise that right as long as the Indians did not accept them, and naturally, the use of force invalidated the legality of the conquests.[38]

His *Tratado de las doce dudas*, the short work written soon after *Los tesoros*, was intended as a response to the doubts expressed by a Dominican preacher about the appalling conditions of the Indians in Peru. The doubts ran the gamut from questioning the legality of the tribute obtained from the last Inca emperor, Atahualpa, to the validity of the titles acquired by the conquerors.[39] Las Casas responded to these doubts with some eight fundamental principles. Among other things, he argued that no matter what the religion or sins of the infidels, they were the legal possessors of their land and their properties, and he further argued that no king or emperor, not even the church, could wage a just war against the Indians. He also maintained that the only authority granted by the papal donation was for the propagation of the faith. After questioning the authority of the crown to ask the natives to pay, against their will, the expenses incurred by Spain in the process of their conversion, he maintained that all the explorations and subjection of the natives carried out by Spaniards beginning in 1492 were evil and tyrannical. In his text outlining the final principle, Las Casas claimed that from 1510 to 1564 there had not been in the Indies a single conqueror or colonist who had acted in good faith.[40]

These two treatises are matched in intensity by a work concerning the right of self-determination of the peoples of the world, *De regia potestate*, published after his death. The literary production of Las Casas's last years lacks the prolix disorder of his *Historia de las Indias* and the *Apológetica historia* that he completed in 1559. Apparently, Las Casas began writing this last treatise between the end of 1555 and the beginning of 1556 and probably revised and amended it between 1563 and 1566.[41] This final work seems the culmination of Las Casas's transformation from the priest-encomendero of the early days into a capable juridical-political scholar. Even more than his testament, *De regia potestate* stands as his last attempt to change the course of relations between Spain and the Indies by a process of careful philosophical disquisition and as his ultimate challenge of the validity of certain aspects of Spain's dominion over the Indies.[42]

In *De regia potestate*, Las Casas argues from the principle that liberty is natural for all human beings and that slavery is an accident rather than a natural condition, and that all prohibitions are opposed to liberty. From his perspective, kings are not the proprietors of private possessions but only have legal jurisdiction over them, and their function is to prevent these properties from being alienated as well as to defend their subjects and their property. Another point that Las Casas raises is that there exists a covenant between a sovereign and the people, thus any tribute or payment to the sovereign is the result of an agreement between both sides. He concludes with the assertion that power is based on the people's will and the sovereign cannot rule by terror or coercion. By ascribing a democratic value to the basis of power, Las Casas challenges the validity of the encomienda. Specifically, this argument represents a continuation of the one against perpetuity. In the conclusion to the treatise, Fray Bartolomé maintains that the king does not have his royal dignity diminished if he abstains from granting cities or any private property in his kingdoms to individual holders, for to do that would be the "equivalent to mutilating them substantially and leaving them without the protection of a just and natural order, transforming the body politic into a monstrosity. To do that, the king has absolutely no power, given that he is not the owner of the goods in his kingdom, but the administrator."[43]

The implications of this conclusion threatened the very essence of the king's power over his whole empire. If he did not have the right to distribute property in the Indies, then the king would be hard pressed to justify his authority to sell towns throughout Castile, as well as his other overseas domains.

In addition to the *Tratado de las doce dudas*, Las Casas wrote a petition to Pope Pius V, at approximately the same time, asking him to have *De unico vocationis modo* examined so it could be published. He also asked the pope to excommunicate those who supported waging war against the Indians and those who claimed that the Indians were not the lawful owners of their possessions, or those who proclaimed that the Indians were incapable of receiving the faith.[44]

The last significant document produced by Las Casas during the final period of his life is his last will and testament, where he legated to the Colegio de San Gregorio of Valladolid all his writings and his files. In this document, Las Casas reaffirmed his belief in the fact that he, like Columbus before him, had only been an instrument in carrying out God's divine work in the New World,

> because thanks to the kindness and mercy of God, who deemed fit to choose me as his minister, without my being worthy of it, to be the universal procurator of those peoples, from the place we call the Indies, rightful owner and possessors of those kingdoms and lands, to redress the grievous and unparalleled harm and hurt received from us Spaniards contravening all justice and reason . . . to free them from the violent deaths they are suffering . . . I have worked in the court of the kings of Castile, coming and going from the Indies to Castile and from Castile to the Indies many times, for nearly fifty years, since the year of fifteen hundred and fourteen, only to serve God and out of compassion from seeing the death of such multitudes of people, rational, domestic, humble and most gentle and simple, and so disposed to receive our Holy Catholic Faith.[45]

After summarizing his labor on behalf of the Indies and its inhabitants, he reverts to the accusatory and apocalyptic tone evident in his *Brevísima relación* and fulminates against Spain, predicting its decline and fall caused by the unstoppable wrath of God as punishment for its participation in the bloody despoiling of the Indies.[46] Having written his testament in 1564, and having made his peace with those around him as well as he could, and being prepared for meeting his Maker, the Universal Procurator of All the Indians, Bartolomé de Las Casas, died in the convent of Our Lady of Atocha in Madrid, sometime between the seventeenth and eighteenth days of July, 1566.

149

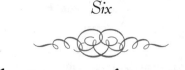

Six

The Legacy of Las Casas

Decolonization never takes place unnoticed, for it influences individuals
and modifies them fundamentally. It transforms spectators crushed
with their inessentiality into privileged actors with the grandiose glare
of history's floodlight upon them.
                              —Frantz Fanon, *The Wretched of the Earth*

THE FINAL FIFTY-TWO YEARS of Las Casas's life, the period between
his conversion in 1514 and his death in 1566, can be characterized as a
mosaic with a single theme binding it together, the friar's endless struggle
for the "restoration" of the Indies.

Crises and Reform

As a representative of the reforming Christian vanguard in America, Las
Casas saw the Indies as a continent in the process of being destroyed by
the Spanish invasion and occupation, just as Spain had been destroyed
by the invasion of the Moors. This perspective had been colored by his
country's experience with nearly eight centuries of Moorish occupation,
the Reconquista and the destruction-restoration (*destrucción-restauración*)
dichotomy prevalent at the time. In keeping with his messianic orientation,
Las Casas saw himself as an individual chosen by God to act as the providential instrument capable of bringing about the restoration of the ravaged and decimated Spanish possessions overseas, and as such he was fully
conscious, at all times, of his role as the leader of the reform movement.
As Juan Friede points out, "Las Casas was more than a historian, jurist,
theologian, or moralist; he was above all the head of a political movement and the organizer of an activist party—the only pro-Indian party

in Spain and America that exerted a strong influence on Latin America's reality."[1]

As the head of such an important social, cultural, moral, and political movement Las Casas faced the necessity of providing viable alternatives to counteract existing Spanish policies in America. His first attempt to restore the Indies found him proposing a plan to alleviate the plight of the natives in the Antilles. This was the aforementioned "Memorial de remedios" of 1516.[2] Because of his suggestion, the royal administration attempted to create a quasi-theocratic form of government in the Antilles under the leadership of a junta of Jeronymite friars working out of Española. The failure of the religious men to implement a successful policy to improve conditions in the islands is widely acknowledged. The Jeronymite experiment won Las Casas the enmity of that order, given his public denunciation of their efforts in favor of the colonizers. The intense feelings were further exacerbated by the accusation of the friars themselves, who had been convinced by the encomenderos of Santo Domingo not to free the Indians as they had been ordered by royal decree but, on the contrary, to vouch that the encomienda was an absolute necessity for the successful exploitation of the island.[3] Las Casas's charges against the Jeronymites led to a series of acrimonious incidents in which charges and countercharges flew back and forth, causing the cleric to lose the support of Cardinal Regent Ximénez de Cisneros and other important personages at court.

Although Las Casas's attempts at restoring the Indies through the intervention of the church failed in that instance, he nevertheless was named universal procurator and protector of the Indians, by none other than Cardinal Regent Cisneros. This was a powerful-sounding official title, with no defined responsibility, that he proudly bore until his death. A second attempt to find an alternative for the restoration of the Indies consumed the next four years of his life, from 1518 to 1522. This was the formulation and implementation of a revolutionary plan for the peaceful conversion of the natives of Tierra Firme from an encampment on the coast of Venezuela. However, once again lacking the cooperation of the officials directly responsible for the affairs of the Indies, Las Casas's second venture also failed.

After his conversion to the Dominican order and a hiatus of some nine years spent behind the walls of Dominican monasteries in Española, Las Casas emerged once again to wage his battles. Facing renewed resistance from the colonizers-encomenderos, Las Casas opted to move his base of operation to a different terrain. Given that all his attempts to restore the

Indies had failed in the actual locality where events were unfolding with unusual celerity, he had himself transferred to Spain, where he could use his proximity to the court to present his now more sophisticated proposals to transform the state of American affairs. When he finally returned to Spain in 1540, he undertook one of the most formidable tasks of his life, the lobbying of the crown for the passage of a comprehensive body of laws that would curb the power of the encomenderos and allow the Indians enough breathing space to begin to recover from the onslaught of the conquest.

As on previous occasions, Las Casas discovered that there was much more to be gained by appealing to the sovereign and his advisors than by trying to influence the colonists to change. By choosing to work with the king and his representatives, Las Casas placed himself on the side of the imperial policymakers and, by default, against the colonizers in America. By opposing the colonizers' interests and their aspirations to create semiautonomous colonies and individual fiefdoms, Las Casas can be recognized as "a precursor of anti-colonialism."[4] Nonetheless, his anti-colonialism must be tempered by an understanding of the particular relations obtaining at the time between the central authority of the Castilian king and the entrepreneurs in the New World. At the time, Spain was in the process of formulating a political theory of empire for the first time in its history and its policies tended to be reactive to specific pressures rather than providing the basis for long-range policies that anticipated the development of a new society under unique conditions.

As I have observed, Las Casas's characterization as an anti-colonialist is a valid one, considering his opposition to the colonial aspirations of the conquistadores and encomenderos. At the same time this in no way diminishes or alters the significance of his role as an instrument of imperial power and domination, one who advocated "the sovereignty of a powerful ruler over numerous territories, whether in Europe or overseas."[5]

The colonizers in America ascribed to themselves the privileges of which they had dreamed in the Old World and saw themselves as part of a new aristocracy that the crown could not afford to alienate.[6] To do so would have meant the loss of income and privileges gained by the crown in the New World merely by granting permission to various entrepreneurs to undertake, sometimes at grave risk, the discovery and settlement of the new territories. The profitable colonial beachheads established by these independent agents contributed substantially to the economic survival of a crown dependent on every possible available means of support. In this context, Las

Casas's activism to restore the Indies, "destroyed" by the colonists, was not only tolerated but tacitly, and often overtly, encouraged by the sovereign and his advisors.

The Dominican's attempts to protect the Indians invariably served to reinforce the imperial authority through the enactment of regulatory legislation. This allowed the crown to gain a measure of control over the colonists without risking its relations with them, for it could always deflect attention to their most visible opponent, Bartolomé de Las Casas, who willingly assumed the role of lightning rod. It is only in the last years of his life that the first manifestations of the transformation of the friar's approach to petition the crown become evident. At last, his traditional approach of presenting profitable schemes to the crown was forsaken in favor of a more polemical style, such the preparation of the infamous *Brevísima relación de la destruición de las Indias* and *De regia potestate.* Although the specifics are subject to discussion, we can assume that the *Brevísima* had some tangential influence in the enactment of the New Laws aimed at curbing the power of the encomenderos and gaining, at least in theory, a greater regulatory role in the government of the Indies.

His *Brevísima relación* was intended as a warning to Spain about possible divine retribution if it did not mend its ways in the Indies. It prophesied the destruction of Castile and the whole of Spain, much like the devastation had suffered under the Moors. This conception, which was not atypical at the time, helps to explain partially his dedication to the cause of restoring the Indies, which from his perspective had been destroyed by the surviving victims and inheritors of another destructive process.

As in most of his proposals, Las Casas argued that the horror and destruction could always be stopped, and the consequences of the conquest could be minimized if his remedies for restoration were implemented and no more encomiendas granted, with the Indians who until then had been held in encomienda becoming free vassals of the king.[7] This proposal meshed perfectly with the crown's desire to limit the power of its subjects in the American kingdoms, thus Las Casas either advisedly or inadvertently once again ended up serving as the battering ram of an imperialist center against emerging colonial elites in the kingdom's peripheral societies. The crown, which by this time could not overlook the significant decrease in native population and the resulting economic losses, seized the opportunity provided by Las Casas's attack on the encomenderos to attempt to enforce the New Laws.[8] However, the laws, instead of providing a remedy to restore the

Indies, created further social and political dislocations among the natives and colonizers in the New World. They produced a climate of animosity against the reformers and caused the civil wars in Peru, which ultimately translated into greater political, social, and cultural hardships for the Indians and political and economic losses for the crown.

In view of the failure of the crown to put in place a viable mechanism to implement the laws, Las Casas accepted the bishopric of the diocese of Chiapa, hoping to use his episcopal power to persuade the encomenderos of the need to adhere to the dictates of the laws emanating from the motherland. Opposition to the law included open manifestations of hatred against Las Casas, who, fearing for his safety, was forced to return to Spain and eventually to resign his see. The failure of his efforts to restore the Indies to their pre-Spanish status forced him to once again modify his approach to attempt to accomplish his goals by returning to his writing and lobbying efforts in the imperial capital.

His practical attempts to use his episcopal office had come to nothing, but he could still challenge the crown from a moral, juridical, theological, and theoretical perspective. This he did with a deluge of books, memorials, and letters, defining, suggesting, and proposing new ways to restore the Indies and gain some modicum of decency for the original inhabitants of the continent. During this period of his life, he put forth some rather "revolutionary democratic concepts" proposing that colonial authorities appointed by the royal power were subject to the approval of the people being ruled while having the sovereign serve in a tutelary capacity.[9]

Las Casas's entire life as procurator and protector of the Indians was characterized by an inordinate faith in the viability of the imperial system's effectiveness in resolving the problems of the New World. Although his faith in the system was somewhat shaken in his latter years, he never stopped demanding that changes for the Indies should take place from the top down.

The history of the Indies is littered with the failures of ambitious laws aimed at protecting the Indians. The Laws of Burgos were enacted, even before Las Casas's first conversion, under the regime of Ferdinand and Isabel, but they brought no relief for the natives. Under Cardinal Cisneros and Charles V, even more legislation affecting the Indies had been approved. The enactment of more laws became a counterproductive exercise given that, with so many laws aimed at regulating the Indies, it was difficult to decide which to enforce. While many laws had been approved, a viable process of implementation was never effected to lend them practical validity. It was idealistic and unrealistic to expect that as Las Casas's challenges to the legitimacy of Spain's dominion over the New World increased, King Philip would be willing to risk anywhere from one fifth to one quarter of the crown's income to satisfy the humanitarian demands of a religious reformer.[10]

By establishing Spain's relationship with the Indies within the dichotomous context of destruction-restoration and perpetrator-victim, Las Casas ultimately failed in his quest to bring about any measurable restoration of the New World. From the perspective of this absolute dichotomy, the answer to destruction was total restoration, and nothing less was acceptable. Even within the structure of the perpetrator-victim dichotomy, Las Casas's efforts at restoration were carried out independently of the aspirations of the natives in the absence of a meaningful dialogue between Las Casas, in Spain and America, and the "victims" he was supposed to represent.

As he became more immersed in his role of protector and spokesman of the Indians, on whose behalf the changes were being sought, Las Casas continued to lose contact with the changing everyday reality of the natives. It was as if his efforts on behalf of the natives rested on the premise that these were powerless victims devoid of will and condemned to a life of permanent dependence on the goodwill of charitable members of the dominant group to intercede for them. During Las Casas's lifetime, the natives, with very rare exceptions in Mexico and Peru, were never present in the process of deliberation resulting in policies affecting their lives, just as they were absent from the determination of any legal or juridical process relating to the enforcement of the laws affecting them.[11] Despite his long experience in American territory, he never became a part of that dynamic American society so immersed in the process of creating a new world. He was always the outsider straddling two worlds, unwilling to forsake his alterity. He opted to work in the sophisticated, lettered, metropolitan center where the court met, rather than attempting to lessen the distance between himself and the people whose causes he advocated. At no time was this more apparent than in his removing himself to Spain permanently without attempting to seek refuge among, and accept support from, the indigenous people whom he so professed to love.

Followers and Disciples

At the beginning of the sixteenth century, Spanish statesmen were absorbed by the process of formulating a political theory of empire for the first time in the history of the country. In the absence of a clearly defined theory of government, Spain's policies tended to be reactive and of short duration; they were not designed to provide the basis for long-range processes that could anticipate or manage the creation and development of a uniquely different world.

Las Casas's role as a benevolent agent of Spanish political and ecclesiastical imperialism began at the time of his conversion, when as a cleric he denounced the conditions in Española during the first decades of occupation. After the failure of Jeronymite rule in the island, the cleric's proposal for the colonization of Tierra Firme provided the king with an opportunity to establish a beachhead on the mainland where he could have absolute authority and become the main recipient of native tribute. The cleric made the enterprise attractive to the crown by guaranteeing profits and political power to the king who was slated to become the sole encomendero of Tierra Firme. To this end he presented an alternative proposal for rational exploitation to gain control of Tierra Firme for the crown that would mark the demise of the colonists' unregulated and anarchic striving for profits at all costs. The plan was intended to increase profits for the crown while accomplishing the transfer of the main characteristics of Spanish culture to the newly conquered people through the teachings of the vanguard of the army of God embodied by members of various Spanish religious orders.

The new proposal, curtailing the privileges of private entrepreneurs in favor of the crown, was rooted in Las Casas's early experience with the encomenderos of Española, an experience that colored his perception of the whole Spanish colonial enterprise. Throughout his long career, the friar's inability to differentiate the events and processes that had taken place in the Antilles from the particularities of the conquest of Mexico, Peru, and the rest of the American mainland became increasingly evident. It was this inability to assimilate the new complex dimension of the encounter between Europe and the high civilizations of mainland America that prevented him from implementing truly effective reforms, as evidenced by the failure of the New Laws and the resulting internecine wars, which brought if anything a worsening of the already dismal conditions of the natives' existence.

During his lifetime, the bishop of Chiapa made numerous enemies, but he also had numerous followers who continued his struggle on behalf of the Indians, even after his death. Notable among this latter group was the lay chronicler Pedro Cieza de León, who shared with Fray Domingo de Santo Tomás a grave preoccupation about the quickly dwindling native population of Peru.[12] It was Santo Tomás who kept Las Casas's struggle on behalf of Peruvian natives alive after the friar's death. From the time of his arrival in Peru in 1540, Santo Tomás had earned a well-deserved reputation as champion of Indian rights and as an enemy of the encomienda and the abuses of the encomenderos. Unlike Las Casas, Santo Tomás was well acquainted with the language and the cultural practices of the Indians, and he was capable of achieving great closeness with the subjects of his affection and work.[13] His familiarity with the Andean worldview and power structure led him to suggest that upon the abolition of the encomienda, the crown should discourage new Spanish immigration to Peru and have the native lords begin retaking control of their country as soon as the last encomendero had vanished. However, the accession of Philip II changed the nature of relations between the imperial center and the colonial periphery, and by the late 1560s "Fray Domingo and his allies were fighting a rear-guard battle. There was no longer any talk of returning the country to its natural rulers; there may be vehemence in the language of some friars like Francisco de Morales, but the battle had been lost."[14]

Santo Tomás, like Las Casas before him, was also appointed to a bishopric. In his case, it was the see of Charcas [La Plata], and from the time of his appointment in 1562, he used the visibility and prestige of his office to continue his unequal struggle in favor of the natives. By the time of his death in 1570, he had incurred the wrath of powerful enemies, including some of the canons of his own cathedral. The animosity aroused by his reformist zeal led his enemies to attempt to discredit him by writing a letter to the king claiming that he was a half-Jew-half-Muslim who was using a fictitious last name to which he had no right.[15] The death of Santo Tomás gravely weakened the indianist movement in the Americas, but far from disappearing, it managed to gain new converts, in the face of mounting odds against it. Prominent among the newcomers was Alonso de la Vera Cruz, an Augustinian monk, a close friend and collaborator of Las Casas during the last days of his life. There was also Alonso Maldonado de Buendía, a Franciscan who continued to question the legality of armed conquest and the forceful domination of the natives, and Luis Sánchez, a disciple of Juan del Valle, bishop of Popayán, who like his mentor also dedicated his life to the defense of the Indians.[16] Unquestionably, Bartolomé de Las Casas blazed a new trail, and his followers kept it operational, but unlike him, most of the disciples and followers lived out their existences in America, in the heart of the contradictions against which they struggled, rather than attempting to fight in the relative safety of the imperial center.

The disciples' contact with the immediate reality of everyday existence in the Americas, and their empirical, as opposed to theoretical, experience lent particular poignancy to their struggle in favor of reforms. This in no way implies that Las Casas lacked experience in America, but one has only to peruse his *Historia* or the *Brevísima* to realize that despite his knowledge and experience of America, there were profound voids in his knowledge of the nuanced relationships between colonizer and colonized obtaining in the New World. The authority he might have derived from his condition as an eyewitness and participant was diluted by his desire to "minimize the differences between Europe and America."[17]

At the same time, his inability to translate his theoretical postulates into concrete gains for the natives was exacerbated by his peripatetic activism. It has been well illustrated that he rarely remained in any one place long enough to acquire a sufficient degree of familiarity with the native inhabitants. Furthermore, he never demonstrated much of an inclination to deal with the anonymous and tedious details of trying to implement beyond their original stages the imperial decrees resulting from his lobbying efforts and the programs he proposed. His effectiveness was hampered further by his constant need to respond to his detractors and the inordinate amount of time he dedicated to protecting his own physical integrity against the ever-present threats to his life. Not surprisingly, much of the animosity and polemical contradictions surrounding Las Casas during his lifetime became an integral part of the legacy he left to his followers.

Early Myths and Mythmakers

A half-century after the death of Las Casas, the Dominican friar Antonio de Remesal received permission from the censors in Spain to publish his *Historia general de las Indias Occidentales y particular de la gobernación de Chiapa y Guatemala*.[18] After finishing the book, he shipped a substantial number of copies to Guatemala, hoping to sell them to recover his original investment and even make a small profit while gaining some recognition for his efforts.

Instead, as a result of his efforts, he found himself involved in a tortuous nightmare that culminated in his premature death only a few years later.

Remesal's ordeal began with the confiscation of his book by the Spanish authorities in the New World, who used the absence of proper paperwork as an excuse to sequester the book. When the friar arrived, in April of 1621, and although he was bearing the proper license and the censor's seal of approval for the books, he was greeted with a peremptory order to leave Guatemala or risk being imprisoned. Refusing to leave, he was detained in his own convent while even the copies of his book that he had brought with him were impounded. Eventually he was released and had most of his books returned, but when he demanded payment for the missing ones, he incurred the wrath of the local inquisitor, Felipe Ruiz del Corral, who had him thrown in prison once again. This time he was held in solitary confinement with only bread and water for sustenance. Two years later he was released and exiled to the Mixteca region in New Spain. From there, he moved to Guadalajara and Zacatecas. In his last known letter, dated February 9, 1627, he lamented his plight and claimed to have been mistreated by "word and deed; I have been able to preach only three sermons and have confessed only three Spaniards; because [the rest] fled from me considering me as an enemy."[19] It is estimated that he died that same year or shortly thereafter.[20]

The case of Remesal is particularly relevant in view of the fact that his travails did not originate with the writing of a history of the early inhabitants and colonizers of Guatemala itself, a history that could in no way be considered demeaning or offensive. Instead, as it became evident with the passage of time, his main mistake had been to praise the Dominicans and their reform efforts in favor of the Indians. The local Creoles and the local inquisitor were enraged by Remesal's uninhibited support and open advocacy of Bartolomé de Las Casas's opinions about peaceful colonization and his wholesale condemnation of all encomenderos of all times. From the authorities' perspective, Remesal had erred in lavishing praise on Las Casas's performance as bishop of Chiapa from 1545 to 1546. By emphasizing the activist aspects of the bishop's experience, such as his refusal to grant absolution to those encomenderos who refused to give up their Indians, the young Dominican had reopened ancestral wounds that refused to heal even after the main protagonists of the conflict had passed from the scene. Antonio de Remesal, the idealistic seventeenth-century Dominican intellectual who had held such great expectations for the New World, fell victim to the hereditary hatred engendered by the activities of Bartolomé de Las Casas as bishop of Chiapa three quarters of a century earlier.

Ironically, Remesal had not been the first to write in praise of Las Casas. The credit for inaugurating this hagiographic tradition belongs to the Dominican Agustín Dávila Padilla and his *Historia de la fundación y discurso de la Provincia de Santiago de México*. Dávila Padilla's text, from Benjamin Keen's perspective, represented far more an attempt to revive a seriously endangered cause by exalting Las Casas than a conscious effort to mythologize its subject. The work invests the Dominican with a "halo of saintliness, but Daniel Ulloa points out that Dávila Padilla's effort is not so much to write down a history, but rather to 'piously edify' the role of the Dominicans in New Spain. According to Ulloa, Dávila's biography of Las Casas 'is not a call for revival of the struggle of human rights; it is an epitaph on a dead cause.' "[21]

Had it not been for Dávila Padilla's and Remesal's efforts, Las Casas's work might have remained buried indefinitely in the archives and library of the Colegio de San Gregorio. Remesal patiently unearthed many of Las Casas's writings, but in the process of writing the friar's biography he created an exalted mythical personage produced by his own overheated imagination. Not even Las Casas's own accounts of the incidents at Tuzulutlán, by then re-baptized as Vera Paz, are as given to drama as Remesal's. It is Remesal's mythical conception of Las Casas that was later revived by Creole patriots of the nineteenth century and kept alive by generations of reformers and academicians thereafter.

Frequently the creation of a symbol or a larger-than-life myth is more reflective of the needs, aspirations, and expectations of the creators than of any real accomplishment on the part of the symbol or person mythologized. In the absence of true heroic personages, and the abundance of villains and antiheroes during the European collision with America, Las Casas, almost by default, emerges as one of the most sympathetic, benevolent, and attractive characters born at the time of the traumatic genesis of America. It may be that the inordinate attention paid to the Dominican friar evidences more a preoccupation with trying to find recuperable elements in the dark and bloody origins of American society than a primary interest in Las Casas himself.

Remesal's history of Las Casas was widely circulated after the writer's death, but that appears to have been more a response to Remesal's own tragic end than an appreciation of his highly imaginative and hagiographic treatment of Las Casas. As Marcel Bataillon explains:

Remesal invents and deforms without any other passion or design other than inventing. A narrator, a storyteller, does not lie; he simply invents, always invents. And Remesal is one of them. He has an imagination eminently realistic. When he likes an episode, he likes to describe it in time and space with the colors of life.[22]

Without fear of exaggeration or equivocation, the same can be said of most of the myriad admirers and detractors of Las Casas throughout the centuries.

Although Remesal's death did not result directly from his romantic portrayal of Las Casas, it nevertheless was a result and a reflection of the spirit of a time when no one was willing to retreat or compromise. At the time of Remesal's writing, the controversy surrounding the colonization of America had assumed its own well-defined characteristics and a momentum. Antonio de Remesal was caught in a mortal crossfire resulting from the ongoing controversies unleashed by or against Las Casas concerning the salvation of the Indians and an emerging colonial oligarchy and its conflictive relations with the power of the imperial crown.

Contested Legacy

Seven years after the death of Las Casas, Philip II signed into law the "Ordenanzas para descubrimientos" (Ordinances for Discoveries), which represented the most comprehensive sets of laws regulating new discoveries of territory in the New World since Columbus encountered the American continent.[23] Most importantly, the document spelled out the manner in which Spanish colonists were supposed to deal with the Indians. The specificity of the laws reflected Philip's fascination with detail. The norms to be followed by "explorers" coming to new American territories by land and sea were so carefully outlined, so inclusive, and, ostensibly, so respectful of Indian rights, at least as far as the letter of the law was concerned, that full authorship could have been certainly attributed to Las Casas had he still been alive.

The ordinances contained more than one hundred clauses stating, among other things, that "no person of any state or condition can by his own authority undertake a discovery or exploration of any new territory . . . *under penalty of death*."[24] They also specifically instructed the discoverers not to "become engaged in war nor conquest of any kind, nor help one group of

Indians against another." In an absolute turnaround from previous practice the ordinances decreed that the *"discoveries will not receive the title of conquests, since they will be carried out with as much peace and charity as we want,* we do not want the name [conquest] to provide occasion or opportunity to use force or injure the Indians."[25] This clause would have satisfied even Las Casas's most exacting demand, as exemplified in his argument against the title of "conquest" in his sixth treatise of 1552.[26]

The emphasis that the ordinances placed on peaceful colonization and catechization, prompted the historian J. H. Parry to compare their scope and impact to Charles's New Laws.[27] Lewis Hanke added that "the standard law of 1573 on new discoveries probably was drawn up in such generous terms because of the battle Las Casas fought at Valladolid."[28]

Although no official winner had emerged out of Valladolid, Hanke goes to great lengths to demonstrate that Philip's policy closely adhered to the principles expressed by Las Casas throughout his life, and particularly in the debates. At the same time, there are glaring contradictions in Philip's actions that the North American historian ignores in order not to detract, even minimally, from the perceived benign influence that Las Casas had on all things having to do with the Indies. In his quest to demonstrate the beneficent nature of sixteenth-century Spanish rulers, insofar as their struggle to bring justice to their kingdoms is concerned, Hanke pays no attention to the consequences that the laws had on the American kingdoms. He ignores the fact that despite the crown's ambitious aspirations for the Laws of Burgos, the New Laws, and the ordenanzas of 1573, it never put in place a mechanism to enforce them nor did this massive corpus of legislation ever translate into tangible benefits for the Americans.

Most admirers of Father Las Casas tend to ignore the ironic and tragic consequences of the friar's proposals and the coincidence between some of them and different variations of the same applied in the subjugation and exploitation of the indigenous people. They also ignore that almost all of Las Casas's utopian aspirations and proposals failed to materialize in the positive manner in which the framer had intended. Among the ironies of the Dominican's utopian quest was the negative application in colonial Peru of one of his earliest proposals to protect the natives. These recommendations, as noted earlier, were applied by Viceroy Francisco Toledo in Peru and constituted a distorted mirror image of the early remedies for the Indies, which Las Casas had suggested to the crown in 1516. At that time Las Casas had called for the Indians to be congregated in villages close to Spanish settle-

ments where they could be protected from random abuses from the encomenderos, receive Christian indoctrination, and become part of crown-
administered labor pools from which the colonists could draw their work
forces. These were measures that Toledo took to heart and implemented in
Peru in 1569.

As a corollary to his proposal to have Indians congregated in villages
under the supervision of the Spaniards, Las Casas had suggested a system
whereby Indians could work on a rotational basis during certain periods of
time per year so they would be allowed time to rest and recover and be more
productive without being worked to death.[29] Upon arriving in Peru in 1569,
Toledo congregated the Indians in reducciones (essentially indigenous reservations), imposed a system of rotational work, *mita*, and delegated some
responsibilities on Indian caciques (*curacas*) to act as intermediaries between
the Spaniards and the Indians.[30] Las Casas had suggested his policies to the
crown as a benevolent form of systematizing the exploitation of the land and
its inhabitants and as a form of preventing the decimation of the Indians.
Conversely, the application of Toledo's policies was designed to increase the
imperial sphere of influence and to maximize the crown's profits regardless
of the human cost. Although his policies resulted in a considerable incre-
ment in the profits of the crown, they also contributed greatly to the demographic disaster decimating the indigenous population.

Toledo and Las Casas represent two faces of the same empire. The
Dominican advocated the creation of a utopian world, a benevolent paternalistic empire, where the Indians could thrive. The royal official was concerned with establishing, at all costs, Spanish hegemony in the New World.
Despite their differences, both Spaniards were bound by their belief in
Spain's right to dominion over America. In the case of Las Casas, it found
justification from a juridical-theological perspective that accepted the hegemonic right of an imperial church to bring all infidels under its mantle. In
the case of the viceroy, it meant being free to act as an imperial agent of
Spain freed by the Valladolid debates of the 1550s. As a direct outcome of
the debates, the question of whether or not Spain had the rights to be present in America had been tacitly recognized in favor of the Iberian nation,
and no other individual, not even Las Casas, had ever publicly questioned
it again.

As Keen points out, there is a contradiction implicit in Hanke's paradoxi-
cal position about the history of Spanish colonial domination. On the one
hand, he champions the thought and work of Las Casas, and on the other he

attempts to rationalize some of the most glaring injustices committed by
official representatives of the crown in the New World. But Hanke is not
alone in holding this contradictory position; there are many of the proponents of the Golden Legend who want to find redeemable elements in the
policies of sixteenth-century Spanish monarchs, despite irrefutable evidence
to the contrary. However, as Keen writes, "Despite the lip service paid to Las
Casas' ideals by the general ordinances of 1573, the essence of Philip's Indian

policy was profoundly anti-Lascasian. During his reign, Indian tribute and
labor burdens increased and Indian living standards decreased."[31] This observation acquires more poignancy if we take into consideration that before,
during, and after the promulgation of the ordenanzas, the war and enslaving raids against the Chichimeca continued unchallenged in the northern frontier of New Spain under the supervision of Viceroy Martín Enríquez.[32] In Peru, at about the same time, the reducciones, along with the
insalubrious and ominous working conditions in the mines, caused the
native tribute-paying population to decrease by half in the fifty years between 1580 and 1630.[33]

The ordinances of 1573 fully represent the complexity and ambivalence
of the work and legacy of Bartolomé de Las Casas. As an exemplar of a
medieval tradition of belief in the justice and authority of the sovereign and
the efficacy of the law, the Dominican deposited his trust in the imperial
authority to enact legislation aimed at "restoring" the world his compatriots
had encountered and "destroyed." Despite the practical limitations of his
exaggerated trust in the power of the king and the law, he gained a measure
of success by obtaining, in isolated instances, the temporary halt of conquests
and attacks against the Indians while new legislative projects were studied
and discussed by different juntas or deliberating bodies capable of influencing the king.

In the case of all legislation governing the Indies, there existed a close
relationship between the complexity of the law and the absence of mechanisms to enforce it, as well as the unwillingness of Spaniards living in the
colonies to obey. The more complex and demanding the law, the more
difficult it was to enforce and translate into viable terms. Once again, in the
absence of articulate enforcement, the ordenanzas remained a collection of
idealistic postulates that served only to gloss over the demands of the reformers; in practice they reflected the complete divorce between the letter of
the law and the crown's ability to achieve significant results from its remote
seat of power. They also served to illustrate the ability of the colonizers to

reject any law that affected their interests. Despite the efforts of the crown and the reformers, the entrepreneurial spirit of the colonizers brought about the partial destruction of the continent they had found at the time of the first Spanish foray into America in 1492.

Bartolomé de Las Casas's impulse to attempt to address and resolve immediate problems of logistics often distracted him at the most crucial moments of his life from seeing his programs though to their final implementation. This was further complicated by the urgency to fend off simultaneous attacks from different quarters. His desire to see his plans and expectations transformed into laws aimed at protecting the Indies and its inhabitants often brought him into conflict with multitudes of people in the colonies and the imperial center. His enmity with the king's representatives in charge of the Indies was legendary. However, it was his constant struggles with the encomenderos, their supporters and associates, and all those who felt their very livelihoods threatened by his relentless demands for justice for the Indians, that consumed the greater part of the friar's labor on both sides of the Atlantic.

Ironically and significantly, one of the most memorable attacks against the Dominican came from within the ranks of the men of the cloth. The Franciscan Toribio Benavente, called Motolinía ("the barefoot one") by the natives out of respect for his humility, was one of the senior members of Spanish missionary efforts in New Spain and a member of the legendary "twelve apostles," Motolinía's criticism of Las Casas reached a climax in a letter written to Charles V in which Toribio depicted Las Casas as a meddler full of sound and fury lacking knowledge of the Indies and the subjects he was most fond of attacking: the encomienda and the encomenderos. This attack occurred at the height of the struggle for perpetuity, around the time of the London junta and Las Casas's Carta grande to Bartolomé de Carranza asking him to intercede before the king in the campaign against perpetuity. The letter was the culmination of a feud exacerbated by the passage of time. As Motolinía himself confessed in the letter, it was he who had collected and given Viceroy Antonio de Mendoza copies of Las Casas's manuscript of the Confesionario to be burned.[34] The vitriolic attack by the Franciscan focused on what he perceived as Las Casas's abrasive personality, his restlessness, as well as on a carefully selected collection of the Dominican's writings.

The missive gave voice to an accumulated fifteen years of ill will between the two men of the cloth. In essence, the dispute represented the two aspects of Spanish occupation: on one side stood the idealistic, reform-minded Las Casas, and on the other the pragmatic-minded Motolinía, who, by sharing the daily life of the colonists, had come to accept their outlook concerning the natives and the relationship of the colonies to the crown. Inevitably, as was the case in all polemics in which Las Casas was involved, the argument devolved to the question of the encomienda and the encomenderos. Motolinía argued in favor of the encomienda by shifting the onus of responsibility

from the individual encomenderos to the king. He claimed that since the king was the ultimate beneficiary of the encomienda, to declare it illegal would be to go not only against the crown's own interests but to contravene its own authority as well. Furthermore, the Franciscan argued that at the time of his writing the letter, the encomienda was subject to such legal restrictions and scrutiny as to render Las Casas's charges of abuses null and void.[35]

Motolinía further charged Las Casas with being guilty of violating some of the most basic tenets of the very laws whose passage he had engineered; he accused him of unlawfully using *tamemes* (private indigenous carriers), which the New Laws clearly forbade. He indicated, in the letter, that when Las Casas had returned from Spain to assume his duties as bishop, he had his belongings carried by "one hundred and twenty Indians without paying them."[36]

Aside from the question of the tamemes, Motolinía further painted Las Casas as an inconsistent member of a religious order who preached in favor of the Indians and then refused to grant them the most elementary spiritual succor. To support his claim, he alluded to the time when the bishop of Chiapa refused to baptize a native who had walked several days to receive the sacrament. As Motolinía told the story, the Dominican only relented after the native complied with his demands to purchase the proper garments to wear in order to be baptized.[37] Motolinía seized this apparent contradiction in Las Casas's behavior to attempt to expose what he characterized as outright hypocrisy. The Franciscan could not reconcile his opponent's use of tamemes and his refusal to baptize a native because he lacked the proper clothing with Las Casas's declarations and protestations of love for the natives. The letter went on to condemn the Dominican's inability, or implied unwillingness, to learn any native languages. It also challenged the Dominican's claims about the peaceful conversion of Indians in Guatemala, arguing that soon after the settlement of Tuzulutlán, Las Casas had departed for Spain without regard for the fate of his newly acquired native parishioners.[38]

Las Casas never responded officially to the Franciscan's accusations, but the incident illustrates the difference in approaches to the problem of the Indian between two different missionary orders and two different individuals. In addition to Motolinía's approach to the wholesale administering of sacraments (he boasted that on one occasion he had baptized fourteen thousand Indians in one day with the assistance of only a single companion), there were profoundly irreconcilable differences in their conception and approach to what constituted true support and affection for the natives.[39]

Concretely, Motolinía was closer to the elementary reality of America and its native inhabitants than the peripatetic Dominican could ever be. As Silvio Zavala has indicated, the Franciscan lived and worked as an apostle attempting to bring the Christian Gospel to the natives of New Spain for more than thirty years. While the one was concerned with evangelizing, the immediate task at hand, the other was preoccupied with the more abstract issues of liberty and justice for the same people. Unlike Motolinía, who felt compelled by his praxis to remain in America, Las Casas felt the need to be at court, close to the centers of power, even if this implied being removed from the people most affected by his acts. While Las Casas approached the question of the Indian from a theoretical and philosophical perspective, Motolinía's contact with the everyday, commonplace reality of ministering to the downtrodden found no benefit or use for the Dominican's lofty idealistic aspirations.[40] These differences between the two missionaries were clearly delineated in the Franciscan's letter to the king. He challenged Las Casas to emulate the example of those who lived every day with the contradictions present in the New World. As he expressed in his letter, he thought little of the Dominican's praxis: "I would like to see the aforementioned Las Casas, persevering for fifteen or twenty years, confessing ten to twelve sick Indians covered with sores everyday."[41] Ultimately, the two friars represented two different aspects of humanitarian affection for the Indians, but, at the same time, they incarnated two different faces of sixteenth-century Spanish ecclesiastical imperialism and its ultimate aim of imposing Christianity and its values on the American "infidels."

Motolinía was only one of a multitude of enemies that Las Casas accumulated during his long life. Las Casas's splenetic disputes with the chroniclers Gonzalo Fernández de Oviedo and López de Gómara are amply documented in their works. Not content with criticizing the accuracy of Oviedo's facts in his *Sumario de la natural historia de las Indias* and his *Historia general y natural de las Indias*, Las Casas attacked the chronicler's perception of the natives and his attitude toward the conquest and the conquerors. Oviedo considered the natives to have barely evolved above the level of animals, an outlook conforming to the old Aristotelian concept that some individuals are inferior and thus condemned to be slaves by nature, a view antithetical to everything that Las Casas upheld.[42] The enmity was further exacerbated by the friar's depiction of the "official" chronicler of the Indies as "a conquistador, robber, and killer of Indians."[43] Aside from the demeaning portrayal of the natives and his exaltation of the role of the conquerors, Oviedo used his *Historia* to mock Las Casas's attempt at peaceful colonization of Cumaná, blaming him directly for the failure of the venture.[44] The Dominican never forgave him for it, nor did he forgive Oviedo for providing the depiction of the Indians that lay at the core of Sepúlveda's argument in Valladolid. Consequently, Las Casas became instrumental in blocking the publication of the remaining volumes of Oviedo's *Historia*.[45]

Las Casas also engaged in a running feud with Francisco López de Gómara, a close friend of Fernando Cortés, a chronicler of the Indies and New Spain, and the author of the *Historia general de las Indias*, which he eventually expanded into the *Historia de las Indias y conquista de México*. Gómara, like Oviedo, also took issue with Las Casas's participation in the fiasco of Cumaná and his alleged role in the promulgation of the New Laws, which were directly responsible for the Peruvian civil wars led by Gonzalo Pizarro. By way of illustration, he described in the *Historia* the reception of the laws by Peru's inhabitants and their condemnation of Las Casas: "Some were saddened, fearful of their application, others cursed, and everyone damned Bartolomé de Las Casas, who had instigated them. Men lost their appetite, women and children cried, the Indians grew haughtier, and this brought fear."[46]

Las Casas, in his own *Historia de las Indias*, retaliated by calling Gómara a servant of the Marqués del Valle (Cortés) and challenging the accuracy of Gómara's account of Cortés's true relationship with Diego de Velázquez, his campaign against the Cempoalans, and his behavior toward the Aztec emperor Moctecuzoma.[47] He also questioned the accuracy of Gómara's charges against him, claiming that all his historical distortions came from Oviedo and that he had no knowledge of what he spoke.[48]

The polemics with Motolinía, López de Gómara, Ginés de Sepúlveda, and Fernández de Oviedo, among many others, allow an insight into the intensity of the friar's controversial impact on the imperial venture of Spain in the New World. They are also indicative of the level of passion that the Dominican could arouse among his contemporaries. At the core of the conflicts surrounding Las Casas we find a single-minded pursuit of his objectives concerning the fate of the natives, and a characteristic inability to change his mind once he had decided on a course of action. It is largely his unwillingness to change, or even retreat partially, that defines Las Casas's existence and is greatly responsible for his inability to accomplish any unqualified victories in his struggle in favor of the Indians or, even, against his most dedicated opponents.

Legend and Reality

Like the legislation he inspired and the historical struggles he fought, Las Casas's legacy is complex and difficult to evaluate in absolute terms. Through five centuries, that legacy has been interpreted from a multitude of perspectives. As a uniquely multifaceted individual, Las Casas is remembered in a multilayered context, as priest, writer, politician, theologian, prophet, and jurist, among other things, but above all he is remembered as a reformer and a defender of the Indians and their rights.[49] As a writer he left a considerable body of work ranging from small memorials and letters to multivolume histories.[50] His value as a historian, anthropologist, politician, and political theoretician has been examined by a multitude of modern scholars in Indoamerica, the United States, and Europe who have dedicated significant time and space to the study of the Dominican and his contribution to the history of Indoamerica and Spain in the sixteenth century.

Although there are different interpretations of Las Casas and his work, there is unanimous agreement in recognizing his labor as an avowed defender of the Indians and a reformer of the Indies as the defining characteristic of his life and work. As a reformer, he was directly responsible for implementing a multitude of changes and additions to the corpus of laws governing the Indies. Although the mechanisms to enforce these laws were often lacking, these reforms slowed down the extermination of natives.

Las Casas's claim that the authority and support for his legal and juridical arguments came from his experience as a colonist, cleric, preacher, and bishop in the New World exemplified the type of experience that no one else in the political, theological, and juridical circles of sixteenth-century Spain could claim. However, in the process of constantly struggling against the colonists, he ultimately became a priceless ally of the crown against the encomenderos' feudal aspirations rather than an agent responsible for gaining specific advantages for the natives.

Despite his early failures at court, experience taught Las Casas that any possibilities of accomplishing his visions of paternalistic benevolent domination for America and its inhabitants could only be attained by appealing to the sovereign and his advisors in Spain. Conversely, he saw the futility of trying to influence the colonists to change, although he never abandoned his efforts to do so. At the same time, he never seems to have contemplated the possibility of organizing any resistance among the natives against the palpable exploitation they were suffering in America.

His decision to work with the crown and its representatives decidedly placed Las Casas on the side of the imperial policymakers against the colonizers in America. However, this must never be equated with his being anti-imperialist. His opposition to the manner in which the colonizers were exploiting the New World and its inhabitants did not call for the end of imperial Spanish rule or the empire's withdrawal from the New World; rather, it suggested the removal of the encomenderos as intermediaries between the crown and its Indian subjects.[51] In the absence of a clearly formulated colonial policy, the Dominican openly sided with the imperialist project of the Castilian king.

The end of the sixteenth century saw a shift in the priorities of the imperial crown as Spain became entangled in various conflicts in the Netherlands, France, and Britain. As a result, America and the question of the legitimacy of Spain's rule became a secondary issue, particularly in the absence of one single defender of Indian causes who could approach the activism or stature of Las Casas. As we have seen, only a few years after Las Casas's death, the military conquest of Peru initiated by Francisco Pizarro was complemented by the bureaucratic and political conquest of Peru by Viceroy Francisco de Toledo, who served in that capacity from 1569 to 1581. Toledo effectively put an end to the resistance of both encomenderos and lascasistas in South America. In Mexico the encomienda began to die a natural death prompted by the transformation of the means of production and the need to depend on a semi-organized work force subject to the payment of wages.

Las Casas's career abounds with instances in which his quest to improve the conditions of the natives helped to consolidate the position of the imperial power of Spain over colonists and the natives. One such instance was the writing of the *Brevísima relación de la destruición de las Indias*. The small tract served as a tool to attack the semi-feudal aspirations of the colonists while providing the crown with an authoritative, "factual," eyewitness testimony that could help it justify the passage of new laws. The legislation instigated by Las Casas and some of his fellow men of the cloth afforded Charles V a unique opportunity to check the growing ambition of the encomenderos by limiting the scope of the encomienda and thus circumscribing their power.

Remarkably, but not surprisingly, it was outside Spain where the influence of Las Casas was felt the most in the period between the end of the sixteenth and the beginning of the seventeenth centuries. It was then that the *Brevísima relación* was published in France, Antwerp, and England. The virulent treatise offered the enemies of Spain an incomparable opportunity to attack that nation's integrity on the basis of the Dominican's denunciations. In this period lay the genesis of the infamous *leyenda negra*, although it would not be referred to by that name for another three hundred years. The name of the legend was first coined by Julián Juderías, writing in the aftermath of the last Spanish defeat in American soil, the Cuban-Spanish-American war of 1898. While calling for Spain to engage in a new form of imperialism, Juderías used the term *leyenda negra* to describe the perception that the rest of the world had of the Spanish conquest and colonization of the Americas: "According to Juderías, the outside world had long viewed Spain and her past through prisms that distorted the Spanish reality."[52]

Juderías was not alone in his "defense" of the enterprise of the Indies; he was only the predecessor of a powerful bicontinental movement that set out to sanitize the role played by Spain during the traumatic days of the birth of the New World. Some of Juderías's followers have characterized the Black Legend as a fable fabricated to create the illusion that

> a truly inhuman spirit had presided over the whole enterprise beginning with the discovery and occupation of the territories by Colón and those who completed his work, which became a form of mismanagement characterized by intolerance and contempt for the offspring of the peninsular trunk, born in the faraway territories of the possessions overseas.[53]

From the perspective of the practitioners of the Golden Legend, anything that was even mildly critical of the Spanish enterprise in America, beginning in the fifteenth century and ending with its expulsion at the end of the nineteenth, was construed as an attack on Spain and an integral part of the Black Legend. This sweeping generalization affecting any critical evaluation of Spain had as a result the emergence of a generation of academicians who undertook the task of revising the history of Spain in America, gilding over the darkest passages of Spain's history in the New World and providing us with a white, or, more appropriately, a gilded, legend. Members of this school of thought in Latin America produced vitriolic works questioning Las Casas's veracity, while attacking the inaccuracy of his numerical account of dead natives in the *Brevísima*. At the same time, they purposefully omitted from their histories some of the most significant acts of genocide committed during the conquest, such as the massacre at Cholula or the killing of thousands of Atahualpa's guards in Cajamarca or the widespread demographic disaster among the natives throughout the continent.[54]

The Argentine historian Romulo Carbia, an assiduous defender of Spanish colonialist and imperialist practices in America, maintained that the conquest was the "execution of a highly and judiciously prepared plan, whose motives have nothing to bring shame to the people who undertook it and carried it out."[55] His defense of Spain's actions can be summed up as a barefaced attempt to support and defend the view that the conquest was nothing short of a blessing, while ignoring the accompanying genocide perpetrated on all natives of America by the Europeans. José Vasconcelos in Mexico, emulating Ricardo Levene in Argentina, maintained that "prior to the coming of the Spaniards, Mexico did not exist as a nation," and that "Spain did not destroy anything, because there existed nothing worth keeping when she came to these territories."[56] If the best form of defense was to attack, the defense of Spanish colonial practices reached an apotheosis of sorts in the unbridled attack against Las Casas orchestrated by the Spanish historian Ramón Menéndez Pidal. Aside from his claim that Las Casas suffered from paranoid delusions, he characterized the Dominican's ideological postulates as antiquated and out of touch with the reality of Spain, tacitly implying a lack of patriotism and love for the mother country. Las Casas's criticism of Spain, despite its harshness, never revealed a lack of patriotism, disloyalty, or disaffection for his country. Las Casas himself on numerous occasions emphasized that it was his love for Spain and the desire to prevent harm from coming to the country that motivated his actions.[57] As Father Vicente Carro wrote in response to Menéndez Pidal: "Las Casas is a Spaniard, a *sevillano*, in his human qualities and his defects which he has like all other mortals. Who could, vaingloriously, claim always to be right?"[58]

A cursory review of the fears and anxieties, often bordering in paranoia, of many "Hispanophile" proponents of the Golden Legend will reveal that the source of their fear originates in the perception of a Spanish nation under attack from all sides. Thus it is not surprising to find the declarations of the likes of the Spaniard Luciano Pereña characterizing the Black Legend as a "sophism that has served as a political weapon to combat Spain and on more than a few occasions the Catholic Church."[59] Pereña's definition of the Black Legend as a piece of sophistry is accurate, not because it serves as a starting point for attacking Spain and the Catholic Church, but because the proponents of the Golden Legend greatly exaggerate the extent and influence of the attack. They seem always ready to label any criticism of early modern Spain as an unqualified attack arising from the exaggerated perspective of the Black Legend. They ignore in the process that there has been widespread universal condemnation, since at least 1789, of the "practices of conquest, colonization and slavery which characterized the Spanish enterprise of the Indies."[60]

Undoubtedly, the original intention of the publication of the *Brevísima* at the end of the sixteenth century by Spain's political enemies was to attack the integrity of Spain's moral character and to weaken its international standing. At the same time, the dissemination of Las Casas's short tract also served to reveal the darkest aspect of imperial and colonialist expansion, which Spain was attempting to gild over and move on.

During the nineteenth century a group of Protestant Nordic historians revived the criticism of Spanish imperialism. We find in this number Francis Parkman, George Bancroft, John Lothrop Motley, and William H. Prescott, who were largely responsible for fashioning the nineteenth- and early-twentieth-century global perceptions of Spain.[61] In response the proponents of the Golden Legend felt, and in some instances continue to feel, justified in mounting an inordinately intense and multifaceted defense of Spain as the hapless victim of unwarranted attacks through the indiscriminate use of the Black Legend. Attacking the Black Legend as a way to justify their exuberance in praising Spain's conquest and colonization of America, the proponents of the Golden Legend can then proceed to exonerate Spain of any wrongdoing during four hundred years of occupation.

The proponents of the Golden Legend found numerous adepts among twentieth-century historians in the United States who felt compelled to initiate revisionist reconsiderations of the Spanish role in the subjugation of America. North American historians like Eugene Bolton, L. B. Simpson,

E. G. Bourne, Irving Leonard, John T. Lanning, and Lewis Hanke, among others, are important components of this group.[62] Ironically enough, when it comes to the question of Las Casas's life and works, some of them deviate from the pattern of support for all things Spanish to attack Las Casas, whose pronouncements were used by Spain's enemies to attack the nation's moral integrity. This is evident in the critical position adopted by Simpson in his attack against Las Casas in the first edition of his book on the encomienda in New Spain.[63]

At the other end of the spectrum of the Golden Legend, Lewis Hanke built a considerable reputation as one of Las Casas's most conscientious biographers and hagiographers. Ironically, Hanke, who was perhaps the best-informed American biographer of Las Casas and the one person responsible "for the re-discovery of the man,"[64] was caught in an interesting paradox concerning two faces of Spanish imperialism in the New World. Hanke was thoroughly familiar with the Dominican's lifelong struggle to obtain justice for the Indians and the frustrations he suffered in his attempts to "restore" the Indies so ravaged by Spain. Yet, at the same time that he exalted the friar's fervor in fighting oppression, he mounted an all-out defense of Spanish attitudes and institutions during the sixteenth century, which he claimed were born out of a desire to make justice prevail among the conquered peoples:

> In the written history of America the undeniable courage and spectacular daring of the conquistadores have hitherto been emphasized, as well as the impressive stability of the far flung empire which Spain brought within the orbit of European civilization and ruled for over three hundred years. There is more, however, to Spain's contribution to the New World, noteworthy as these aspects of her work will always be. Other nations sent out bold explorers and established empires. But no other European people, before or since the conquest of America, plunged into such a struggle for justice as developed among Spaniards shortly after the discovery of America and persisted throughout the sixteenth century.[65]

For Hanke to praise imperial Spain for plunging "into such a struggle for justice" is akin to praising a pyromaniac for calling the firefighters after setting a building on fire. Although Hanke extols Las Casas's attempts to obtain better conditions for the Amerindian, he does not hesitate in praising Viceroy Toledo as a "wise lawgiver, energetic administrator and the greatest ruler that Spain ever sent to Peru, who laid the basis for Spanish dominion there during the years 1569–82."[66]

What the American historian avoids mentioning is that the basis for "Spanish dominion" came at a high price for the indigenous population that Las Casas had so defended. In Hanke's narrative, there is nothing identifying Francisco Toledo as the person responsible for the institution of forced labor known as the mita in Peru. Nor is there any reference to his responsibility for the dislocation of the last vestiges of established native society and the wholesale death of Indians in the mines of Potosí and Huancavelica. Lewis Hanke does not differentiate between the man guilty of regicide, responsible for the execution of Tupac Amaru I, the last surviving Inca, and the *defensor universal de los indios*, Bartolomé de Las Casas. It is ironic and oddly fitting that the two personages who represented two antithetical elements of a contradictory society that allowed perpetrators and victims to coexist side by side would be joined posthumously in a work exalting the system of "justice" imposed by imperial Spain in its American colonies.

175

In the debates of Valladolid, Las Casas had argued that while waging war against the American "infidels" was not acceptable from any perspective, the Spanish crown nonetheless had the moral and religious obligation to carry out the evangelization of the natives by peaceful means. Thus the rights of Spain to be in America could be justified in terms of it being expected to fulfill its duty as a Christian nation to disseminate the true faith and to assume the tutelage of the infidels while taking over their temporal possessions. It is worth reiterating that after Valladolid the question of whether Spain had the right to have dominion over the New World was never raised again.

As we have seen, in the aftermath of the debate against Juan Ginés de Sepúlveda, royal authority was further revalidated with the emergence of the issue of perpetuity pitting the encomenderos against some of the reformers and the Peruvian Indian elite. Resorting to the king to determine whether or not the perpetuity of the encomiendas should be abolished implied the recognition of his absolute authority to decide the fate of the New World. Although the debate had never been resolved in favor of either party, it served to reaffirm the ultimate authority of the king in all affairs of the Indies. Las Casas's intervention in the debates about perpetuity, like his participation in Valladolid, also contributed to the consolidation of the power of the imperial crown over the colonizers' aspirations in the New World.

The certainty afforded by Valladolid provided Viceroy Toledo with the moral and political certainty to implement his politico-economic plans to consolidate Spain's grip on Peruvian territory. What Las Casas accepted from a religious perspective, Toledo accepted and implemented from a political one. It is in this context of conflicting aspects of Spanish imperialism that Las Casas's legacy must be measured, not only in terms of his legislative struggle for the Indians and its consequences, but in terms of his total contribution to the transformation and development of the sixteenth-century Spanish imperial venture in America.

Conclusion

Bartolomé de Las Casas: A Man for All Seasons?

Today, into this house,
Father, come in with me
I will show you the letters,
the torment
of my people, of man
persecuted.
I will show you the ancient
sorrows.

—Pablo Neruda,
"Fray Bartolomé de Las Casas"

FROM THE TIME HE FOUND his "road to Damascus" in 1514, until his death in 1566, Father Bartolomé de Las Casas waged an unparalleled struggle to obtain legislation to protect the well-being of the indigenous people of the Americas. The cleric, who first presented his grievances and his remedios to the king in 1516, evolved into the elder bishop-statesman who in 1566 wrote Pope Pius V asking him to order the king to improve the treatment of the Indians. The last years of his life showed a Las Casas no longer bent on prescribing but someone still trusting that those in power would act in the best interest of even their poorest subjects. That was why he asked the pontiff to excommunicate and anathematize those who declared war on the Indians. Ironically, Las Casas, who never learned any native languages, also asked that the pope should require the bishops to learn the native language of the people in their American dioceses. He also asked the pontiff to order the bishops to take personal care of the natives and to defend them even with their own lives.[1] This image of Las Casas, as a benevolent advocate of human rights before the powerful of the world, is the one that has remained imbedded in the collective memory of Indoamerica.

Bartolomé de Las Casas's elevation to mythological dimensions responds, in part, to a need to recreate the Indoamerican past as part of a kinder, gentler, compassionate New World, its people the descendants of an advocate of human rights instead of the children of *la chingada*, as some modern Mexican literary figures have characterized the mestizo inhabitants of America.[2] The mythologizing of Las Casas also responds to a need to find a heroic redeemer, even an imported one, to save Indoamericans from the shame resulting from the inability of its native inhabitants to resist the European onslaught. Las Casas has been transformed into an "autochthonous American" savior. Additionally, the veneration of an individual heroic figure such as Las Casas helps us assuage many of our own feelings of inadequacy about transforming existing reality. As Sara Castro Klarén has indicated, when we are faced with a fragile, imperfect, and unacceptable reality, "we can only write the past from the sense of one's own present," and creating myths and adopting symbols from the past makes our present more bearable.[3]

Inheritors

By exalting the value of a historical figure like Las Casas, a man with a reputation as a pugnacious fighter, we proclaim ourselves the inheritors of such a personage and rationalize our present inability to rid ourselves of the contradictions and paradoxes originating more than five hundred years ago. It is as if whole generations had renounced the search for a defining praxis today and instead had found refuge in a utopian past, which incarnated resistance. In our desire to create an idealized past we tend to find virtue in even the most insignificant act, as John Chasteen tells us: "Recently and for readily understandable reasons, interpreters of Latin America have preferred to dwell on the story of popular resistance within this larger picture. Resistance studies offer the stirring and salutary message that the people of Latin America have often tenaciously defied exploitative rule."[4]

By anointing Las Casas as a symbol of resistance and as savior of the Indians, all of us can share in his accomplishments. In our desire to gloss over our own historical inadequacies we often fail to see that the Dominican's benevolent paternalistic attitude toward the Indians is symptomatic of a person who saw himself as coming from a culturally superior world with a divine mandate to impose a set of ideas and beliefs on the less privileged colonized.

The main difference between Las Casas and the other colonists was his deeply seated belief that the implementation of imperialism—political, economic, and ecclesiastical—could be accomplished through nonviolent means, a departure in form but not in essence from the basic beliefs of his contemporaries. Ultimately, the friar, like many modern intellectuals, failed to address the natives' alienation and socio-cultural dislocation implicit in the forced process of conversion to an alien faith and an alien way of life. This characterization of Las Casas is not mere speculation but is grounded in the reading of his primer for peaceful conversion and his constant calls for the natives to conform to the authority of the European king as a way of escaping subjection to the encomenderos.

By placing the natives in reducciones and shattering their way of life, by replacing their traditional belief system with the alien system of the occupying forces, he contributed to the destruction of the world as they knew it, instead of the creation of a better world, as many claim he did. This is one of the contradictions implicit in Las Casas's role that his biographers and hagiographers are either unable to see or unwilling to accept.

The effect that Las Casas's legacy has had on Indoamerica is so profound that it is impossible to define it with a single phrase, concept, label, or even an academic monograph. This is a legacy that reaches into the political and philosophical foundations of modern Indoamerican nation-states, even though, in terms of concrete gains for indigenous Americans, the result of his life work is rather limited. Yet, given the dearth of heroic figures, he has become a symbol of protest and resistance dating back to the days of Indoamerican patriots fighting for independence from Spain.

During the wars of independence, the name of Las Casas became synonymous with resistance; his voice was appropriated by the patriots to denounce the wrongs perpetrated on Indoamerica by a remote and voracious master. The rebel leaders, who were largely Spaniards born in America, *criollos*, adopted as symbols a multitude of figures prominent in anti-Spanish resistance throughout colonial times. They resurrected the images and deeds of indigenous heroes of resistance, the likes of Lautaro in Chile, Guarionex in the Caribbean, Tupac Amaru in Peru, and Cuauhtémoc in Mexico, but Las Casas, who was culled from the ranks of the colonizers, offered a powerful non-indigenous symbol with which Creoles could easily identify without bringing up the specter of a potential race war.

A Man for All Seasons?

The adoption of the Dominican's image by Creole patriots was an integral part of their quest to define their identity as "Americans." The bishop of Chiapa was the best-known advocate of the natives through colonial times, and his reputation as a symbol of resistance turned him into a natural ally. Aside from creating a symbolic bridge to the native population, the Dominican was also a Spaniard who, like the creoles, was unhappy with certain aspects of Spanish rule. Thus, he figures prominently in the writings of nineteenth-century patriots across the continent, from the Mexican Servando Teresa y Mier to the Venezuelan Simón Bolívar. The Mexican, in a spirited defense of the Dominican against the charges that he was responsible for initiating the African slave trade in America, referred to Las Casas as "the father of the Indians par excellence."[5] In South America, Bolívar saw him not just as the "father of America" but the one true voice of Spain, brave enough to denounce the atrocities committed against the Americans by his countrymen.

This admiration, bordering on hagiographic adoration for Las Casas, has carried over into latter centuries, and some theologians find enough recuperable elements to ascribe the paternity of the theology of liberation to him. As an alternative to the power struggle between a centralized monarchy and an antagonistic periphery made up by the colonizers and their godless oppression of the Indians, Las Casas posited a third alternative that would not to do away with the colonies or the colonizers but would transform the nature of the relationship between the crown and its possessions. He proposed to attain a working relationship with the natives through the peaceful preaching of the Gospel and their conversion to Christianity. As a result of the conversion of the natives by the religious representatives of the empire, an economic understanding between the crown and the Indians would follow, and, to mitigate their losses, the colonizers would be hired by the crown as administrators and in other positions such as imperial overseers. Like Las Casas, liberation theologians of today are seeking a third way between the heartless exploitation of godless regimes and the violent response of the oppressed. That is, they advocate a reformist model of obtaining a measure of power by peaceful means to create an economic, social, and political order in the context of the terms stipulated in the Gospel. Hence Las Casas as a symbol of nonviolent reform emerges as a powerful role model for liberation theology.[6]

Many of his supporters characterize him as the "father of America," like Bolívar before them, because of his labor with Native Americans. However, the element of accountability is absent from such a characterization: paternity implies the creation of, and the responsibility for, an offspring, and the America and its native inhabitants that Las Casas left behind in 1547 was neither his creation nor in any way his direct responsibility. The America that existed during his lifetime and after his death was a continent in the process of gestation, birth, and development shaped by different cultural, socioeconomic, and political forces. The alternative he advocated was a reformist one which responded more to the needs of an absolutist Spanish regime than to the needs of the large indigenous population. Nevertheless, even accepting the friar's influence in the recognition of the needs of the indigenous and the poor of our continent, it is difficult not to recognize the level of paternalism evident in Las Casas's actions.

In his fifty years of struggle, Las Casas exhausted all available legal means to reform and change the corpus of legislation affecting the natives. Nevertheless, by relying on the existing dichotomous standard of the republic of Indians separated from the republic of Spaniards, exploiter-exploited, perpetrator-victim, Las Casas contributed to placing the Indians in the unmovable and inescapable position of victims, a condition from which they could not emerge on their own without the paternalistic intervention of European authority figures. This dichotomous premise has been rescued by some theologians, among them the respected Gustavo Gutierrez, who reinterprets Las Casas's belief of "assimilation through conversion" into "salvation through evangelization" as the hope of the poor, as evidenced by the following passage:

> Thus, for Las Casas "the only way" to evangelize is by persuasion and dialogue . . . Seeing things "as if we were Indians". . . makes us more sensitive to the injustice of the treatment being inflicted on the autochthonous population, as well as to the rejection of evangelical values that this violation of their rights implies.[7]

Like Las Casas before us, we, the general population, are called on to empathize and sympathize with the indigenous, but the call retains the same level of separation that Las Casas advocated. That is, we are called to sympathize and empathize with the downtrodden, but from a privileged position, without integrating with the cause of the exploited, and without bridging the chasm that separates these disparate segments of society. Identifying the problem, empathizing with the poor from afar, is tantamount to once again abandoning them, leaving them alone and isolated, feeling pity for them rather than actively taking part in their process of liberation. Nevertheless, after the failure of the revolutionary utopian proposals of transformation of the late twentieth century, it has become evident that one of the remaining sources of hope is that offered by some of the profoundly committed theologians of various backgrounds.

Some of these theologians have broken down the barriers that Las Casas left standing and have cast their fate with the downtrodden and the poor, who invariably constitute the totality of the indigenous population of our continent.

In the colonial world of Las Casas's time, indigenous people remained unprotected, and in order for their rights to be recognized they were forced to embrace an alien culture with its alien god and its alien religion. Bartolomé de Las Casas envisioned utopias resulting from his proposals, but ultimately he was defeated by the economic dependence of the crown on the contributions coming from the colonies and the inevitable sway of capital, which transformed those utopian dreams into inescapable and unforgiving dystopias.

Despite his lobbying efforts in favor of the Indians, who constituted the poorest segments of colonial society, the liberation he advocated for them was conditioned by the natives' agreement to renounce their own cultural and religious practices and embrace Christianity, a simple question of trading cultures. It was only by becoming like their oppressors, like the "other," that they could be welcomed as Spanish subjects, which in theory entitled them to a modicum of royal protection. Furthermore, his proposals for peaceful evangelization constitute a clear form of ecclesiastical imperialism, insofar as the only difference between the proposals for colonization that he put forth and those carried out by the Spanish entrepreneurs differed in the use of force. While the colonizers advocated and preferred military conquest, the Dominican consistently called for the peaceful evangelization and colonization of the natives.

Ironically, and despite the friar's advocacy of peaceful colonization, there were numerous occasions when his desire for expediency came in contradiction with his avowed principles in favor of a measured and benevolent transformation. This was evident, in cases where Spanish catechizing efforts encountered native resistance (as in the case of the coast of Paria). On occasions like these, he saw no contradiction in calling for the creation of fortresses to establish military *entradas* to put an end to native resistance so the Gospel could be safely preached among the natives.

During the first century of Spanish domination, Las Casas, thanks largely to his self-promotion, emerged as the most visible champion of Indian rights and the most dedicated opponent of the encomenderos. This degree of visibility, more than any specific accomplishment on behalf of the natives, is the basis of his long-standing reputation as an activist. Perhaps his most significant contribution to the historical reality of Indoamerica was his tenacity in defending that most important of human rights, the right to life. Thus, in a very concrete sense, he must be recognized as an important precursor of the prevailing move toward a wider understanding and application of the doctrine of human rights, or as Paolo Carozza has called him, "the midwife of human rights talk."[8] Las Casas's repeated attempts to limit the prerogatives of the encomenderos led him to emphasize the humanity of the Indians and the importance of this humanity in granting them the natural rights intrinsic to all humans. As we have seen, Las Casas came to these conclusions through empirical experience rather than through the theoretical construct of contemporary theologians in Salamanca and other learning centers in Spain. In the context of reexamining Las Casas, we must recognize that being a representative of his times, he could not break totally with the established strictures controlling societal behavior, and as such we must accept his limitations. The contradiction arises when modern intellectuals make Las Casas into a mythological being divorced from the milieu in which he existed.

Despite the enthusiasm that many Indoamerican, Spanish, other European, and North American academicians might feel in proclaiming Las Casas as a paradigmatic champion of justice and precursor of human rights, the creation of a *lascasista* myth of liberation must be tempered with caution and examined in its every dimension. This examination must serve the purpose of reevaluating and redimensioning the mythological scope of Las Casas's accomplishments, not out of a desire to diminish them but rather to produce a historical narrative that goes beyond distortion and mythological creation.

In our days, the bishop of Chiapa has become the patrimony of the intellectual members of white and mestizo society in Indoamerica more than of the Indian masses. Among the vast majority of Indians, most of whom are unaware of his existence and his work, he is at best a mythical footnote whose legendary exploits are similar to those imputed to saints, vaguely familiar, but not specific enough to be identifiable. What is ignored in the process of constantly refueling the myth is the fact that in his drive to restore the Indies, destroyed by the predatory cruelty and greed of the conquerors, Las Casas ultimately became an active agent of Spanish imperialism who contributed to the subjugation of the Amerindians under more paternalistic and benevolent conditions than his contemporaries.

Missing from the hagiographic body of work about Las Casas is precisely the fact that his efforts rarely resulted in tangible, measurable gains for the natives. Such were the cases in the Caribbean, Mesoamerica, and South America. While it is undeniable that his later body of work has been influential in the drafting of universal declarations of rights, it must be recalled that, at the same time, a great deal of it was dedicated to the attempt to rationalize the imperialistic occupation of America by Spain and to propose ways in which these opposing powers could coexist. It also appears that he never saw the contradiction in maintaining that there was no incompatibility between the political authority of the native lords and that of the Spanish crown as long as the former accepted the lordship of the Spanish monarch of their own free will.

In Las Casas's worldview, the two levels of political authority, the one brought by the colonizer and the one possessed by the colonized, were compatible. He saw this condition as a state where natural rights and the grace of the Gospel conjoined "in the free self-determination of the native peoples and nations. The image is that of a humanitarian and evangelizing empire, mediated by the consent of the vassals. [Las Casas's] schema excludes the authority of colonizers and encomenderos, which does not correspond to natural right nor to the needs of evangelization."[9] In essence the world that Las Casas envisioned was a construct where disembodied rulers could live in harmony with the faceless masses of indigenous people without the participation of corruptible and corrupted intermediaries, a veritable but nonexistent, utopian state of grace.

Many of his biographers, hagiographers, and admirers have labeled him an apostle of the Indians, and although the title is given in the context of his work on behalf of the natives, this is a groundless exaggeration. An apostle, by one definition, is one who performs an active missionary role attempting to convert unbelievers to one's faith. Las Casas engaged in little active missionary work. During his forty-five years in America, he spent time in the proximity of the natives on only four occasions. The first was the time he spent as a doctrinero in the conquering campaigns of Española and Cuba. The second was the short time he spent in the mountains of Española with Enriquillo.[10] A third occasion was the time he spent coordinating the pacification campaign at Tuzulutlán, and the last was the time he visited the Indian districts in his bishopric of Chiapa. Consequently, to call Las Casas an apostle contradicts the available evidence, given that Las Casas's apostolic work among the Indians was almost nonexistent. More than apostle, Las Casas was an organizer of missions and missionaries. More than missionary, he was a theoretician and a tactician of a benevolent ecclesiastical imperialism, insofar as one of his overriding preoccupations was the conversion of American infidels to Christianity even from a distance. Nowhere is this more apparent than in his unwillingness to learn native languages in order to more fully understand the natives' individual and collective problems, aspirations, and expectations.

185

The admiration and respect for Las Casas that emerged during the wars of independence from Spain in the nineteenth century have carried over into our times and he has become a heroic figure and a symbol of hope in desperate times. However, many of those who exalt the paradigmatic role of a Christian Las Casas ignore that in his case Christianity indeed becomes a religion of pity. They embrace an anachronistic perspective, ignoring how pity "stands in antithesis to the tonic of emotions: [that] it has a depressive effect."[11] Indoamericans have experienced a depressive effect that they have not been able to eradicate despite the lip service paid to liberation and transformation. In this light, Bartolomé de Las Casas must be remembered as one of the most important actors in the drama of the gestation and birth of the New World. At the same time, he must also be remembered as an active and willing participant in the ecclesiastical and political imperialist domination of Indoamerica by Spain and as one of the best-known representatives of benevolent Spanish imperialism in the formative century of our continent.

~⊙~ Notes ~⊙~

SHORT TITLES HAVE generally been used to cite works in the notes. A few works are identified by the following short forms:

DII	*Colección de documentos ineditos*
DIM	*Colección de documentos para la historia de México*
Opúsculos	Las Casas, *Obras escogidas de Fray Bartolomé de Las Casas: Opúsculos, cartas y memoriales*

Introduction

1   The character of the territory that we know as Latin America is determined by its indigenous culture. However, the term "Latin America" only acknowledges the European component of the continent's name. If in addition we consider that the French, because of political motivations, adopted the name "Latin" America during the second half of the nineteenth century, then the term "Indoamerica" comes closer to integrating the native people into the mestizo reality of America. At the very least, despite Columbus's erroneous conviction, the term incorporates, if only partially, the indigenous and European components of the continent. "Indoamerica" is not a new term; it was frequently used by two different but important Indoamerican political thinkers of the twentieth century, Victor Raúl Haya de La Torre and José Carlos Mariátegui.

2   In the aftermath of his third voyage, Columbus identified the world he had encountered an appendage of Asia or a manifestation of the Terrestrial Paradise. Morison, *Admiral of the Ocean Sea*, 384, 547.

3   Elliott, *The Old World and the New*, 7.

4   As noted above, because of Columbus's ignorance about his landing place, the term "Indian" has become a descriptor for the natives of Indoamerica and often carries strong negative racial implications. Its use in the context of this work carries no pejorative connotation. On the contrary, as a mestizo of "Indian" and Spanish extraction, I would like to see the term stripped of any pejorative connotations and to revalidate the pride and the integrity of our indigenous ancestors. I believe that the use of euphemistic neologisms to describe the natives of the continent encountered by Columbus has done little to alter their living conditions, and it does little to remove the urgency to transform the abject reality that the indigenous people have been forced to endure for the last five hundred years. However, to avoid breaking with the patterns of customary usage, the terms "Indian," "indigenous," and "native," and the neologisms "Native American" and "Amerindian" will be used interchangeably throughout this book.

5 Montesinos's first name appears in various guises; Las Casas calls him Antón Montesino, Lewis Hanke Antonio de Montesinos, and Patricia Seed, among others, Antonio Montesinos. Since this last one seems to be the most widely accepted use, I have adopted it.

6 Bennassar, *The Spanish Character*, 80. Bennassar depicts Las Casas as an early Quixotic figure, although Las Casas's praxis when dealing with the legal realities of his time would more suggest a hybrid between Quixote and the realist Sancho.

7 Hanke, "Bartolomé de Las Casas historiador," xi. I claim sole responsibility for any errors of interpretation in the translation of original Spanish or French texts.

8 There are more than one thousand printed works, including more than three hundred authored by Las Casas himself.

9 Keen, "The Black Legend Revisited," 703.

10 Ibid., 704–6.

11 For sources on this topic, see Gibson, *The Black Legend* (the introduction is particularly enlightening); Keen, "The White Legend Revisited," 336–55; Hanke, "A Modest Proposal for a Moratorium on Grand Generalizations, 112–27; Levene, *Las Indias no eran colonias;* Carbia, *Historia de la Leyenda Negra hispano-americana*, among others.

12 Gustavo Gutierrez, a Peruvian pioneer of the movement of liberation theology, dedicated a significant amount of work to the examination of Las Casas's contribution to the same. See in particular *En busca de los pobres de Jesucristo*.

13 The wording was contained in a resolution passed at a meeting of the Congress of Americanists in Seville in 1935; the characterization also surfaces in Hanke's "Bartolomé de Las Casas historiador."

14 Gonzalo Fernández de Oviedo, Juan Ginés de Sepulveda, and various conquistadores and encomenderos in his own day, and, recently, Roberto Levene, José Vasconcelos, and many others.

15 Ramón Menéndez Pidal, *El padre Las Casas*, xiv.

16 Pagden, "*Ius et Factum*," 89–90.

17 Marcel Bataillon, "The *Clérigo* Casas, Colonist and Colonial Reformer," 353.

18 It seems that other than his early experiences as a *cura doctrinero* in the Caribbean, Las Casas never played a direct role in the Spanish evangelizing effort in subsequent years. The closest he came were his activities in Paria, later with the cacique Enriquillo in Española, and still later as the leader of the missionary operation in Tuzulutlán.

19 Las Casas, *Historia de las Indias*, 1:15. Emphasis added.

20 Gutierrez, *En busca de los pobres de Jesucristo*, 102.

21 This is the pseudo-humanism exhibited by colonial powers throughout the underdeveloped world. On this point, see Cesaire, *Discourse on Colonialism*, 15.

22 Las Casas, *The Only Way*, 63. Emphasis added. For an approximation of when *De único modo* was written, see chap. 3, n. 91 of this book.

23 The *encomienda*, from the Spanish verb *encomendar*, "to entrust," implied that

in exchange for the tribute received from the natives, the conquistador was responsible for the material and spiritual well-being of the natives thus entrusted to him.

24 Las Casas, "Memorial de remedios para las Indias, 1516," in *Opúsculos*, 5.

25 Las Casas, *A Short History of the Destruction of the Indies*, 6.

26 One of Charles's early preoccupations had been to curb the power of the colonizers. The semi-feudal prerogative adopted by the encomenderos was, according to Parry, "inevitably repugnant both to a centralised monarchy and to autocratic missionary orders" as long as it represented private authority over the Indians. Parry, *The Spanish Theory of Empire in the Sixteenth Century*, 43. Throughout this book I will refer to the king who ruled officially as Carlos I of Spain as Charles V or Charles the king of Spain. The title "Charles V" refers to his status as Holy Roman Emperor and is commonly used to identify him both in Spain and in the English-speaking world.

27 Hanke, *The Spanish Struggle for Justice in the Conquest of America*, 8.

28 Angel Rama, in his seminal work, *La ciudad letrada*, illustrates the cultural divide between the two conflicting worlds forcefully integrated into the so-called New World: the city and the countryside, the city of letters and the rural world of "darkness." For a concise and penetrating analysis of the concept of the "Lettered City," see Rama, *La ciudad letrada*.

29 Wagner and Parish, *Life and Writings*, 85. Benavente, "Carta del Padre Fray Toribio de Benavente Motolinía a Carlos V," in *DII* 22:175–213. Also see Las Casas, *Apologética historia*, 1:322, 447.

30 Rivera Pagán, *Evangelización y violencia*, 105.

31 Simón Bolívar refers to him as "apostle of the Americas," in his famous "Reply of a South American Gentleman," in *Selected Writings*, 104. Arthur Helps also labels him as an apostle of the Indians in the title of his 1868 book, *The Life of Las Casas: Apostle of the Indies*.

32 This paternalism became even more evident in later centuries as European imperialism increased its domination of the rest of the world. For a detailed and thorough discussion of this topic, see Said, *Orientalism*, 7.

33 Freire, *Pedagogy of the Oppressed*, 53.

Chapter One Defining and Possessing

1 Pagden, *European Encounters with the New World*, 21.

2 Zamora, "Christopher Columbus's 'Letter to the Sovereigns,' " 5.

3 Ibid, 7. Emphasis added.

4 The term "bestial Indians" is a direct translation of Gonzalo Fernández de Oviedo's text in his *Historia general y natural de las indias, islas y tierra firme del mar océano* published in Madrid in 1547. Pagden, *European Encounters with the New World*, 21. Emphasis added.

5 Greenblatt, *Marvelous Possessions*, 9. Emphasis added.

6 Parish, "Introduction," 9.

7 Simpson, *The Encomienda in New Spain*, vi.

8   López de Gómara, *Historia general de las Indias*, 8. The quote in Spanish reads: "La mayor cosa después de la creación del mundo, sacando la encarnación y muerte del que lo crió, es el descubrimiento de Indias; y así las llaman Nuevo Mundo."

9   Pagden, *European Encounters with the New World*, 51.

10   Las Casas, *A Short History*, 3. Emphasis added.

11   Elliott, *The Old World and the New*, 7.

12   Milhou, *Colón y su mentalidad mesiánica*, 7–8. Spain had just expelled the Moors and the renewed religious fervor demanded a high degree of orthodoxy and a constant watchfulness that excluded other faiths. Although it was only the halfway mark of the second millennium, the time was ripe to dream of a Second Coming.

13   MacLachlan, *Spain's Empire in the New World*, x.

14   Elliott, *Imperial Spain*, 57–58.

15   Gibson, *Spain in America*, 5.

16   Hernáez, ed., *Colección de Bulas*, 824–25.

17   Fiske, *The Discovery of America*, 1:455, n. 2.

18   Molina Meliá, *Iglesia y estado en el Siglo de Oro Español*, 36.

19   In the twelfth century, Gratian and John of Salisbury heralded the supremacy of ecclesiastical over secular power. They maintained that the Church was responsible for granting temporal power at the same time that it was "reserving spiritual authority for the papacy." Salisbury, *Policraticus*, 32. This was reaffirmed in the thirteenth century in the writings of Henricus de Segusia, cardinal of Ostia (Ostiensis), who continued to espouse the principles of universal dominion of the papacy over temporal and spiritual matters. Although his writings preceded Spain's appropriation of the New World by two centuries and dealt essentially with the "infidels" of the Near East, they nevertheless resurfaced in the writings of sixteenth-century Spanish jurists and theologians. See Zavala, *Las instituciones jurídicas en la conquista de América*, 15–17.

20   Fiske, *The Discovery of America*, 1:454.

21   There is some controversy as to the exact dates of the bulls. Hernáez dates both May 4; Fiske dates them on consecutive days, May 3 and 4, as do Hanke, Zavala, and numerous other historians. The will of the majority has been respected.

22   From the bull *Inter Caetera* cited in appendix 1 of Las Casas, *Tratados de Fray Bartolomé de Las Casas*, 2:1278–79. Emphasis added.

23   Tobar, *Compendio Bulario Indico*, 11–16.

24   Parry, *Spanish Theory of Empire*, 4.

25   Hernáez, *Colección de Bulas*, 16.

26   From *Dudum Siquidem*, in Las Casas, *Tratados*, appendix 4, 2:1288–90.

27   Elliott, *The Old World and the New*, 80.

28   Tordesillas defined a line of demarcation, placing the new line for Portuguese domination 370 leagues west of the Cape Verde Islands. Because of their limited geographical knowledge, the Spaniards had granted the Portuguese a

significant portion of the eastern coast of South America. See Gibson, *Spain in America*, 15–16.

29 Zavala, *Las instituciones jurídicas*, 42. Those who supported this second perspective came from varied backgrounds and occupations; prominent among them were Juan López de Palacios Rubios, Juan Ginés de Sepúlveda, Gregorio López, and Antonio de Herrera.

30 Juan Friede, "Las Casas and Indigenism in the Sixteenth Century," 134.

31 Mackenthun, *Metaphors of Dispossession*, 12.

32 Pagden, *The Fall of Natural Man*, 27.

33 Ibid., 28.

34 Dante Alighieri, *On World Government*, 69.

35 Zavala, *La filosofía política en la conquista de América*, 31. Also see Parry, *Spanish Theory of Empire*, 16–18.

36 Urdanoz, "Sintésis teológico-jurídica de la doctrina de Vitoria," xcii. Not surprisingly, one of the most devoted followers of Major's doctrine of imperial dominion and the natural slavery of the Indians was none other than the humanist philosopher and adversary of Las Casas at Valladolid, Juan Ginés de Sepúlveda.

37 Zavala, *Instituciones jurídicas*, 60. There is an uncanny resemblance between Major's proposal for the edification of armed outposts and some of the early proposals put forth by Las Casas for the colonization of Tierra Firme. See Las Casas's earliest memorial to the crown, "Memorial de remedios para las Indias (1516)," in *Opúsculos*, 5–27.

38 Major's *Sententiae* in the appendix printed in P. Leturia, *Maior y Vitoria ante la conquista de América*. Cited in Parry, *Spanish Theory*, 18.

39 García-Pelayo, "Juan Ginés de Sepúlveda y los problemas jurídicos de la conquista de América" in Sepúlveda, *Tratado sobre las justas causas*, 13.

40 Sepúlveda, *Tratado sobre las justas causas*, 171, 173. Emphasis added.

41 Parry, *Spanish Theory of Empire*, 38.

42 As well as the encomenderos and their representatives, he enjoyed the support of Grand Inquisitor Fernando de Valdés and the head of the Council of the Indies Cardinal García de Loaysa.

43 Pagden, *Spanish Imperialism*, 5.

44 The original *lecciones* from which his *Relectio de Indis* were derived took place between 1539 and 1542. Beltrán de Heredia, " Personalidad del Maestro Francisco de Vitoria y trascendencia de su obra doctrinal," in Vitoria, *Relectio de Indis*, xxi.

45 MacLachlan, *Spain's Empire in the New World*, 5.

46 Parry, *Spanish Theory*, 20.

47 Reginaldo Di Agostino Iannarone, "Genesis del Pensamiento Colonial en Francisco de Vitoria," in Vitoria, *Relectio de Indis*, xxxi.

48 Vitoria, *Relectio de Indis*, 1.

49 Ibid., 11.

50 Pagden, *Spanish Imperialism*, 20.

51 Ibid., 16. The word *dominium* traditionally implied possession of real property. In the sixteenth century the term's usage expanded to include the right over peoples, as in the case of the American possessions. From the Spanish perspective, *dominium* implied absolute control, not just over material property, but also over the minds and wills of the natives of the colonized territory.

52 Vitoria, *Relectio de Indis*, 78.

53 Ibid., 100, 107.

54 Ibid., 126.

55 Vitoria, *Relección sobre los Indios*, in Hernández Martín, ed., *Francisco de Vitoria y su "Relección sobre los Indios,"* 18.

56 Pagden, *Spanish Imperialism*, 20.

57 Vitoria, *Relectio de Indis*, 99. Emphasis added.

58 "Carta de Francisco de Vitoria al P. Arcos sobre negocios de Indias." In ibid., 137–39.

59 Parry, *Spanish Theory of Empire*, 25.

60 See appendices 5 and 6 in the *Relectio*, "Carta de Carlos V al prior de San Esteban de Salamanca," and "Carta de Carlos V a Francisco de Vitoria," 152–55.

61 Most prominent among these proponents are the Argentines Ricardo Levene and Rómulo Carbia, the prominent Mexican politician and postrevolutionary minister of education José Vasconcelos, and the North American historian Lewis Hanke.

62 Pagden, *The Fall of Natural Man*, 28.

63 Foucault, "Truth and Power," 122.

64 In addition to the Dominicans in the Caribbean, the defenders of the Indians were represented by Bishop Juan de Zumárraga, the Franciscans Bernardo de Sahagún and Toribio Benavente (Motolinía) in Mexico; in Peru they were represented by the Jesuit José de Acosta and the Dominican Domingo de Santo Tomás. Among the lay supporters in South America we find the Spanish chronicler Pedro Cieza de León and the Indian chronicler Felipe Guamán Poma de Ayala taking up the cause of the natives.

65 Chasteen, introduction to Rama, *The Lettered City*, xiii.

66 The distortion had a great deal to do with the reformers' own ignorance of native languages and the cultural divide between themselves and the natives. See Plato, *The Republic*, in *Great Dialogues of Plato*, 312.

67 Friede, "Las Casas y el movimiento indigenista," 344.

68 Gonzalo Fernández de Oviedo y Valdés, *Historia general y natural de las Indias*, 3:111.

69 López de Gómara, *Historia general de las Indias*, 48. The Spanish text reads: "Facilísimamente se juntan con las mujeres, y aun como cuervos o víboras, y peor; dejando aparte que son grandísimos sodomíticos, holgazanes, mentirosos, ingratos, mudables y ruines."

70 Las Casas, *Apologética historia sumaria*, 1:171. Emphasis in original.

71 Ibid, 1:175–81.

72 Las Casas, prologue to *A Brief History*, 5.

73 Pagden, *European Encounters*, 51–52.

74 According to Isacio Fernández Pérez's *Inventario Documentado de los Escritos de Fray Bartolomé de Las Casas*, there are 369 known works by Las Casas. These include letters, memorials, treatises, a primer for peaceful evangelization, works on history and anthropology, and works of political theory.

75 Lewis Hanke, *Las teorías políticas de Bartolomé de Las Casas*, 26.

76 Las Casas, *De regia potestate*, 16. Written between 1556 and 1559, this is one of Las Casas's seminal political treatises.

77 The original suggestions appeared in the *Remedios* written in 1516 for Cardinal Regent Ximénez de Cisneros. References to the topic also appear throughout the last part of his *Historia de las Indias*. See Las Casas, *Historia de las Indias*, book 3, chapters 85, 102, and 129, among others.

78 Las Casas, "Tratado comprobatorio del Imperio Soberano," in *Tratados de 1552*, 10:397–410.

79 Las Casas, *Historia* 1:28. For a colorful narrative of the legend of Saint Christopher, see Morison, *Admiral of the Ocean Sea*, 10.

80 Bourne, *Spain in America, 1450–1580*, 47–49.

81 "Instructions of Queen Isabella's to Nicolás de Ovando, Comendador de Lares, December 20, 1503." Cited in Simpson, *The Encomienda*, 13. Emphasis added.

82 "First Letter," in Cortés, *Letters from Mexico*, 36.

Chapter Two American Crucible

1 Díaz del Castillo, *Historia verdadera de la conquista de la Nueva España*, 584. Emphasis added.

2 Las Casas, "Este es el primer viaje," in *Diario del primer y tercer viaje de Cristobal Colón*, 113. In the diary entry corresponding to December 17, 1492, Columbus reiterates his faith that God would show him the place "*donde nasce* [*sic*] *el oro*" ("where gold is born").

3 Todorov, *The Conquest of America*, 9. For Columbus's complex attitude about gold as a transforming force, see Pagden, *European Encounters*, 20–21. Alejo Carpentier provides a provocative version of Columbus's ambivalent attitude about his penchant for writing about gold in a fictionalized version of Columbus's deathbed soliloquy: "I become indignant with myself to see, for instance, that on December 24, in which I should have meditated like a Franciscan about the Divine Occurrence of the Nativity, I print five times the word GOLD in ten lines that seem to come out of an alchemist's crucible. Two days later, St. Stephen's day, instead of thinking about the blessed death. . . of the first martyr of our religion… I write twelve times the word GOLD, in a text where I only mention the Lord only once—and that, only to fulfill a daily usage of the language. Because a routinized use of the language is the fact that I mention the name of the Almighty only fourteen times in a general text where the references to GOLD are more than two hundred" (Alejo Carpentier, *El arpa y la sombra*, 139).

4 Las Casas, "La historia del viaje qu'el Almirante Don Cristobal Colón hizo la terçera vez que vino a las Indias cuando descubrió la tierra firme," in *Diario del primer y tercer viaje*, 14:190, 193; *Historia*, 43–45.

5 Lockhart, "Trunk Lines and Feeder Lines," 90.

6 Taylor, "Landed Society in New Spain," 393.

7 Phillips and Phillips, "Spain in the Fifteenth Century," 19.

8 Pike, *Enterprise and Adventure*, 15.

9 Ibid., 20–47.

10 Altman, *Emigrants and Society*, 44.

11 Hanke, *Aristotle and the American Indians*, 13. Emphasis added.

12 Morison, *Christopher Columbus, Mariner*, 84. Emphasis added.

13 Las Casas, *Historia*, 2:205.

14 Cited by Keen in the introduction to Bennassar, *The Spanish Character*, ix.

15 Oviedo y Valdés, *Historia general y natural de las Indias*, 1:54.

16 Las Casas, *Historia*, 1:137, 438. Herrera y Tordesillas, *Historia general de los hechos de los castellanos*, 1:304.

17 For a description of the dramatic voyage, see Las Casas, *Historia*, 2:215. Cortés cancelled passage at the last minute, following an accident he suffered before departure. An illustrative study of Extremadura emigrants, among them Ovando, Cortés, and the Pizarro brothers, is provided in Altman's *Emigrants and Society*.

18 Schäfer, *El consejo real y supremo de las Indias*, 1:30–31.

19 Isabel and Ferdinand's royal cédula naming Ovando as governor of the Indies. "Instrucción al Comendador de Lares, Frey Nicolas de Ovando," *DII*, 30:14. Emphasis added.

20 Ibid., 14–15.

21 Ibid.

22 Simpson, *The Encomienda*, 12.

23 Zavala, *La encomienda indiana*, 14–16.

24 Las Casas, *Historia*, 1:416–19.

25 Las Casas, *Historia*, 2:86–87, 104.

26 Ibid., 204.

27 Simpson, *The Encomienda* 7–12. It seems almost incomprehensible that a group of individuals with a hard-earned reputation as the saviors of Christianity, in the war against the Muslim infidel, could starve to death in a land which Columbus himself had likened only a few years before to the Earthly Paradise.

28 Friede, "Las Casas y el movimiento indigenista," 348.

29 Simpson, *The Encomienda*, 13.

30 "Real Cédula para que los vecinos de "La Española" sirvan a los cristianos en la labranza e granxería, e les ayuden a sacar oro, pagandoles sus jornales," *DII*, 31:209–12. A significant part of the text used appears in translation in Simpson, *La Encomienda*, 12–13.

31 Fernández de Oviedo, *Historia general y natural*, 1:30, 133. According to the chronicler, the failure of administrators was predicated on the fact that the

Indians' *incapacidad y malas inclinaciones* (incapacity and evil inclinations) prevented them from being of any use to the Spaniards. At times, he continued, "they behave even worse than lowly vipers." By placing the onus of the failure of the imperial enterprise on the Indians, Oviedo could then justify the Spaniards' insensitivity and cruelty.

32 Schäfer, *El Consejo Real*, 1:31.

33 Friede, "Las Casas y el movimiento indigenista," 349.

34 The real value of a horse became evident after the conquest of Peru, when every horseman's share was double that of the infantryman fighting alongside him. By 1534, the price of a horse (2500 ducats) was nearly ten times the price of a basic war galley without artillery. Guilmartin, "The Cutting Edge," 54, 67, n. 50.

35 García Bernal, *Población y encomienda en Yucatán bajo los Austrias*, 193.

36 Cited in ibid., 186.

37 Zavala, *La encomienda indiana*, 16.

38 Aimé Césaire, *Discourse on Colonialism*, 13.

39 Las Casas, *Historia de las Indias*, 2:523–24.

40 Quote from ibid., 2:523.

41 Burkholder and Johnson, *Colonial Latin America*, 39.

42 Bernal Díaz del Castillo, cited in Thomas, *Conquest*, 87.

43 Popularly known as the "Twelve Apostles," they arrived in Mexico in 1524 because of a conjunction of circumstances, requests from Cortés, Charles V's suggestions, and orders from popes Leo X and Adrian VI. Ricard, *The Spiritual Conquest of Mexico*, 21–22.

44 Bernardino de Sahagún, *Historia de las cosas de Nueva España*, cited in León-Portilla, *Aztec Thought and Culture*, 62–63.

45 Guilmartin, "The Cutting Edge," 53–60. The combination of technology and cultural and religious factors gave the Spanish an insurmountable advantage. In the case of Peru, once the ruling Incas had been removed, the compulsion that had forced many *ayllus* to recognize their legitimacy as rulers disappeared and the ensuing entropy greatly facilitated their work.

46 Braudel, *Capitalism and Material Life, 1400–1800*, 55.

47 Las Casas, *Historia*, 3:113.

48 Las Casas lists the aboriginal population remaining in Española in 1508 as 60,000, a decrease of three million since 1494; *Historia*, 3:346. Simpson, on the other hand, disputes Las Casas's figure of over three million and places the total number of natives in Española at 500,000 at the point of contact, but by 1514, he points out, there were only 29,000 people left; see *The Encomienda*, 30, n. 1. Cook and Borah, *Essays in Population History*, 1:376–400, suggest a range from 3,700,000 to possibly eight million, a population reduced by one half in 1496 and further reduced to 30,000 by 1514.

49 *Historia*, 2:523.

50 Montesinos, "Sermón de Adviento, 20 de diciembre, 1511," cited in Las Casas, *Historia*, 2:441.

51 Pagden, *Spanish Imperialism*, 14.

52 "Alfonso de Loaysa a los padres Domínicos en Española," in Serrano y Sanz, *Orígenes de la dominación española en América*, 1:349–50. There is some confusion as to the exact date of this letter; Serrano y Sanz dates it mid-1511, because he places the time of Montesinos's sermon during Lent of 1511 instead of the last Sunday of Advent, as Las Casas did in his *Historia*, 2:440–41.

53 Preceding Vitoria's *Relectio de Indis* by nearly twenty years, Loaysa could affirm without any compunction that the Indies belonged to the Spanish sovereign because of the laws of just war. In case these reasons were not sufficient, he fell back on the popes' prerogative of adjudicating earthly domains to whomever they saw fit.

54 Quoted in Serrano y Sanz, *Orígenes de la dominación española*, 1:350.

55 "Real Cédula al Almirante Colón," *DII*, 32:375.

56 Ibid., 378. Emphasis added.

57 Zavala, *La encomienda*, 18.

58 Hanke, *The Spanish Struggle*, 23; Simpson, *The Encomienda*, 31. A contemporary version of these events is also found in Las Casas, *Historia*, 2:448–49.

59 Simpson, *The Encomienda*, 32.

60 Simpson, *The Laws of Burgos of 1512–1513*, 29.

61 See Isabel's cédula, *DII*, 32:209.

62 Zavala, *La encomienda indiana*.

63 MacLachlan, *Spain's Empire in the New World*, 30.

64 For the complex rituals of possession practiced by different colonialist powers, see Seed, *Ceremonies of Possession in Europe's Conquest of the New World*, 70.

65 For the complete text of the Requerimiento, see Las Casas, *Historia*, 3:26–27; *DII*, 20:311–14.

66 Hanke, *The Spanish Struggle for Justice*, 34–35.

Chapter Three Ecclesiastical Imperialism

1 Giménez Fernández, "A Biographical Sketch," 69.

2 Helen Rand Parish has established the date of his ordination in Rome as March 3, 1507; see her "Introduction," 15.

3 See Las Casas, *Historia*, 2:441–45.

4 The only extant testimony of Las Casas's relations with his Indians is provided by himself in the *Historia*, 3:93–94.

5 Cited in Parish, "Introduction," 20. The original citation in Latin appears in *Historia*, 3:92.

6 Las Casas, *Historia*, 2:536. Serrano y Sanz thought of the incident at Caonao as the catalyst of the cleric's conversion, although he mistakenly refers to the place as Cibao. Serrano y Sanz, *Orígenes de la dominación española*, 340.

7 *Historia*, 3:93.

8 Giménez Fernández, "A Biographical Sketch," 74.

9 Simpson, *The Encomienda in New Spain*, 59.

10 Friede, "Las Casas and Indigenism," 135–36.

11 For an account of the deliberation of the junta and the text of Mesa's propositions, see Las Casas, *Historia*, 2:448–62.

12 Greenleaf, introduction to *The Roman Catholic Church in Colonial Latin America*, 1.

13 Las Casas, *Historia*, 3:95.

14 Ibid., 3:102.

15 Fabié, *Vida y escritos de Fray Bartolomé de Las Casas*, 1:45. Fabié seems to accept this as a plausible explanation for his actions. Wagner also suggests as much, but in the absence of hard and fast documentation, there is no way of knowing with certainty if this was the cleric's intention. See Wagner and Parish, *Life and Writings*, 19.

16 "Representación hecha al Rey por el clérigo Bartolomé de Las Casas," *DII*, 7:5–12.

17 Ibid., 11.

18 Despite his argument against Sepúlveda's justification of the subjection of the Indians because they were inferior, making them subject to being natural slaves, Las Casas's attitude at times conveys the impression that he considered himself morally and intellectually superior to those around him.

19 Wagner and Parish, *Life and Writings*, 18.

20 "Representación," *DII*, 7:11.

21 Las Casas, "Memorial de remedios para las Indias, 1516," in *Opúsculos*, 5. Emphasis added.

22 Wagner and Parish, *Life and Writings*, 20–23.

23 Hanke and Giménez Fernández, *Bibliografía crítica*, 6.

24 For a detailed monograph comparing Las Casas and More, see Baptiste, *Bartolomé de Las Casas and Thomas More's "Utopia."*

25 Las Casas, "Memorial de remedios," in *Opúsculos*, 6.

26 Andrien, "Spaniards, Andeans and the Early Colonial State in Peru," 124–27. See also Brading, *The First America*, 133.

27 Las Casas, "Memorial de remedios," in *Opúsculos*, 7. In the closing statement of this proposal, Las Casas informs the king that he is attaching a separate sheet with the specific conditions required for the communities. Unfortunately, this document, if it was ever written, is missing.

28 Las Casas used this concept as the cornerstone of his Tierra Firme proposal.

29 Las Casas, "Memorial de remedios," in *Opúsculos*, 9. This is the first instance in which Las Casas suggested the use of black slaves to replace Indians. At the time, African slaves, because of their high cost, were treated better than the Indians by the Spaniards. Black slaves had demonstrated a greater capacity than indigenous people to survive the rigor of working in the gold mines. The practice of using black slaves in the New World had been initiated in 1510 by order of Ferdinand.

30 Ibid., 17; Las Casas, *Historia*, 3:177–78.

31 The Lucayo islands were the main source of Indian slaves. Friede, *Bartolomé de Las Casas*, 33.

32 Ibid., 15.

33 Wagner and Parish, *Life and Writings*, 19.

34 *Bibliografía crítica*, 18. Emphasis added.

35 One of Charles V's early preoccupations had been to curb the power of the encomenderos in the New World; see Parry, *Spanish Theory of Empire*, 43.

36 Bataillon and Saint Lu advanced this concept of the "goose" and the aspiring caretakers, which is apparent to any student critical of the colonization of America, in *El padre Las Casas y la defensa de los indios*, 11.

37 The choice of a specific religious order or individual over others was also dependent on whether the order or the individuals were members of the conventuals or reformers in the struggle to reorganize the church in Spain. As a reformer, Cisneros had a tendency to side with kindred spirits, even if they belonged to another order. This would in a sense explain his sympathy for Montesinos and Pedro de Córdoba, Dominican reformers, as opposed to the Franciscan representative of the encomenderos, Espinar, who was identified with the conventuals. See Giménez Fernández, *Bartolomé de las Casas: Delegado de Cisneros*, 1:151–59; Martínez, *Fray Bartolomé de Las Casas*, 59.

38 Las Casas, *Historia*, 3:117.

39 *Historia*, 3:123–35; Wagner and Parish, *Life and Writings*, 26–27.

40 Giménez Fernández, *Las Casas: Delegado*, 168–71.

41 There are several versions of the conflicts between the Jeronymites and Las Casas. Some of the detractors of the latter blame his irascible temper, his abrasiveness, and his exalted manner for the break. See Serrano y Sanz, *Orígenes de la dominación española en América*, 1:403.

42 Las Casas, *Historia*, 3:136.

43 Simpson, *The Encomienda*, 43–44.

44 Zavala, *La encomienda indiana*, 28–32.

45 Simpson, *The Encomienda*, 55.

46 This portion of the continent had first been explored by Columbus in 1498, during his third voyage, and had gained a reputation for its abundance of pearls and the willingness of the natives to trade for cheap Spanish *rescates*; Morison, *The European Discovery of America*, 153.

47 Giménez Fernández, *Las Casas: Capellán*, 675.

48 By being elected Emperor of Germany under the title of Holy Roman Emperor Charles V in 1509, the young sovereign Charles I of Spain became, in effect, the "most important ruler in Christendom." See Lynch, *Spain 1516–1598*, 51–52.

49 Las Casas, *Historia*, 3:188.

50 In Las Casas's words: "Bien librado estaría el rey dar cien leguas que sin provecho alguno suyo las tuviesen ocupadas los frailes." Ibid.

51 The heading of the letter sent by Las Casas to the king does not specify a place where the plan of peaceful colonization could be implemented. Nevertheless, it can be surmised that it was intended to be applied throughout the Indies, not only the already settled Antilles but also the mainland. See Fabié, "Carta de Bartolomé de Las Casas Esponiendo [*sic*] las ventajas que se seguirían al

estado, adoptando lo que propone se debía hacer en las Indias," in *Vida y escritos de Fray Bartolomé de Las Casas*, 2:49–57.

52   Giménez Fernández, *Las Casas: Capellán*, 613.

53   Giménez Fernández points out the importance of the possibilities of monetary gain for a young king whose high standard of living and need to meet costly ceremonial expenses meant going further and further into debt. Giménez Fernández, *El estatuto de la tierra de Casas*, 11.

54   *DII*, 7:102. Wagner pointed out the discrepancy between the figures appearing in the *DII* and those in Las Casas's own summary in the *Historia*, 3:178. In the first, the number of Christians appears as one hundred, but in the second, it is only thirty per fortress. See Wagner and Parish, *Life and Writings*, 47, n. 4.

55   Parry, *The Spanish Theory of Empire in the Sixteenth Century*, 16; chap. 1, n. 29.

56   Giménez Fernández, *Las Casas: Capellán*, 627.

57   Ferdinand and Isabel created the Casa de Contratación in 1503 to regulate all passage and trade with the colonies.

58   *Historia*, 3:374.

59   Giménez Fernández, "A Biographical Sketch," 80–82.

60   *Historia*, 3:279.

61   By the time Las Casas ended his negotiations with the crown, his original request for one thousand leagues had been reduced to two hundred and sixty leagues along the coast, but it was unlimited toward the interior. Wagner and Parish, *Life and Writings*, 57.

62   Giménez Fernández, *El estatuto de la tierra*, 38.

63   The original date was May 15, 1520. Ibid., 53–54.

64   This particular privilege, specifically the fact that the knights were allowed to dress in colorful white tunics with red crosses, has been the object of numerous satirical and insulting commentaries by Las Casas's critics, particularly Gonzalo Fernández de Oviedo and Ramón Menéndez Pidal. Las Casas claimed that the original style of dress of the knights was supposed to impress on the Indians their difference from all other Spaniards. For a detailed description, see the *Historia*, 3:279–80. For a copy of the original grant to Las Casas, *DII*, 7:74–75.

65   Bataillon, analyzing Las Casas's own version of events in the *Historia*, points out that in the partnership between Las Casas and Pedro de Rentería, before the former's "conversion" in 1514, it was Las Casas who had demonstrated true business talent which made their holdings prosper. Ironically, the layman was more inclined to spiritual practices than the religious partner; see Bataillon, *Estudios sobre Bartolomé de Las Casas*, 49. Furthermore, Las Casas had managed to survive in court until 1520 by virtue of the proceeds from the sale of his and Rentería's business enterprises at the time of his conversion. See Giménez Fernández, *Las Casas: Capellán*, 835.

66   The consulta was one of the advising bodies of the audiencia of Santo Domingo that presented Las Casas with a four-point proposition about conducting punitive expeditions against the natives of Tierra Firme responsible for the death of some Dominican and Franciscan missionaries in the settlement of

Chiribichí. The third and fourth proposals specifically called for the enslaving of the Indians captured in war. *Historia*, 3:371.

67 Giménez Fernández, "A Biographical Sketch," 83.

68 "Memorial de Don Diego Colón . . . a S. M. . . . ," in Hanke and Giménez Fernández, *Bibliografía crítica*, 40.

69 *Historia*, 3:178.

70 Wagner and Parish, *Life and Writings*, 48.

71 *Historia*, 3:381.

72 Ibid., 3:382.

73 Pedro de Córdoba had first suggested to Las Casas to request a sanctuary of sorts for the Indians of Tierra Firme. It is very likely that without the Dominican's suggestion, Las Casas would have never begun the project.

74 Parish, "Introduction," 31. According to Parish, at the time of his entering the order, Las Casas was unaware of Betanzos's attitude toward the Indians, an attitude Bentanzos apparently recanted on his deathbed in 1549. For a detailed account of his recantation, see Parish, *Las Casas en México*, 75–76.

75 *Historia*, 3:387.

76 According to Giménez Fernández, he must have solicited admission toward the end of 1522 and made his preliminary vows at the beginning of 1523 and his permanent vows at the end of that year. Giménez Fernández, *Las Casas: Capellán*, 1222.

77 Bataillon, "The *Clérigo* Casas, Colonist and Colonial Reformer," in Friede and Keen, *Las Casas in History*, 414.

78 The question concerns the nature of Las Casas's education in his long quest in defense of the Indians. Whether Las Casas actually received a degree in jurisprudence, or a *licenciatura*, as Rolena Adorno and Helen Rand Parish claim, is almost irrelevant. On the basis of the available evidence, it should be sufficient to consider the autodidactic nature of Las Casas's education in addition to the formal but irregular training he received at different points in his life: at court, with his Dominican brethren, and at Salamanca. Manuel Giménez Fernández's assertion, that "it was almost certain that [Las Casas] never received a degree from any University School," seems to be the most widely accepted claim about Las Casas's educational status. See Giménez Fernández, "A Biographical Sketch," 83–84, also his *El estatuto de la tierra*, 8–9.

79 Courses in the Scriptures, patristics, and theology were obligatory for all newcomers. Parish, "Introduction," 28.

80 Hanke, "Bartolomé de Las Casas historiador," xvii.

81 Hanke and Giménez Fernández, *Bibliografía crítica*, 43.

82 Las Casas, "Carta al Consejo de Indias," in *Opúsculos*, 43–44.

83 Bataillon, "The *Clérigo* Casas," 414.

84 Las Casas, "Carta al Consejo de Indias," 48a-b. Translated from a Spanish transcript of the original Latin version. The size of the population of Española has been estimated never to have exceeded 500,000 at the point of contact.

85 Completed in 1542 and published in 1552.

86 Bataillon and Saint Lu, *El padre Las Casas*, 163.

87 Las Casas, "Carta al Consejo de Indias," *Opúsculos*, 52a.

88 Wagner and Parish, *Life and Writings*, 73.

89 Bataillon, "The *Clérigo* Casas," 414.

90 The title in English differs somewhat from the titles in romance languages, but this is the title given to the translation of the Latin text by Patrick Sullivan in the version edited by Helen Rand Parish.

91 According to Remesal, when Las Casas came to Guatemala in 1537, he already had a copy of the book with him. Pérez de Tudela claims that the book was written somewhere between 1522 and 1526. Saint Lu argues that Las Casas probably wrote the tract when he was prior at La Plata in 1527. Parish has reconstructed a complex chronological chart, which would indicate that the book was written in 1534; see Las Casas, *The Only Way*, 212–14. Giménez Fernández's and Hanke's bibliography lists 1537 as a possible date; see *Bibliografía crítica*, 50–55. The exact date of the writing of *The Only Way* is particularly relevant in the context of Las Casas's work in Tuzulutlán and the pacification of the "Land of War."

92 Las Casas, *The Only Way*, 68. Emphasis added.

93 Hanke and Giménez Fernández, *Bibliografía crítica*, 51; Las Casas, *The Only Way*, 68–116.

94 Las Casas, *The Only Way*, 117–18.

95 Borges, *Quién era Bartolomé de Las Casas?* 159, 165.

96 His "providentialism" was evident innumerable times, as in the case of his self-analysis after the failure at Paria and his decision to join the Dominicans (*Historia*, 3:382, 387); or when in 1545 he expressed in a letter to Prince Philip the belief that it was God who prompted him to act as the voice of the Indians ("Carta al príncipe Don Felipe," *Opúsculos*, 231b). The same providentialism emerges in the "Tratado comprobatorio del imperio soberano," where he claims that all he wanted was to "follow his conscience in carrying out the ministry bestowed upon me by Divine Providence"; see "Tratado comprobatorio," *Tratados de 1552 impresos por Las Casas en Sevilla*, 10:398.

97 Las Casas explains in the *Historia* that the diminutive form of the name of the cacique, Enriquillo, was used by those who knew him from childhood, but it seems to have been a common practice among Spaniards to call natives who had been baptized by the diminutive form of their names, perhaps in keeping with a perception of the Indians as little more than overgrown children. A good example of this practice is offered by Pedro Pizarro in his chronicle of the conquest of Peru, where all the *lenguas* used by the Spaniards were known for the diminutive form of their names: *Francisquillo, Felipillo, Martinillo*; see Pizarro, *Relación del descubrimiento y conquista de los reinos del Perú*, 32, 38, 58. To avoid confusion, the diminutive form of the name of the cacique of Española will be used in all references to this event.

98 Fernández de Oviedo dates the initial confrontation to 1519 in his *Historia general y natural de las indias*, 1:140. Las Casas provides a detailed account of the process from the beginning of the uprising to the peace signing in *Historia*, 3:259–70.

99　The Council of the Indies was established in 1524. "It ranked below the Council of Castile or Royal Council but above all other councils in Spain. Like the Older Royal Council for Castile, [it] oversaw every kind of government activity in the colonies." Burkholder and Johnson, *Colonial Latin America*, 81.

100　Although there is no hard evidence that this was the case, according to Las Casas, Parish, and other biographers of the Dominican, this was a precarious peace.

101　English version in Wagner and Parish, *Life and Writings*, 76–78. The Spanish text appears in *Opúsculos*, 57.

102　Las Casas, *Historia*, 3:263–64.

103　Las Casas, *Opúsculos*, 57b.

104　Menéndez Pidal, *El padre Las Casas*, 78–79.

105　See the detailed account of the various native rebel leaders and their pattern of operations in Utrera, *Polémica de Enriquillo*, 227–32. The book provides one of the most detailed examinations of this particular story.

106　Wagner, "Three Studies on the Same Subject," 168.

107　Pagden, "*Ius et Factum*," 90.

108　Las Casas, *Historia*, 2:385.

109　Wagner was convinced that Las Casas had not learned any native languages despite Remesal's claim to the contrary. Wagner's evidence is based on Las Casas's own assertions in the *Apologética*, Motolinía's letter to the emperor, and various other bits of information provided by Las Casas himself. See Wagner and Parish, *Life and Writings*, 85–86.

110　Las Casas, "Carta a un personaje de la corte," in *Obras escogidas*, 90:62b. The personage at court was ostensibly Juan Bernal de Luco; see Borges, *Quién era Bartolomé de Las Casas?* 178. Giménez Fernández gives the name as Juan Bernal Díaz de Luco, concilor of the Indies; see "A Biographical Sketch," 92.

111　"Carta a un personaje," 59b.

112　Giménez Fernández, "Biographical Sketch," 87.

113　"Informaciones hechas en la ciudad de León de Nicaragua, a pedimento del señor gobernador de aquella provincia," in *DII*, 7:118.

114　Giménez Fernández, "Biographical Sketch," 88.

115　For an extensive and detailed examination of this and other episcopal meetings in Mexico, see Parish and Weidman, *Las Casas en México*.

116　Bull *Sublimis Deus* in Las Casas, *The Only Way*, 115. Emphasis added.

117　His accomplishments in Tuzulutlán have contributed greatly to the creation of a mythical Las Casas, thanks largely to the story narrated by the Dominican Remesal and interpreted by later biographers. However, Bataillon and Menéndez Pidal, although for entirely different motives, set out to correct prevailing misconceptions about this event.

118　Remesal, *Historia general de las Indias*, 175:212a, b.

119　Hanke, *The Spanish Struggle for Justice*, 77.

120　There are numerous accounts of this agreement, as well as of the number and names of the missionaries present for the occasion. These versions range from the highly detailed and imaginative narration of Remesal, to the careful attempt by Bataillon to separate fact from fiction in Remesal, to the soberly objective and sketchy one of Pedro Borges.

121 Borges, *Quién era Bartolomé de Las Casas?* 185–86.
122 Giménez Fernández, "Biographical Sketch," 91.
123 Bataillon, *Estudios sobre Bartolomé de Las Casas*, 204–5.
124 Ibid., 203.
125 Borges, *Quién era Bartolomé de Las Casas?* 186–87.
126 Quintana, *Vida de fray Bartolomé de Las Casas*, quoted in Martínez, *Fray Bartolomé de Las Casas*, 67.
127 Martínez, *Fray Bartolomé de Las Casas*, 217. It is ironic that one of the letters came from Bishop Marroquín, who at the time was one of the objects of Las Casas's attacks.
128 Giménez Fernández, *Las Casas: Capellán*, 663.
129 Lovett, *Early Habsburg Spain, 1517–1598*, 133.
130 "Carta del cabildo secular al emperador, 20 de abril de 1540," cited in Bataillon, *Estudios*, 208–9. For the full text, see *DII*, 7:149–56.
131 Remesal, *Historia general*, 175:248–52.
132 Ibid., 256, a, b.
133 "Carta al emperador, 15 de diciembre de 1540," *Opúsculos*, 68a-b, 69a.
134 Schäfer, *El consejo real y supremo de las Indias*, 1:60.
135 Under the terms of the visita, the members under investigation did not have to be suspended but could continue working until a judgment had been rendered. Ibid., 62.
136 There are different versions of this event. While various biographers of Las Casas attribute the visita of the council to Las Casas's denouncing some councilors for venality and extortion, Schäfer in his history of the council claimed that the investigation was the result of an accumulation of numerous complaints about the council's handling of various affairs, one of the most important cases being that of the trial conducted against Hernando Pizarro for the death of Diego de Almagro in Peru. As a result of the visita, councilors Diego de Beltrán and Juan Suárez de Carvajal were found guilty of accepting bribes and other charges. Both were expelled from the council and made to pay heavy fines. According to Schäfer the replacement of Cardinal Loaysa by Sebastián Ramirez de Fuenleal was the result of his old age and infirmity rather than of the charges brought before the king by Las Casas and others. For a sampling of versions of these events, see Giménez, "A Biographical Sketch," 94–97; Hanke, *Spanish Struggle*, 94; Borges, *Quién era Bartolomé de Las Casas?* 190–91; Keniston, *Francisco de los Cobos*, 254; Schäfer, *El comsejo real*, 1:60–75.

Chapter Four Theory and Praxis

1 "Representación hecha al Rey por el clérigo Bartolomé de Las Casas, en que manifiesta los agravios que sufren los indios de la isla de Cuba de los españoles," in *DII*, vol. 7.

2   Aside from the *Brevísima* the most commonly read of his works are the multivolume *Historia de las Indias*, the two-volume *Apologética historia sumaria*, the eight treatises published in 1552, his primer for religious conversion, *The Only Way*, and his treatise on self-determination, *De regia potestate o derecho de autodeterminación*, published posthumously in 1571.

3   Aside from its literal meaning, which is "report," the term *relación* also means "narrative," "retelling," or "memorial."

4   The requirement for official permission, though not always enforced, could serve as a form of censorship. Wagner and Parish, *Life and Writings*, 187.

5   Ibid., 267.

6   The term also refers to the anti-Spanish critique by Germany and the Netherlands in the sixteenth century. Keen, "The Black Legend Revisited," 703.

7   Foucault, *The Archaeology of Knowledge and the Discourse on Language*, 7.

8   Las Casas, *A Short Account*, 6.

9   Ibid., 5.

10 Ibid., 3.

11 Cited in Hanke, "Bartolomé de Las Casas historiador," in Las Casas, *Historia de las Indias*, 1:xxxviii.

12 "Carta que escribieron varios padres de la Orden de Santo Domingo, residentes en la isla Española a Mr. de Xevres," *DII*, 7:397–430.

13 Ibid., 399.

14 Milhou, "De la destruction de l'Espagne à la destruction des Indes," 25–47.

15 Ibid., 25.

16 Las Casas, *A Short History*, 15.

17 Hanke, *Spanish Struggle*, 89–90.

18 MacLachlan, *Spain's Empire in the New World*, 13.

19 Ibid., 53.

20 Oviedo listed the number of people killed by Pedrarias at Castilla del Oro as two million, when from modern accounts the population could not have been one tenth of that; see *Historia general y natural de las Indias*, 3:241. López de Gómara, echoing Oviedo, claimed that the heads of the Indians of Española were so hard that swords broke when the conquistadores hit them; see, *Historia general de las Indias*, 1:66. Díaz del Castillo, recounting the escape from Tenochtitlán, wrote that there were so many dead that the Spanish soldiers could walk over the dead men and horses in the water; see *Historia verdadera de la conquista de la Nueva España*, 257a.

21 Las Casas, "Entre los remedios," in *Opúsculos*, 93b.

22 The New Laws were signed in November 1542, and the *Brevísima* was dated December of that same year.

23 Simpson, *The Encomienda*, 129.

24 Hanke, *Spanish Struggle*, 91.

25 In the case of the New Laws, as was the case of the Visigoth legacy mentioned above, the fact that the law was supposed to be a reflection of justice rather than a result of it was very evident: the laws emanated from the bountiful, kind, and just sovereign who was there to administer justice. Ibid., 59.

26 Cited in Simpson, *The Encomienda*, 130.

27 Simpson lists this as article 35, *The Encomienda*, 132. Zavala lists it as article 30, *La encomienda indiana*, 80. My use reflects widespread habit rather than a specific preference.

28 Parry, *The Spanish Theory of Empire*, 27.

29 MacLachlan, *Spain's Empire*, 58.

30 Friede, *Bartolomé de Las Casas, precursor del anticolonialismo*, 143. Francisco Roldán, one of the early settlers of Española, rebelled in 1498 against the authority of the Columbus brothers in an attempt to seize control from the "foreigners," Genoa-born Christopher and Bartholomew. Morison, *Admiral of the Ocean Sea*, 563–67.

31 Losada, *Fray Bartolomé de Las Casas a la luz de la historia moderna*, 193–94.

32 On a curious note, Giménez Fernández insists that Las Casas was not so much against the encomenderos as he was against the authorities that allowed the encomenderos to carry on at their own discretion. See "A Biographical Sketch," 94.

33 There is no certainty about the date of the actual nomination of Las Casas. Remesal, in his highly imaginative biography, places it as the Sunday after the signing of the New Laws; *Historia general*, 175:301b–302. According to Menéndez Pidal, the emperor signed the laws in Barcelona on Monday, November 20, 1542, and the next day left for Valencia. This would have made it impossible for Las Casas to see the emperor before his departure for Valencia (Menéndez conveniently ignores the fact that it was not Charles himself who presented Las Casas with the nomination, but the emperor's secretary). He assumes that Charles sent the nomination on Sunday, December 10, two days after Las Casas had completed the text of the *Brevísima*. See Menéndez Pidal, *El padre Las Casas*, 158. Borges, without providing a reason, sets the date as November 12, 1542; Borges, *Quién era Bartolomé de Las Casas?* 199.

34 A possible reason for his refusal might have been his sense of Peru's instability after the long civil wars in reaction to the New Laws. Perhaps he believed that he was being bought off with one of the richest bishoprics in the Spanish world, or perhaps he feared the possibility of being personally attacked or killed for his alleged role in the enactment of the laws. See Friede, *Bartolomé de Las Casas, precursor del anticolonialismo*, 160.

35 In colonial times the province was known as Chiapa. Only in the last century was the name changed to Chiapas.

36 Parish, *Las Casas as a Bishop*, xi.

37 Ibid., xii.

38 "El Obispo electo Bartolomé de Las Casas al Emperador Carlos V," in Parish, *Las Casas as a Bishop*, 18.

39 Menéndez Pidal, *El padre Las Casas*, 159.

40 Las Casas, cited in Parish, *Las Casas as a Bishop*, 18–23.

41 Wagner and Parish, *Life and Writings*, 125–28.

42 Giménez, "A Biographical Sketch," 99.

43 "The Atlantic Crossing of Father Tomás de la Torre," in Leonard, *Colonial Travelers in Latin America*, 26.

44 José Alcina Franch, *Bartolomé de Las Casas*, 109.

45 Leonard, *Colonial Travelers*, 25

46 Wagner and Parish, *Life and Writings*, 129.

47 Ibid., 129–30.

48 Remesal, *Historia general de las Indiàs*, 175:357b–359b.

49 This accusation was based on the bishop's request to define the geographic boundaries of his diocese.

50 This last, very subjective charge coincided with the charges contained in the letter sent by Toribio de Benavente to the king; see Friede, *Las Casas, precursor*, 162.

51 Wagner and Parish, *Life and Writings*, 132.

52 Fabié maintained that in this proclamation resided the seeds of the *Confesionario* that the bishop would later prepare. Fabié, *Vida y escritos*, 1:179.

53 Friede, *Las Casas, precursor*, 164.

54 Brading, *The First America*, 69.

55 Las Casas, *Tratados de Fray Bartolomé de Las Casas*, 2:857–59.

56 Ibid., 883.

57 Giménez Fernández, *Biographical Sketch*, 102.

58 Wagner and Parish, *Life and Writings*, 137.

59 Remesal, *Historia general*, 175:412a-b–413a-b.

60 Biermann, "Bartolomé de Las Casas and Verapaz," 472.

61 Wagner and Parish, *Life and Writings*, 135.

62 Ibid., 148.

63 Zavala, *La encomienda*, 89.

64 Ironically, the Mercedarians had pleaded with him on behalf of the colonists to modify his views in the matter of confession and the enforcement of the New Laws in general but to no avail. At one point in his bishopric, Las Casas had petitioned the king not to allow any more Mercedarian friars to travel to his dioceses.

65 Moscoso Pastrana "Fray Bartolomé de Las Casas en Ciudad Real, Chiapa," 273.

66 Giménez Fernández, "Biographical Sketch," 104.

67 Ibid., 103.

68 Parish, *Las Casas en México*, 58–59.

69 Pagden, *The Fall of Natural Man*, 109.

70 Although the titular president of the Council of the Indies at the time was still García de Loaisa. See Hanke, *Aristotle and the American Indians*, 30.

71 Las Casas, "Aquí se contiene una disputa," in *Tratados de Fray Bartolomé de Las Casas*, 1:221.

72 The book had appeared in abbreviated form in Rome in 1550 as an apologia. It was first translated and published in Spanish in its fuller form in 1892 in an edition prepared by Marcelino Menéndez y Pelayo with the title of *Tratado sobre las causas justas de la guerra contra los Indios*. The book was also variously known as *Democrates II, Democrates Alter*, or *Democrates Secundum*. Sepúlveda in his *Apología* denies the fact that his book had been refused approval at Alcalá and Salamanca: "No se trató realmente de un juicio de la Universidad,

sino de un artificio amañado por unos cuantos corruptores." Sepúlveda, *Apología de Juan Ginés de Sepúlveda contra Fray Bartolomé de las Casas*, 45.

73 Hanke, *Aristotle and the American Indians*, 30–31.

74 Losada, "The Controversy between Sepúlveda and Las Casas in the Junta of Valladolid," 279.

75 Borges, *Quién era Bartolomé de Las Casas?* 213–14.

76 Martinez Bulle Goyri, "El encuentro entre Fray Bartolomé de Las Casas y Juan Ginés de Sepúlveda," 234.

77 Parry, *Spanish Theory of Empire*, 55; Losada, *Las Casas a la luz de la historia*, 247.

78 See Sepúlveda, *Tratado sobre las justas causas de la guerra contra los indios*.

79 Sepúlveda, *Apología*, 61–71.

80 Las Casas, *Apología contra Sepúlveda*, 132.

81 Ibid., 127–38.

82 Ibid., 145–246.

83 Parry, *Spanish Theory of Empire*, 34.

84 Las Casas, *Apología*, 247–313. As in the case of the *Apología*, Las Casas devoted considerable space to the question of human sacrifices in his *Apologética historia*. In the second volume he dedicated six chapters to an analysis of sacrifices and rituals in Mesoamerica. See *Apologética historia*, 2:184–213.

85 Las Casas, *Apología*, 315–57.

86 Apparently Las Casas did not consider the imposition of Christianity as a form of oppression.

87 Hanke, *All Mankind Is One*, 63.

88 Las Casas, *Apología*, 349–51, 375.

89 Novalín, *El inquisidor general Fernando de Valdés*, 356.

90 In 1546 Melchor Cano had written against Sepúlveda's book, and the latter maintained that Cano had been one of the theologians voting against him in the debate's aftermath. The enmity between fellow Dominicans Melchor Cano and Carranza is legendary, as is the inquisitorial process begun by Inquisitor General Valdés against Carranza in 1559, resulting in the latter spending seventeen years in prison and being released only a few days before his death in 1576. For more details on Cano and Sepúlveda, see Hanke, *All Mankind Is One*, 113, and *Aristotle and the American Indians*, 31; Pagden, *The Fall of Natural Man*, 110–11. For Carranza and Valdés, see Tellechea, *Carranza y su tiempo*, and Novalín, *El inquisidor general Fernando de Valdés*.

91 Parry, *Spanish Theory of Empire*, 43.

92 Pagden, *The Fall of Natural Man*, 137.

93 Queralto Moreno, *El Pensamiento filosófico-político de Bartolomé de Las Casas*, 90.

94 Hanke, *Spanish Struggle*, 8–9.

95 Martinez Bulle Goyri, "El Encuentro entre Fray Bartolomé de Las Casas y Juan Ginés de Sepúlveda," 237.

96 Hanke and Giménez Fernández, *Bibliografía crítica*, 141.

97 MacLachlan, *Spain's Empire in the New World*, 60.

98 The conditions of the contract signed with the superiors of the convent were extraordinarily good for any member of a religious order. They received "three new cells—one of them presumably for the large collection of books and manuscripts Las Casas had amassed—a servant, first place in the choir, freedom to come and go as they pleased, and burial in the sacristy." Hanke, *Aristotle*, 75.

99 Giménez Fernández, "A Biographical Sketch," 107.

Chapter Five Toward a Restoration of the Indies

1   Wagner and Parish, *Life and Writings*, 171.

2   Both treatises appeared as part of the collection published in 1552.

3   Las Casas, "Aquí se contienen treinta proposiciones muy jurídicas," in *Tratados*, 1:467.

4   Las Casas, "Proposición XXIX," in *Tratados*, 1:493.

5   Las Casas, "Proposición XXX y última," in ibid., 499.

6   Zavala, *La encomienda*, 146.

7   Friede, "Las Casas and Indigenism," 183.

8   Ibid., 194.

9   Wagner and Parish, *Life and Writings*, 185. See also Remesal, *Historia general de las Indias*, 189:298a-b, for the manner in which these objects arrived to the Indies.

10 Las Casas, *Tratados*, ed. Carlo and Moreno. This version of the *Tratados* includes the fragment of a letter, "Lo que sigue es un pedazo de una carta y relación . . ." that Las Casas included as a faithful description of the conquest of the Indies by an anonymous captain, which Alcina Franch, concurring with Giménez, claims as an appendix to the *Brevísima*; see Franch, *Bartolomé de Las Casas*, 131. Currently there is a newer, more manageable edition of the *Tratados* in circulation, part of an ambitious collection aiming to publish all Las Casas's works; see Hernández and Galmés, eds., *Tratados de 1552*. The four principles that constitute the last treatise seem to be an excerpt of a longer treatise, *Erudita et elegans explicatio*, printed posthumously in Frankfurt in 1571. See Hanke, *Las teorías políticas de Bartolomé de Las Casas*, 23–24. At present the original *Erudita explicatio* has been published as a single text under the title *De regia potestate o derecho de autodeterminación*, edited by Pereña et al.

11 Las Casas, *A Short Account*, 43.

12 For a study on the importance of books during the conquest and the colonial period, see Leonard, *Books of the Brave*, 330–31.

13 Losada, *Las Casas a la luz de la historia*, 161. Emphasis in the original.

14 Interestingly, despite the multitude of books about Las Casas, there are very few references to this incident or the earlier one when he was charged with "high treason" because of the *Confesionario*. Parish's choice of words like "high treason" seems like a bit of verbal pyrotechnics to further enhance the figure of the bishop of Chiapa. See Parish, "Introduction," 45–47. For the charges presented to the Inquisition, see Wagner and Parish, *Life and Writings*, 187–88.

15 Very likely the *Erudita elegans explicatio* (see Friede, "Las Casas and Indigenism," 183). Juan Antonio Llorente, *Histoire critique de L'Inquisition d'Espagne*, quoted in Wagner and Parish, *Life and Writings*, 187.

16 Wagner and Parish, *Life and Writings*, 189. The only reference to the possibility of Sepúlveda being the accuser of Las Casas appears in the text of appendix 25 in Fabié's study of Las Casas, "Proposiciones temerarias, escandalosas y heréticas que notó el doctor Sepúlveda." See Fabié, *Vida y escritos*, 2:543–69.

17 Borges, *Quién era Las Casas?* 235. 209

18 Díaz del Castillo, *Historia verdadera*, 587–89.

19 It is difficult to ascertain the exact quantity of money offered by the Peruvian encomenderos. In the "Estudio Preliminar" of *De regia potestate*, Pereña and the others list the amount as "*cinco millones de ducados de oro*," ix, xlvii. Giménez Fernández mentions the sum of "8,000,000 pesos," "A Biographical Sketch," 113. Wagner mentions a sum of "some seven to nine million ducats, *Life and Writings*, 214. David Brading lists the amount as "four million ducats," *The First America*, 71.

20 Pereña, "Estudio Preliminar," xlviii–xlix.

21 Zavala, *La encomienda indiana*, 146–47.

22 Schäfer, *El consejo real*, 2:285.

23 Las Casas, "Carta al Maestro Fray Bartolomé Carranza de Miranda," in *Opúsculos*, 431a–b.

24 Ibid., 434a–b.

25 Ibid., 449b–450a-b. The Indian caciques would be responsible to the Spanish authority appointed by the crown.

26 Ibid., 448a-b, 449a-b.

27 Pereña, "Estudio preliminar," lii.

28 Schäfer, *El consejo real*, 2:287.

29 Pereña, "Estudio preliminar," ci–cvi.

30 "Memorial del obispo Fray Bartolomé de Las Casas y Fray Domingo de Santo Tomás," in *Opúsculos*, 466a.

31 Ibid., 466b–467a-b.

32 Schäfer, *El consejo real*, 2:289.

33 "Memorial al consejo de Indias," *Opúsculos*, 536a-b–538a-b.

34 Schäfer, *El consejo real*, 292–94.

35 Tellechea Idígoras, *El Arzobispo Carranza y su tiempo*, 2:26–29.

36 Las Casas testified twice before the Inquisition, in 1561 and 1562. On both occasions he defended his friend against the charges of heresy and unorthodoxy. Ibid.

37 Las Casas, "Carta a los Domínicos de Chiapa y Guatemala, 1563," in *Opúsculos*, 469a–477b.

38 See Las Casas, *Los tesoros del Perú*.

39 Most likely the author expressing the doubts was Domingo de Santo Tomás, with whom Las Casas had represented the Indians in the famous controversy on perpetuity.

40 Las Casas, "Tratado de las doce dudas," in *Opúsculos*, 478a–536b. The eight principles with which Las Casas responds to the twelve doubts are contained in the middle section of his treatise, 486a–501a.

41 Pereña, "Estudio preliminar," cxxvi–cxxvii.

42 It is very likely that after his previous experience with the publication of the treatises in 1552, Las Casas was unwilling to tempt the wrath of the censors and the Inquisition, particularly in light of the *pragmáticas* of 1556 and 1558. The first forbade the publication of any texts about the Indies without the approval of the Council of the Indies; the second, as we have seen, called for the death penalty for those who disobeyed the prohibition. The pragmática ordered that "no book nor work of any kind, written in Latin or romance, nor any other language will be printed in these kingdoms without said book or work being presented in our Council and seen and examined by the person or persons that our Council will determine . . . And whoever prints or allows, or gives out to be printed a book or another work without being preceded by said examination and approval, and our license in the stipulated manner will incur the death penalty and the loss of all his goods and the books and works will be publicly burned." Cited in Pereña, "Estudio preliminar," cxix–cxx.

43 Las Casas, *De regia potestate*, 113–15.

44 Las Casas, "Petición de Bartolomé de Las Casas a Su Santidad Pio V sobre los negocios de las Indias," in *Opúsculos*, 541–42.

45 Las Casas, "Claúsula del testamento que hizo el obispo de Chiapa, Don Fray Bartolomé de Las Casas," in *Opúsculos*, 539b.

46 Ibid., 540a.

Chapter Six The Legacy of Las Casas

1 Friede, "Las Casas and Indigenism," 133.

2 It is widely assumed that his proposal for the peaceful colonization of the New World influenced the thinking of Thomas More and his *Utopia*. The reasons for this assumption are largely based on various points of coincidence between the two works. Las Casas made his own work, "Entre los remedios," public in March 1516 and More published his treatise in December of the same year. It is distinctly possible that More had an opportunity to see Las Casas's proposal, which was circulating widely among crown officials, many of whom were More's acquaintances. In addition, there is the correspondence of geographical descriptions and the sizes of towns and households. Las Casas's proposal concerned an island; More's *Utopia* was likewise featured an island of similar characteristics. Further evidence is manifested in the cases where More's descriptions conform to Las Casas's own descriptions of minor places or events, as well as similarities between the proposals for work programs that Las Casas formulated and those that appear in More's work. See Baptiste, *Bartolomé de Las Casas and Thomas More's "Utopia,"* 61–67.

3 Las Casas, *Historia*, 3:146.

4 One of Friede's most significant works, *Bartolomé de Las Casas precursor del*

anticolonialismo, is entirely dedicated to the study of the friar's work as an anticolonialist.

5   Mommsen, *Theories of Imperialism*, 3.

6   Simpson, *The Encomienda*, 132.

7   Las Casas, "Entre los remedios," in *Tratados*, 2:645.

8   Modern studies have demonstrated that the native population of Mexico alone had been reduced by 34 percent in the first decade after the conquest. See Borah and Cook, *The Aboriginal Population of Central Mexico*, 4.

9   The term "democratic" is used advisedly in this context. It refers to a government that despite its intentions to safeguard the interests of the popular masses was, nevertheless, being imposed from the outside: "[Spanish rule] must meet with the approval of the natives in order to be legitimate," wrote Las Casas in "Principio 6" in *Doce dudas*, 11.2:65, 67. Throughout *De regia potestate* he reaffirms the concept of the king acting as the guardian of the well-being of his subjects and their possessions.

10 Elliott, *The Old World and the New*, 87.

11 The exceptions include, most notably, a group of Mexican notables headed by Pedro Motecuhzoma Tlacahuepatzin who wrote to Philip asking the king to maintain Las Casas as the protector of the Indians, and the caciques meeting in Peru in 1559 who asked that Las Casas and Santo Tomás represent them before the court.

12 Pedro Cieza de León was the earliest chronicler of Peru to attempt to capture the history of the Incas and to study their contribution to the evolution of high culture in South America. He seemed to have been familiar with the writings of Las Casas, and he is supposed to have requested from his executors that if any problems arose in having the second part of his *Crónicas del Perú* printed, Las Casas should be asked to do it for him. Keen, "Approaches," 5.

13 As a result of his work, Santo Tomás produced a grammar and dictionary of Quechua usage in Peru in 1560, *Grammática o arte de la lengua de los indios de los reynos del Perú y Lexicón o vocabulario de la lengua general del Perú*.

14 Murra, "Nos hazen mucha ventaja," 84.

15 They charged him, among other things, with having appropriated the name Navarrete, which he added to his name after becoming a bishop. Ibid., 84.

16 Saint Lu, "Vigencia histórica de la obra de Las Casas, 22.

17 Pagden, *European Encounters*, 58.

18 Remesal, *General History of the Occidental Indies, and in Particular of the territory of Chiapa and Guatemala*. Conscious of the absence of historical writings on Guatemala and Chiapa, Remesal wanted to be known as the first historian of the spiritual conquest of Guatemala. Originally he had 1500 copies printed, of which he seems to have shipped at least 800 to America. Saénz de Santa María, "Estudio preliminar," in Remesal, *Historia general*, 175:46.

19 MacLeod, "Las Casas, Guatemala and the Sad but Inevitable Case of Antonio de Remesal," 64.

20 There is no exact date available, since at the time of his death he was so far from any of his brethren. Saénz, "Estudio preliminar," 29.

21 Keen, "Approaches to Las Casas," 6–7. See also Ulloa, *Los predicadores divididos*, 93, 96–100.

22 Bataillon, *Estudios*, 193.

23 "Ordenanzas de su Magestad hechas para los nuevos descubrimientos, conquistas y pacificaciones. Julio de 1573," *DII*, 16:142–87.

24 Ibid., 143, 147, 149, 152. Emphasis added.

25 Ibid., 152. Emphasis added.

26 See "Entre los remedios," "Tratado Sexto," in *Tratados de Fray Bartolomé de Las Casas*, 2:643–849.

27 See Parry, *The Spanish Theory of Empire*, 26.

28 Hanke, *Aristotle and the American Indians*, 86–88.

29 Las Casas, "Memorial de remedios," in *Opúsculos*, 5b–6a.

30 For the Toledan regime in Peru, see Andrien, "Spaniards, Andeans and the Early Colonial State"; Aranibar, "El principio de la dominación," 41–62; Brading, *First America*, 128–46. Also see Levillier, *Don Francisco de Toledo*.

31 Keen, "The Black Legend Revisited," 704, n. 2.

32 Powell, *Soldiers Indians and Silver*, 105–7.

33 Andrien, "Spaniards, Andeans and the Early Colonial State in Peru," 129.

34 "Carta del Padre Fray Toribio de Motolinía a Carlos V, 2 de enero, 1555," *DIM*, 1:256.

35 Ibid., 260–61.

36 Ibid., 259.

37 Ibid., 258. Las Casas had gone on record in the ecclesiastical conference in Mexico in 1539 as supporting the position of the majority against mass baptism or the administration of other important sacraments without proper preparation. This seems to be the original point of conflict between Las Casas and Motolinía. See Wagner and Parish, *Life and Writings*, 98–100. It is important to note that despite Las Casas's opposition to baptism without adequate preparation, during the time he spent with Enriquillo in the mountains he administered confession and other sacraments to the rebels without obviously having had enough time to prepare them adequately. *Opúsculos*, 57.

38 "Carta del Padre Fray Toribio de Motolinía," 259–60.

39 Fray Toribio de Benavente, Motolinía, *Historia de los indios de la Nueva España*, cited in Wagner and Parish, *Life and Writings*, 99.

40 Zavala, *Recuerdo de Bartolomé de Las Casas*, 15–17.

41 "Carta del Padre Fray Toribio de Motolinía," *DIM*, 270.

42 For a more detailed account of the enmity with Oviedo, see Hanke, "Bartolomé de Las Casas historiador," and Bolaños, *Panegírico y libelo del primer cronista de Indias Gonzalo Fernández de Oviedo*.

43 Las Casas, *Historia de las Indias*, 2:518.

44 Fernández de Oviedo, *Historia natural*, 2:199–201.

45 Hanke, "Las Casas historiador," 1:xxix.

46 López de Gómara, *Historia general de las Indias*, 220.

47 Las Casas, *Historia*, 3:251–52.

48 Ibid., 3:321.

49 It must be remembered that the title of *protector universal de todos los indios*, a resounding title with rather nebulous prerogatives and powers, was granted to him by the imperial authority of Cardinal Ximénez de Cisneros, acting as regent of Castile, in 1516 at a time when it was thought possible to establish a theocracy in the Antilles. Later, he was once again named official procurator of the Indians, from the time of his nomination to the bishopric of Chiapa until the time of his resignation.

50 For the most detailed catalogue of Las Casas's works, see Pérez Fernández, *Inventario documentado de los escritos de Fray Bartolomé de Las Casas*. This is in addition to the massive compilation by Giménez Fernández and Hanke, *Bibliografía crítica*.

51 Rivera Pagán, *Evangelización y violencia*, 105.

52 Keen, "The Black Legend Revisited," 706. Judería's book was first printed in 1914 and then revised in 1917. The popularity of such views is reflected in the fact that in twelve years the book went through twelve editions.

53 Carbia, *Historia de la leyenda negra hispano-americana*, 14–15.

54 One has only to take a cursory look at Leon-Portilla's *The Broken Spears*, as well as Borah and Cook's *The Aboriginal Population of Central Mexico on the Eve of the Spanish Conquest*, to realize what important historical aspects are being omitted by the proponents of the Golden Legend.

55 Carbia, *Historia de la leyenda negra*, 54–55.

56 Vasconcelos, *Breve historia de Méjico*, cited in Carro, *España en America*, 73, 74.

57 The prologue to his *Historia de las Indias* and several of his treatises from 1516 to his testament in 1564 attest to this.

58 Carro, "Carta abierta a D. R. Menéndez Pidal," 6. Appended to D. Carro, *España en America*.

59 Pereña, *Proceso a la leyenda negra*, 9.

60 See Goytisolo, "Menéndez Pidal y el padre Las Casas," in *El furgón*, 218.

61 Sánchez, "The Spanish Black Legend," 21.

62 Keen, "The Black Legend Revisited," 707.

63 The original L. B. Simpson book on the encomienda, published in 1929, dismissed much of Las Casas's *Brevísima* as an exaggeration and fell into many of the stereotypical accusations against the Dominican. Simpson accused Las Casas of beginning the slave trade and of wild exaggerations and inaccuracies. See Simpson's introduction to the 1929 edition of *The Encomienda in New Spain*. In the revised edition (1950), the author toned down his earlier criticism of Las Casas.

64 Keen, "The White Legend Revisited," 338.

65 Hanke, *The Spanish Struggle for Justice*, 1.

66 Ibid., 162.

Conclusion

1 Las Casas, "Petición a Su Santidad Pío V," in *Opúsculos*, 541–42.

2 In this context, *chingada* is interpreted as the "raped one." Concerning the use of the phrase and its implications, see Octavio Paz, *El laberinto de la soledad*, and Carlos Fuentes, *El espejo enterrado*, among many others.

3 Castro-Klarén, "The Nation in Ruins," 165.

4 Chasteen, introduction to Rama, *The Lettered City*, 5.

5 The textual quote reads: "*Este es por antonomasia el padre de los indios.*" Teresa de Mier, "La calumnia de haber sido Casas autor del comercio de esclavos negros," in *Obras Completas*, 86. See also Bolívar, "Reply of a South American gentleman," in *Selected Writings*, 104.

6 See Gutiérrez, *En busca de los pobres de Jesucristo* or its English translation, *Las Casas: In Search of the Poor of Jesus Christ*.

7 Gutierrez, *In Search of the Poor*, 456.

8 Carozza, "From Conquest to Constitutions," 289.

9 Rivera, *Evangelización y violencia*, 107.

10 At most a two-month period. See chapter 3 above for a more detailed description of the time with the rebel chief Enrique on the island of Española.

11 Nietzsche, *The Anti-Christ*, 118.

ᴞ Bibliography ᴞ

Alcina Franch, José. *Bartolomé de Las Casas*. Madrid: Historia 16, 1987.

Altman, Ida. *Emigrants and Society: Extremadura and América in the Sixteenth Century*. Berkeley: University of California Press, 1989.

Andrien, Kenneth J. "Spaniards, Andeans and the Early Colonial State in Peru," in Andrien and Adorno, *Transatlantic Encounters*.

Andrien, Kenneth J., and Rolena Adorno, eds. *Transatlantic Encounters: Europeans and Andeans in the Sixteenth Century*. Berkeley: University of California Press, 1991.

Aranibar, Carlos. "El Principio de la dominación (1531–1580)." In *Nueva historia general del Perú*, edited by Luis Guillermo Lumbreras et al. 5th ed. Lima: Mosca Azul Editores, 1988.

Aristotle. *The Politics*. Edited and translated by Carnes Lord. Chicago: University of Chicago Press, 1984.

Avalle-Arce, Juan Bautista. "Las Hipérboles del Padre Las Casas." *Revista de la Facultad de Humanidades* 2:1 (January–March 1960): 33–55.

Baptiste, Victor N. *Bartolomé de Las Casas and Thomas More's "Utopia": Connections and Similarities: A Translation and Study*. Culver City, Calif.: Labyrinthos, 1990.

Bataillon, Marcel. "The *Clérigo* Casas, Colonist and Colonial Reformer." In Friede and Keen, *Bartolomé de Las Casas in History*, 353–440.

——. *Estudios sobre Bartolomé de Las Casas*. Barcelona: Ediciones Península, 1976. First published in French in 1965.

Bataillon, Marcel, and André Saint Lu. *El Padre Las Casas y la defensa de los indios*. Barcelona: Editorial Ariel, 1976. First published in French, 1971.

——. *Las Casas et la defense des Indiens*. Paris: Julliard, 1971.

Benavente, Motolinía, Toribio de. "Carta del Padre Fray Toribio de Motolinía a Carlos V, 2 de enero, 1555." In *Colección de documentos para la historia de México*, vol. 1, edited by Joaquín García Icazbalceta, 253–77. México: Librería de J. M. Andrade, Portal de Agustinos, 1858–66.

Bennassar, Bartolomé. *The Spanish Character: Attitudes and Mentalities from the Sixteenth to the Nineteenth Century*. Translated by Benjamin Keen. Berkeley: University of California Press, 1979. First published in French, 1975.

Biermann, Benno M. "Bartolomé de Las Casas and Verapaz." In Friede and Keen, *Bartolomé de Las Casas in History*, 443–84.

Bolaños, Félix Alvaro. *Panegírico y libelo del primer cronista de Indias Gonzalo Fernández de Oviedo*. Bogotá: Instituto Caro y Cuervo, 1990.

Bolívar, Simón. *Selected Writings of Bolívar*. Vol. 1. Edited by Vicente Lecuna and Howard Bierck. New York: Banco de Venezuela/Colonial Press, 1951.

Borah, Woodrow. "Representative Institutions in the Spanish Empire in the Sixteenth Century: The New World." *The Americas* 12 (1955–56): 246–56.

Borah, Woodrow, and S. F. Cook. *The Aboriginal Population of Central Mexico on the Eve of the Spanish Conquest*. Berkeley: University of California Press, 1963.

Borges, Pedro. *Quién Era Bartolomé de Las Casas?* Madrid: Ediciones Rialp, S. A., 1990.

Bourne, Edward Gaylord. *Spain in America, 1450–1580*. New York: Harper and Brothers, 1904.

Boxer, C. R. *The Church Militant and Iberian Expansion, 1440–1770*. Baltimore: Johns Hopkins University Press, 1978.

Brading, D. A. *The First America: The Spanish Monarchy, Creole Patriots and the Liberal State, 1492–1867*. Cambridge: Cambridge University Press, 1990.

Braudel, Fernand. *Capitalism and Material Life, 1400–1800*. Translated by Miriam Kochan. New York: Harper and Row, 1973. First published in French in 1967.

Brewer, Anthony. *Marxist Theories of Imperialism: A Critical Survey*. 2nd ed. London: Routledge, 1990.

Burkholder, Mark, and Lyman L. Johnson, *Colonial Latin America*. 4th ed. New York: Oxford University Press, 2001.

Camorlinga Alcaraz, Jose María. *El choque de dos culturas (Dos religiones)*. Mexico: Plaza Valdés Editores, 1993.

Camus, Albert. *The Rebel*. Translated by Anthony Brewer. New York: Vintage International, 1991. Originally published as *L'homme revolté*, 1951.

Carbia, Rómulo D. *Historia de la Leyenda Negra hispano-americana*. Buenos Aires: Ediciones Orientación Española, 1943.

Carozza, Paolo G. "From Conquest to Constitutions: Retrieving a Latin American Tradition of the Idea of Human Rights." *Human Rights Quarterly* 25 (2003): 281–313.

Carpentier, Alejo. *El arpa y la sombra*. 17th ed. Madrid: Siglo XXI de España, 1997.

Carro, Venancio D. "Carta abierta a D. R. Menéndez Pidal: Anotaciones a su conferencia sobre Las Casas (23-XI-1962)." In *España en America . . . Sin Leyendas. . .*

———. *España en America . . . Sin Leyendas . . .* Madrid: Librería Ope, 1963.

———. *La teología y los teólogos-juristas españoles ante la conquista de América*. 2nd ed. Salamanca: Biblioteca de Teólogos Españoles, 1951.

Castilla Urbano, Francisco. *El pensamiento de Francisco de Vitoria: Filosofía política e indio americano*. México: Universidad Autónoma Metropolitana, Unidad Iztapalapa/Anthropos, 1992.

Castro-Klarén, Sara. "The Nation in Ruins: Archaeology and the Rise of the Nation." In *Beyond Imagined Communities: Reading and Writing the Nation in Nineteenth-Century Latin America*, edited by Sara Castro-Klarén and John Chasteen, 161–195. Baltimore: Johns Hopkins University Press, 2003.

Césaire, Aimé. *Discourse on Colonialism*. New York: Monthly Review Press, 1972. Originally published as *Discours sur le colonialisme*, 1955.

Clavero, Bartolomé. *Genocidio y justicia: La destrucción de Las Indias, ayer y hoy*. Madrid: Marcial Pons, Ediciones de Historia, 2002.

Clendinnen, Inga. *Ambivalent Conquests: Maya and Spaniard in Yucatan, 1517–1570*. Cambridge: Cambridge University Press, 1987.

——. " 'Fierce and unnatural Cruelty': Cortés and the Conquest of Mexico." In Greenblatt, *New World Encounters*, 12–47.

Columbus, Christopher. *Libro de las profecias*. Translated by Delno C. West and August Kling. Gainesville: University of Florida Press, 1991.

Colección de documentos inéditos, relativos al descubrimiento, conquista y organización de las antiguas posesiones españolas de América y Oceanía sacados de los Archivos del Reino y muy especialmente del de Indias (DII). 42 vols. Edited by Luis Torres de Mendoza. Madrid, 1864–84.

Colección de documentos para la historia de México (DIM). 2 vols. Edited by Joaquín García Icazbalceta. México: Librería de J. M. Andrade, Portal de Agustinos, 1858–66.

Congreso Teológico Internacional. *Las Casas entre dos mundos*. Lima: Instituto Bartolomé de Las Casas–Rimac–Centro de Estudios y Publicaciones, 1993.

Cook, Noble David. "Population Data for Indian Peru: Sixteenth and Seventeenth Centuries." *Hispanic American Historical Review* 62:1 (February 1982): 73–75.

Cook, Sherburne F., and Woodrow Borah. *Essays in Population History*. 2 vols. Berkeley: University of California Press, 1971–74.

Cortés, Hernán. *Letters from Mexico*. Translated and edited by A. R. Pagden. New York: Grossman Publishers, 1971.

Dante Alighieri. *On World Government (De Monarchia)*. Translated by Herbert W. Schneider. Indianapolis: Bobbs-Merrill, 1959.

Di Agostino Iannarone, Reginaldo. "Genesis del pensamiento volonial en Francisco de Vitoria." In *Relectio de Indis o libertad de los indios*, edited by Luciano Pereña and J. M. Prendes, xxxi–xli. Madrid: Consejo de Investigaciones Científicas, 1967.

Díaz del Castillo, Bernal. *Historia verdadera de la Conquista de la Nueva España*. 14th ed. Edited by Joaquín Ramirez Cabañas. México: Editorial Porrúa, S.A., 1986. First published in Madrid in 1632.

Durán Luzio, Juan. *Bartolomé de Las Casas ante la conquista de América: Las voces del historiador*. Heredia, Costa Rica: Editorial de la Universidad Nacional, 1992.

Elliott, J. H. *Imperial Spain, 1469–1716*. New York: St. Martin's Press, 1964.

——. *The Old World and the New, 1492–1650*. New York: Cambridge University Press, 1972.

Estudios Lascasianos: IV centenario de la muerte de Fray Bartolomé de las Casas, (1566–1966). Sevilla: Facultad de Filosofía y Letras de la Universidad de Sevilla, 1966.

Fabié, Antonio María. *Vida y escritos de Fray Bartolomé de Las Casas, obispo de Chiapa*. 2 vols. Madrid: Imprenta de Manuel Ginesta, 1879.

Fernández Buey, Francisco. "La controversia entre Ginés de Sepúlveda y Bartolomé de las Casas: Una revisión." *Boletín Americanista* 42–43 (1992–93): 301–47.

Fiske, John. *The Discovery of America, with some Accounts of Ancient America and the Spanish Conquest*. 2 vols. Boston: Houghton Mifflin, 1897.

Flores Galindo, Alberto. *Buscando un Inca: Identidad y utopía en los Andes*. Lima: Editorial Horizonte, 1988.

Flores Hernández, Benjamín. "Pelear con el Cid después de muerto: Las *Apologías y*

217

discursos de las conquistas occidentales de Bernardo Vargas Machuca, en controversia con la *Brevísima relación de la destrucción de las Indias*, de Fray Bartolomé de las Casas." *Estudios de Historia Novohispana* 10 (1991): 45–105.

Foucault, Michel. *The Archaeology of Knowledge and the Discourse on Language*. Translated by A. M. Sheridan Smith. New York: Pantheon Books, 1972.

——. "Truth and Power." In *Power/Knowledge: Selected Interviews and Other Writings, 1972–1977*, edited by Colin Gordon. New York: Harvester Press, 1980.

Frank, Andre Gunder. *World Accumulation, 1492–1789*. New York: Monthly Review Press, 1978.

Freire, Paulo. *Pedagogy of the Oppressed*. Translated by Myra Bergman Ramos. New York: Seabury Press, 1968.

Friede, Juan. *Bartolomé de Las Casas*. Bogotá: Carlos Valencia Editores, 1974.

——. *Bartolomé de Las Casas, precursor del anticolonialismo: Su lucha y su derrota*. México: Siglo Veintiuno Editores, 1974.

——. "Las Casas y el movimiento indigenista en España y América en la primera mitad del siglo XVI." *Revista de Historia de América* 34 (December 1952): 339–411.

——. "Las Casas and Indigenism in the Sixteenth Century." In Friede and Keen, *Bartolomé de Las Casas in History*, 127–236.

Friede, Juan, and Benjamin Keen, eds. *Bartolomé de Las Casas in History: Toward an Understanding of the Man and His Work*. DeKalb: Northern Illinois University Press, 1971.

Galeano, Eduardo. *Las venas abiertas de América Latina*. México: Veintiuno Editores, 1987. First published 1970.

García Bernal, Manuela Cristina. *Población y encomienda en Yucatan bajo los Austrias*. Sevilla: Escuela de Estudios Hispano-Americanos de Sevilla, 1978.

Gibson, Charles. *Spain in America*. New York: Harper Torchbooks, 1966.

——, ed. *The Black Legend: Anti-Spanish Attitudes in the Old World and the New*. New York: Alfred A. Knopf, 1971.

Giménez Fernández, Manuel. *Bartolomé de Las Casas: Delegado de Cisneros para la reformación de las Indias (1516–1517)*. Vol. 1. Sevilla: Escuela de Estudios Hispano-Americanos de Sevilla, 1953.

——. *Bartolomé de Las Casas : Capellán de S. M Carlos I, Poblador de Cumaná (1517–1523)* Vol. 2. Sevilla: Escuela de Estudios Hispano-Americanos de Sevilla, 1960.

——. *El estatuto de la tierra de Casas: Estudio histórico y juridico del asiento y capitulación para pacificar y poblar la tierra firme de Paria concedida por Carlos V a su capellán micer Bartolomé de Las Casas*. Sevilla: Editorial Edelce, 1949.

——. "Fray Bartolomé de Las Casas: A Biographical Sketch." In Friede and Keen, *Bartolomé de Las Casas in History*, 67–125.

Goytisolo, Juan. *El furgón de cola*. Barcelona: Biblioteca Breve, Editora Seix Barral, 1976.

Greenblatt, Stephen. *Marvelous Possessions: The Wonder of the New World*. Chicago: University of Chicago Press, 1991.

——, ed. *New World Encounters*. Berkeley: University of California Press, 1993.

Greenleaf, Richard E., ed. *The Roman Catholic Church in Colonial Latin America*. Tempe: Center for Latin American Studies, Arizona State University, 1977.

Guamán Poma de Ayala, Felipe. *Nueva corónica y buen gobierno*. Edited by Franklin Pease. 2 vols. Caracas: Editorial Ayacucho, 1980.

Guilmartin, John F. Jr. "The Cutting Edge: An Analysis of the Spanish Invasion and the Overthrow of the Inca Empire, 1532–1539." In Andrien and Adorno, *Transatlantic Encounters*, 40–89.

Gutierrez, Gustavo. *Dios o el oro en las Indias*. 2nd ed. Lima: Instituto Bartolomé de Las Casas–Rimac–Centro de Estudios y Publicaciones, 1989.

——. *En busca de los pobres de Jesucristo: El pensamiento de Bartolomé de Las Casas*. Lima: Instituto Bartolomé de Las Casas–Rimac–Centro de Estudios y Publicaciones, 1992.

——. *Las Casas: In Search of the Poor of Jesus Christ*. Translated by Robert R. Barr. Maryknoll, N.Y.: Orbis Books, 1993.

——. "Search for Identity." Translated by Fred Murphy. *Latin American Perspectives* 19:3. *Five Hundred years of Colonization Struggles for Emancipation and Identity* (Summer 1992): 61–66.

Hanke, Lewis. *All Mankind Is One: A Study of the Disputation between Bartolomé de Las Casas and Juan Ginés de Sepúlveda in 1550 on the Intellectual and Religious Capacity of the American Indians*. De Kalb: Northern Illinois University Press, 1974.

——. *All the Peoples of the World Are Men*. Minneapolis: Associates of the James Ford Bell Library, 1970.

——. *Aristotle and the American Indians: A Study in Race Prejudice in the Modern World*. Bloomington: Indiana University Press, 1959.

——. "Bartolomé de Las Casas, an Essay in Hagiography and Historiography." *Hispanic American Historical Review* 33:1 (1953): 136–51.

——. *Bartolomé de las Casas, Historian: An Essay in Spanish Historiography*. Gainesville: University of Florida Press, 1952.

——. "Bartolomé de Las Casas historiador." In *Historia de las Indias*, edited by Agustín Millares Carlo, ix–lxxxvi. México: Fondo de Cultura Económica, 1951.

——. *Estudios sobre Fray Bartolomé de Las Casas y sobre la lucha por la justicia en la conquista española de América*. Caracas: Universidad Central de Venezuela, 1968.

——. "More Heat and Some Light on the Spanish Struggle for Justice in the Conquest of America." *Hispanic American Historical Review* 44:3 (August 1964): 293–340.

——. "A Modest Proposal for a Moratorium on Grand Generalizations: Some Thoughts on the Black Legend." *Hispanic American Historical Review* 51:1 (1971): 112–27.

——. *The Spanish Struggle for Justice in the Conquest of America*. Philadelphia: University of Pennsylvania Press, 1959. First published in 1949.

——. *Las teorías políticas de Bartolomé de Las Casas*. Buenos Aires: Publicaciones del Instituto de Investigaciones Históricas, Facultad de Filosofía y Letras n 67, 1935.

Hanke, Lewis, and Manuel Giménez Fernandez, *Bartolomé de Las Casas, 1474–*

1566: Bibliografía crítica y cuerpo de materiales para el estudio de su vida, escritos, actuación y polémicas que suscitaron durante cuatro siglos. Santiago de Chile: Fondo Histórico y Bibliográfico José Toribio Medina, 1954.

Haring, C. H. *The Spanish Empire in America*. San Diego: Harcourt Brace Jovano-vich, Publishers, 1963

Helps, Arthur. *The Life of Las Casas: Apostle of the Indies*. Philadelphia: J. B. Lippin-cott, 1868.

Hernáez, Francisco Javier, ed. *Colección de bulas, breves y otros documentos relativos a la iglesia de América y Filipinas*. 2 vols. Vaduz: Kraus Reprint Ltd., 1964. Origi-nally published in Brussels, 1879.

Hernández Martín, Ramon. *Francisco de Vitoria y su "Relección sobre los Indios": Los derechos de los hombres y de los pueblos*. Madrid: Edibesa, 1998.

Herrera y Tordesillas, Antonio de. *Historia general de los hechos de los castellanos en las islas, y tierra firme de el mar océano*. 2 vols. Asunción del Paraguay: Editorial Guaranía, 1944. First published 1601.

Kamen, Henry. *Spain, 1469–1714: A Society of Conflict*. London: Longman, 1982.

Keen, Benjamin. "Approaches to Las Casas, 1535–1970." In Friede and Keen, *Bartolomé de Las Casas in History*, 3–63.

——. "The Black Legend Revisited: Assumptions and Realities." *Hispanic American Historical Review* 49:4 (1969): 703–19.

——. "The White Legend Revisited: A Reply to Professor Hanke's 'Modest Pro-posal.'" *Hispanic American Historical Review* 51:2 (1971): 336–55.

Keniston, Hayward. *Francisco de los Cobos: Secretary of the Emperor Charles V*. Pittsburgh: University of Pittsburgh Press, 1958.

Las Casas, Bartolomé de. *Apologética historia sumaria*. Vols. 1–2. Edited by Ed-mundo O'Gorman. México: UNAM, Instituto de Investigaciones Históricas, 1967.

——. *Apología o declaración universal de los derechos del hombre y de los pueblos*. Salamanca: Junta de Castilla y León, 2000.

——. *Apología de Bartolomé de Las Casas contra Juan Ginés de Sepúlveda*. In Losada, *Apología*.

——. *Brevísima relación de la destruición de las Indias*. Buenos Aires: Ediciones Mar Océano, 1953. First published in 1552.

——. *De regia potestate o derecho de autodeterminación*. Edited by Luciano Pereña, J. M. Pérez-Prendes, Vidal Abril, and Joaquín Azcárraga. Corpus Hispanorum de Pace, vol. 8. Madrid: Consejo Superior de Investigaciones, 1969.

——. *Diario del primer y tercer viaje de Cristobal Colón*. Edited by Consuelo Varela. Vol. 14. *Obras completas*. Madrid: Alianza Editorial, 1989.

——. *Doce dudas*. Edited by J. B. Lassegue. Vol. 11.2. *Obras Completas*. Madrid: Alianza Editorial, 1992.

——. *Historia de las Indias*. Edited by Agustin Millares Carlo. 3 vols. México: Fondo de Cultura Económica, 1951. Completed 1559. First published 1875.

——. *Los tesoros del Perú*. Edited and translated by Angel Losada García. Madrid: Consejo de Investigaciones Científicas, 1968.

——. *Obras escogidas de Fray Bartolomé de Las Casas*. Edited by Juan Pérez de Tudela

Bueso. Vols. 90, 95, 96, 105, 106, 110 of the Biblioteca de Autores Españoles. Madrid: Biblioteca de Autores Españoles, 1957.

———. *Obras escogidas de Fray Bartolomé de Las Casas: Opúsculos, cartas y memoriales.* Vol. 110 of the Biblioteca de Autores Españoles. Edited by Juan Pérez de Tudela Bueso. Madrid: Biblioteca de Autores Españoles, 1958.

———. *The Only Way: A New Restored Version.* Edited by Helen Rand Parish. Translated by Francis Patrick Sullivan. New York: Paulist Press, 1992.

———. *A Short Account of the Destruction of the Indies.* Edited and translated by Nigel Griffin. London: Penguin Books, 1992.

———. *Tratados de Fray Bartolomé de Las Casas.* Translated by Agustín Millares Carlo and Rafael Moreno. 2 vols. México: Fondo de Cultura Económica, 1965.

———. *Tratados de 1552 impresos por Las Casas en Sevilla.* Edited by Ramón Hernández and Lorenzo Galmés. Vol. 10. *Obras Completas.* Madrid: Alianza Editorial, 1992.

Lassegue, Juan Bautista. *La larga marcha de Las Casas: Selección y presentación de textos.* Lima: Centro de Estudios y Publicaciones, 1974.

Leonard, Irving A. *Books of the Brave: Being an Account of Books and Men in the Spanish Conquest and Settlement of the Sixteenth-Century New World.* New York: Gordian Press, 1964. First published in 1949.

———. *Colonial Travelers in Latin America.* Edited by William C. Bryant. Newark, Del.: Juan de la Cuesta-Hispanic Monographs, 1986.

León-Portilla, Miguel. *Aztec Thought and Culture: A Study of the Ancient Nahuatl Mind.* Translated by Jack Emory Davis. Norman: University of Oklahoma Press, 1990.

———, ed. *The Broken Spears: The Aztec Account of the Conquest of México.* Boston: Beacon Press, 1992.

Levene, Ricardo. *Las Indias no eran colonias.* Buenos Aires: Espasa-Calpe, 1951.

Levillier, Roberto. *Don Francisco de Toledo: Supremo organizador del Perú, su vida, su obra, 1515–1582.* Vol. 1. Madrid: Espasa-Calpe, 1935.

Lockhart, James. "Encomienda and Hacienda: The Evolution of the Great Estate in the Spanish Indies." *Hispanic American Historical Review* 49:3 (August, 1969): 411–29.

———. "Trunk Lines and Feeder Lines: The Spanish Reaction to American Resources." In Andrien and Adorno, *Transatlantic Encounters,* 90–120.

López de Gómara, Francisco. *Historia general de las Indias.* Caracas: Biblioteca Ayacucho, 1978. First published in Spain in 1552.

Losada, Angel. "The Controversy between Sepúlveda and Las Casas in the Junta of Valladolid." In Friede and Keen, *Bartolomé de Las Casas in History.*

———. *Fray Bartolomé de Las Casas a la luz de la historia moderna.* Madrid: Editorial Tecnos, 1970.

———, ed. and trans. *Apología de Juan Ginés de Sepúlveda contra Fray Bartolomé de las Casas y de Fray Bartolomé de Las Casas contra Juan Ginés de Sepulveda.* Madrid: Editora Nacional, 1975.

Lovett, A. W. *Early Habsburg Spain, 1517–1598.* Oxford: Oxford University Press, 1986.

221

Mackenthun, Gesa. *Metaphors of Dispossession: American Beginnings and the Translation of Empire, 1492–1637*. Norman: University of Oklahoma Press, 1997.

MacLachlan, Colin. *Spain's Empire in the New World: The Role of Ideas in Institutional and Social Change*. Berkeley: University of California Press, 1988.

MacLachlan, Colin, and Jaime E. Rodriguez O. *The Forging of the Cosmic Race: A Reinterpretation of Colonial Mexico*. Berkeley: University of California Press, 1990. First published 1980.

MacLeod, Murdo J. "Las Casas, Guatemala and the Sad but Inevitable Case of Antonio de Remesal." *Topic* 2 (Fall 1970): 53–64.

Mariátegui, José Carlos. *7 ensayos de interpretación de la realidad peruana*. 13th ed. Lima: Editorial Amauta S.A., 1968. First published 1928.

Martínez, Manuel M. *Fray Bartolomé de Las Casas: "Padre de America": Estudio biográfico crítico*. Madrid: private printing, 1958.

——. "El padre Las Casas, Promotor de la evangelización de América." In *Estudios Lascasianos: IV centenario de la muerte de Fray Bartolomé de las Casas (1566–1966)*. Sevilla: Facultad de Filosofía y Letras de la Universidad de Sevilla, 1966.

Martínez Bulle Goyri, Victor Manuel. "El Encuentro entre Fray Bartolomé de Las Casas y Juan Ginés de Sepúlveda en la junta de Valladolid, en 1550." In *Symposium: Fray Bartolomé de Las Casas, trascendencia de su obra y doctrina*, 225–38. México D.F.: Universidad Nacional Autónoma de México, 1985.

Marx, Karl, and Friedrich Engels. *The Communist Manifesto*. New York: International Publishers, 1983.

Mélida y Gonzalez-Monteagudo, Monico. *El P. Bartolomé de Las Casas y Valladolid*. Valladolid: Casa-Museo de Colón, 1975.

Menéndez Pidal, Ramón. *El Padre Las Casas: Su doble personalidad*. Madrid: Espasa-Calpe S.A., 1963.

Mignet, M. *Antonio Perez et Philippe II*. Paris, 1854.

Milhou, Alain. *Colón y su mentalidad mesiánica en el ambiente franciscanista español*. Cuadernos Colombinos 11. Valladolid: Casa-Museo de Colón, Seminario Americanista de Valladolid, 1983.

——. "De la destruction de l'Espagne à la destruction des Indes: Histoire sacrée et combats ideologiques." In *Études sur l'impact culturel du Nouveau Monde*, 25–47. Séminaire Interuniversitaire Sur L'Amérique Espagnole Coloniale. Paris: L'Harmattan, 1981.

——. "Las Casas profeta de su tiempo: Profeta para nuestro tiempo." In Congreso Teológico Internacional, *Las Casas entre dos mundos*, 177–205.

Molina Meliá, Antonio. *Iglesia y estado en el siglo de oro español: El pensamiento de Francisco Suarez*. Valencia: Universidad de Valencia, Secretariado de Publicaciones, 1977.

Mommsen, Wolfgang J. *Theories of Imperialism*. Translated by P. S. Falla. Chicago: University of Chicago Press, 1980.

Morison, Samuel Eliot. *Admiral of the Ocean Sea: A Life of Christopher Columbus*. Boston: Little, Brown, 1970. First published in 1942.

——. *Christopher Columbus, Mariner*. New York: Meridian Books, 1983.

——. *The European Discovery of America: The Southern Voyages, 1492–1616*. New York: Oxford University Press, 1974.

Moscoso Pastrana, Prudencio. "Fray Bartolomé de Las Casas en Ciudad Real, Chiapas." In *Symposium: Fray Bartolomé de Las Casas, trascendencia de su obra y doctrina*, 265–77. México D.F.: Universidad Nacional Autónoma de México, 1985.

Murra, John. "Nos hazen mucha ventaja." In Andrien and Adorno, *Transatlantic Encounters*.

Nadel, George H., and Perry Curtis, eds. *Imperialism and Colonialism*. New York: Macmillan, 1964.

Naipaul, V. S. *Among the Believers: An Islamic Journey*. New York: Alfred A. Knopf, 1981.

Nietzsche, Friedrich. *Twilight of the Idols and The Anti-Christ*. Translated by R. J. Hollingdale. London: Penguin Books, 1968.

Novalín, José Luis G. *El inquisidor general Fernando de Valdés (1483–1568): Su vida y su obra*. Oviedo: Universidad de Oviedo, 1968.

Ortega y Gasset, José. *En torno a Galileo*. Madrid: Espasa Calpe, 1996.

——. *History as a System and Other Essays toward a Philosophy of History*. Translated by Helene Weyl. New York: W. W. Norton, 1961. First published in 1941.

——. *Man and Crisis*. Translated by Mildred Adams. New York: W. W. Norton, 1958.

Oviedo y Valdés, Gonzalo Fernández de. *Historia general y natural de las indias, islas y tierra firme del mar océano*. 4 vols. Madrid, 1851: Real Academia de la Historia, 1851–55. First published 1547.

Pagden, Anthony. *European Encounters with the New World: From Renaissance to Romanticism*. New Haven, Conn.: Yale University Press, 1993.

——. *The Fall of Natural Man: The American Indian and the Origins of Comparative Ethnology*. Cambridge: Cambridge University Press, 1988. First published 1981.

——. Introduction to Las Casas, *A Short Account*, xiii–xli.

——. "*Ius et Factum*: Text and Experience in the Writings of Bartolomé de Las Casas." In Greenblatt, *New World Encounters*, 85–100.

——. *Spanish Imperialism and the Political Imagination: Studies in European and Spanish-American Social and Political Theory, 1513–1830*. New Haven, Conn.: Yale University Press, 1990.

Parish, Helen Rand. "Bartolomé de Las Casas: A Saga for Today." In *Bartolomé de Las Casas: Liberation for the Oppressed*, edited by Michael Marie Zobelein. Mission San José, Calif.: M. M. Zobelein, Dominican Sisters, 1984.

——. "Introduction: Las Casas' Spirituality—The Three Crises." In Las Casas, *The Only Way*, 9–58.

——. *Las Casas as a Bishop: A New Interpretation Based on his Holograph Petition in the Hans P. Kraus Collection of Hispanic American Manuscripts / Las Casas, Obispo: Una nueva interpretación a base de su petición autografa en la Colección Hans P. Kraus de Manuscritos Hispanoamericanos*. Washington: Library of Congress, 1980.

——. "Las Casas: Una vida redescubierta." In Congreso Teológico Internacional, *Las Casas entre dos mundos*.

Parish, Helen Rand, and Harold E. Weidman. *Las Casas en México: Historia y obra desconocidas*. México, D.F.: Fondo de Cultura Económica, 1992.

———. "The Correct Birthdate of Bartolomé de Las Casas." *Hispanic American Historical Review* 56:4 (1976): 385–403.

Parry, J. H. *The Spanish Theory of Empire in the Sixteenth Century*. Cambridge: Cambridge University Press, 1940.

Parry, J. H., and Robert G. Keith. *New Iberian World: A Documentary History of the Discovery and Settlement of Latin America to the Early Seventeenth Century: The Conquerors and the Conquered*. Vol. 1. New York: Times Books, 1984.

Peña, Juan de la. *De bello contra insulanos, intervención de España en América: Escuela española de la paz, segunda generación*. Corpus Hispanorum de Pace, vol. 10. Madrid: Consejo Superior de Investigaciones Científicas, 1982.

Pereña, Luciano. *Proceso a la leyenda negra*. Salamanca: Universidad Pontificia de Salamanca, 1989.

Pérez Fernandez, Isacio. *Inventario documentado de los escritos de Fray Bartolomé de Las Casas*. Bayamón, Puerto Rico: Centro de Estudios de los Domínicos del Caribe (CEDOC), 1981.

Pérez de Tudela Bueso, Juan. "Estudio Crítico Preliminar." In *Obras escogidas de Fray Bartolomé de Las Casas*, edited by Juan Pérez de Tudela Bueso. Vol. 95 of the Biblioteca de Autores Españoles. Madrid: Biblioteca de Autores Españoles, 1957.

Peter, Anton. "Bartolomé de Las Casas y el tema de la conversión en la Teología de la Liberación." *Paginas* 17:116 (July 1992): 49–63.

Phelan, John Leddy. "The Problems of Conflicting Spanish Imperial Ideologies in the Sixteenth Century." In *Latin American History: Select Problems: Identity, Integration and Nationhood*, edited by Fredrick B. Pike. New York: Harcourt, Brace and World, 1969.

Phillips, William D. Jr., and Carla Rahn Phillips. "Spain in the Fifteenth Century." In Andrien and Adorno, *Transatlantic Encounters*, 11–39.

Pike, Ruth. *Enterprise and Adventure: The Genoese in Seville and the Opening of the New World*. Ithaca, N.Y.: Cornell University Press, 1966.

Pizarro, Pedro. *Relación del descubrimiento y conquista de los reinos del Perú y del gobierno i orden que los naturales tenían y tesoros que en ella se hallaron y de las demás cosas que en el han sucedido hasta el día de la fecha*. 2nd ed. Buenos Aires: Editorial Futuro, 1944. Written in 1571.

Plato. *Great Dialogues of Plato*. Translated by W. H. D. Rouse. New York: New American Library, 1956.

Powell, Philip Wayne. *Soldiers, Indians, and Silver: North America's First Frontier War*. Tempe: Center for Latin American Studies, Arizona State University, 1975.

Prescott, William H. *History of the Reign of Ferdinand and Isabella the Catholic*. Vol. 3. Philadelphia: J. B. Lippincott, 1869.

Queralto Moreno, Ramón Jesús. *El pensamiento filosófico-político de Bartolomé de Las Casas*. Sevilla: Secretariado de Publicaciones de la Universidad de Sevilla, 1976.

En el quinto centenario de Bartolomé de Las Casas (1484–1566). Madrid: Ediciones Cultura Hispánica, Instituto de Cooperación Iberoamericana, 1986.

Quiroga, Vasco de. *La utopía en América*. Edited by Paz Serrano Gassent. Madrid: Historia 16, 1992.

Rabasa, José. *Inventing America: Spanish Historiography and the Formation of Eurocentrism*. Norman: University of Oklahoma Press, 1993.

Rama, Angel. *La Ciudad letrada*. Hanover, N.H.: Ediciones del Norte, 1985.

——. *The Lettered City*. Translated and edited by John Charles Chasteen. Durham, N.C.: Duke University Press, 1996.

Remesal, Antonio de. *Historia general de las Indias occidentales y particular de la gobernación de Chiapa y Guatemala*. 2 vols. Edited by P. Carmelo Saenz de Santa María. Vols. 175 and 189 of the Biblioteca de Autores Españoles. Madrid: Biblioteca de Autores Españoles, 1964, 1966.

Ricard, Robert. *The Spiritual Conquest of Mexico: An Essay on the Apostolate and the Evangelizing Method of the Mendicant Orders: 1523–1572*. Translated by Lesley Byrd Simpson. Berkeley: University of California Press, 1966. First published in French, 1933.

Rivera Pagán, Luis N. *Evangelización y violencia: La conquista de América*. 3rd ed. San Juan: Ediciones CEMI, 1992.

Said, Edward. *Orientalism*. New York: Vintage Books, 1979.

Saint Lu, André. "Vigencia histórica de la obra de Las Casas." In *En el quinto centenario de Bartolomé de Las Casas (1484–1566)*. Madrid: Ediciones Cultura Hispánica, Instituto de Cooperación Iberoamericana, 1986.

Salinas C. Maximiliano. *Historia del pueblo de Dios en Chile: La evolución del cristianismo desde la perspectiva de los pobres*. Santiago de Chile: CEHILA, Ediciones Rehue, 1987.

Salisbury, John of. *Policraticus: Of the Frivolities of Courtiers and the Footprints of Philosopher*. Edited and translated by Cary J. Nederman. Cambridge: Cambridge University Press, 1990.

Sánchez, Joseph P. "The Spanish Black Legend: Origins of Anti-Hispanic Stereotypes." *Encounters: A Quincentenary Review* (Winter 1989): 16–21.

Schäfer, Ernesto. *El consejo real y supremo de las Indias: Su historia, organización y labor administrativa hasta la terminación de la Casa de Austria*. 2 vols. Sevilla: Universidad de Sevilla, 1935, 1947.

——. *Las Casas indigeniste: Etudes sur la vie et l'ouvre du défenseur des indiens*. Paris: Editions L'Harmattan, 1982.

Schneider, Reinhold. *Imperial Mission*. Translated by Walter Oden. New York: Gresham Press, 1948.

Seed, Patricia. "'Are These Not Also Men?' The Indians' Humanity and Capacity for Spanish Civilisation." *Journal of Latin American Studies* 25 (October 1993): 629–52.

——. *Ceremonies of Possession in Europe's Conquest of the New World, 1492–1640*. New York: Cambridge University Press, 1995.

Seminario Americanista de la Universidad de Valladolid. *Juan Ginés de Sepúlveda y su crónica indiana*. Valladolid: Seminario Americanista de la Universidad de Valladolid y Excmo. Ayuntamiento de Pozoblanco, 1976.

225

Sepúlveda, Juan Ginés de. *Apología de Juan Ginés de Sepulveda*. In Losada, *Apología*.
———. *Tratado sobre las justas causas de la guerra contra los indios*. 2nd ed. Edited by Marcelino Menéndez y Pelayo. México: Fondo de Cultura Económica, 1941. First published in 1891.

Serrano y Sanz, Manuel. *Orígenes de la dominación española en América*. Madrid: Nueva Biblioteca de Autores Españoles 25:1.

Shumway, Nicolas. *The Invention of Argentina*. Berkeley: University of California Press, 1991.

Simpson, Lesley Byrd. *The Encomienda in New Spain: Forced Native Labor in the Spanish Colonies, 1492–1550*. Berkeley: University of California Press, 1929.

———. *The Encomienda in New Spain: The Beginning of Spanish Mexico*. Berkeley: University of California Press, 1982. First published in 1950.

———, ed. and trans. *The Laws of Burgos of 1512–1513: Royal Ordinances for the Good Government and Treatment of the Indians*. San Francisco: John Howell Books, 1960.

Smith, Adam. *An Inquiry into the Nature and Causes of the Wealth of Nations*. Abridged with an introduction by Richard Teichgraeber III. New York: Random House, 1985. First published in 1776.

Taylor, William B. "Landed Society in New Spain: A View from the South." *Hispanic American Historical Review* 54: 3 (August 1974): 387–413.

Tellechea Idigoras, José Ignacio. *El Arzobispo Carranza y su tiempo*. 2 vols. Madrid: Ediciones Guadarrama, 1968.

Teresa de Mier, Servando. *Obras completas: La formación de un republicano*. Vol. 4. México: Universidad Nacional Autónoma de México, 1988.

Thomas, Hugh. *Conquest*. New York: Simon and Schuster, 1993.

Tobar, Balthasar de. *Compendio bulario indico*. Edited by Manuel Gutierrez de Arce. Sevilla: Escuela de Estudios Hispano-Americanos de Sevilla, 1954. Originally compiled in 1695.

Todorov, Tzvetan. *The Conquest of America: The Question of the Other*. Translated by Richard Howard. New York: Harper and Row, 1985. First published in French in 1982.

Ulloa, Daniel. *Los predicadores divididos: Los domínicos en Nueva España, siglo XVI*. México: El Colegio de México, 1977.

Universidad Nacional Autónoma de México. *Symposium: Fray Bartolomé de Las Casas, trascendencia de su obra y doctrina*. México D.F.: Universidad Nacional Autónoma de México, 1985.

Urdanoz, Teófilo. "Síntesis teológico-jurídica de la doctrina de Vitoria," In *Relectio de Indis o libertad de los indios*, edited by Luciano Pereña and J. M. Prendes, xlii–cxlii. Corpus Hispanorum de Pace Series No. 5. Madrid: Consejo de Investigaciones Científicas, 1967.

Utrera, Fr. Cipriano de. *Polémica de Enriquillo*. Santo Domingo, R.D.: Academia Dominicana de la Historia, 1973.

Valcarcel, Carlos Daniel. *Rebeliones coloniales sudamericanas*. México: Fondo de Cultura Económica, 1982.

Vicens Vivens, Jaime. *Historia crítica de la vida y reinado de Fernando II de Aragón*. 2 vols. Zaragoza: Institución Fernando el Católico, 1962.

Vitoria, Francisco de. *Relecciones del estado, de los indios, y del derecho de la guerra*. Edited by Antonio Gómez Robledo. México: Editorial Porrúa S.A., 1974.

———. *Relectio de Indis o libertad de los indios*. Edited by Luciano Pereña and J. M. Prendes. Corpus Hispanorum de Pace Series No. 5. Madrid: Consejo de Investigaciones Cientificas, 1967.

Wagner, Henry Raup. "Three Studies on the Same Subject." *Hispanic American Historical Review* (May 1945): 155–211.

Wagner, Henry Raup, and Helen Rand Parish. *The Life and Writings of Bartolomé de Las Casas*. Albuquerque: University of New Mexico Press, 1967.

Weckmann, Luis. *La herencia medieval de México*. 2 vols. Mexico: El Colegio de Mexico, 1984.

Zamora, Margarita, ed. and trans. "Christopher Columbus's 'Letter to the Sovereigns': Announcing the Discovery." In Greenblatt, *New World Encounters*, 1–11.

Zavala, Silvio. *La encomienda indiana*. 2nd ed. México: Editorial Porrúa, 1973. First published in 1935.

———. *Ensayos sobre la colonización española en América*. 3rd ed. México: Editorial Porrúa, 1978. First published in 1944.

———. *La filosofía política en la conquista de América*. 3rd ed. México: Fondo de Cultura Económica, 1977. First published in 1947.

———. *Las instituciones jurídicas en la conquista de América*. 2nd ed. México: Editorial Porrúa, S.A., 1975. First published in 1935.

———. *Recuerdo de Bartolomé de Las Casas*. Guadalajara, Jalisco: Librería Font. S.A., 1966.

227

Index

Acosta, José de, 192 n. 64

Aguirre, Lope de, 2

Alcalá, University of, 127

Alonso islets, 80

Altitudo divino consilii, 99

Alvarado, Pedro de, 2, 100, 102

Angulo, Pedro de, 103

Anti-colonialism, 11, 152

Apologética historia sumaria (Las Casas), 15, 92, 134, 147

Atahualpa, 146; massacre of guards of, 172

Audiencia de los Confines, 124

Ávila, Predrarias de, 2

Ayala, Felipe Guamán Poma de, 192 n. 64

Aztecs, 53–54

Baoruco, 93

Barrionuevo, Captain Francisco de, 94

Beltrán, Diego de, 104

Benavente, Fray Toribio de, Motolinía, 111, 115, 165–66, 168, 192 n. 64

Berlanga, Tomás de, 88

Betanzos, Domingo de, 87

Black Legend (*leyenda negra*), 3–4, 107–8, 171, 173

Bobadilla, Francisco de, 47

Bolívar, Simón, 180

Brevísima relación de la destruición de las Indias (Las Casas), 3, 12, 20, 51, 90, 105–7, 110, 112, 137, 148, 153, 171–72

Buendía, Alonso Maldonado de, 157

Burgos, Laws of, 59–61, 68, 72, 85, 154, 161

Cajamarca, 172

Campeche, 120

Cano, Melchor, 27, 131, 207 n. 90

Caonao, Cuba, 65

Carranza y Miranda, Bishop Bartolomé de, 131, 140, 143, 145

Carro, Father Vicente, 172

Carta grande (Las Casas)*,* 140, 145

Carvajal, Juan Suárez de, 104

Casa de Contratación, 82–83, 119

Castro, Alonso de, 140

Castro, Pedro de, 145

Cédulas de Malines, 124, 126

Charles V, 10, 31–32, 75, 80, 100, 102, 104, 117, 124, 128, 136, 139, 169, 171, 189 n. 26, 198 n. 48

Chiapa, 67, 91, 101, 116–17, 120, 133, 145, 167, 205 n. 35

Chichimeca, 164

Chile, 131

Cholula massacre, 172

Cibao, Española, 47

Cieza de León, Pedro, 111, 157, 192 n. 64, 221 n. 12

Ciguayo, 96

Cisneros, Cardinal Ximénez de, 10, 69, 77–78, 151, 198 n. 37

Ciudad Real, 120, 124

Cobos, Francisco de los, 82, 117

Colegio de San Gregorio, 134, 148, 160

Colón, Diego, 58

Colonial administration, 45

Colonialism, Spanish, 14, 67

Colonial rebellion, 115

Colonists, ambitions of, 42–44

Colonizers, dehumanization of, 51

Columbus, Christopher, 1, 17–22, 38, 42, 63, 198 n. 46; exhumation of remains of, 119

Columbus, Diego, 85

Conchillo, Lope de, 59

Confesionario (Las Casas), 121, 128, 135, 137–38, 165

Contreras, Governor Rodrigo de, 98

Córdoba, Hernández de, 53

Córdoba, Pedro de, 24, 56, 79–80, 198 n. 37, 199 n. 73

Corral, Felipe Ruiz del, 159

Cortés, Fernando, 2, 41, 53, 168

Council of Santiago de los Caballeros, 102

Council of the Indies, 4, 100, 115, 202 n. 99; Las Casas's letter to, 89–91

Council of Trent, 131

Crown Prince Philip, 105, 139

Croy, Gillaume de, 109

Cuauhtémoc, Mexico, 179

Cuba, 51, 65, 68, 75, 106, 111, 113, 185

Cubaguá, 82

Cuban-Spanish War, 171

Cultural subjugation, 53–54

Cumaná, 82–84, 90, 168

Cusco, Perú, 117

Darién, Panama, 52

Del único modo de atraer a todos los pueblos a la verdadera religión (Las Casas), 7, 91–92

De regia potestate (Las Casas), 140, 145, 147, 153

Destruction-restoration dichotomy, 150, 155

De unico vocationis modo omnium gentium ad veram religionem (Las Casas), 7, 91–92

Díaz del Castillo, Bernal, 40–41, 97, 113, 139

Dominican reformers, 55

Donation of Constantine (*Donatio Constantini*), 22

Ecclesiastical imperialism, 13, 21, 63, 67, 156, 182

Encomienda, 9, 47, 49–50, 100, 115, 188 n. 23; admonitions against, 136; effects on Indian population of, 51; end of, 170; in perpetuity, 138, 140, 144

Enríquez, Viceroy Martín, 164

Enriquillo, 185, 188 n. 18, 201 n. 97; pacification of, 93–96

Española, 38, 45, 55–56, 65, 68, 77, 119, 151, 185, 200 n. 84

European colonial attitudes, 18–19

Ferdinand, 58; Isabel and, 22, 46

Fonseca, Juan Rodríguez de, 58, 81–82, 102

Friede, Juan, 34, 115, 150, 210 n. 4

Fuenleal, Sebastían Ramírez de, 104

Garcés, Bishop Julián, 88

Giménez Fernández, Manuel, 72, 199 n. 53, 200 n. 76, 133, 209 n. 19

Gold, 41, 44, 47, 74, 193 n. 3

Golden Legend (*leyenda aurea*), 3, 10, 32, 75, 164, 171, 173; twentieth-century views of, 173–74

Gómara, Francisco López de, 35, 113, 167, 168

Gomera, 119

Granada, 22, 97

graves, pillaging of, 146

Guadalajara, 159

Guadalquivir River, 119

Guarionex, 179

Guatemala, 99–102, 104, 145, 167

Gutierrez, Gustavo, 7, 181

Guzmán, Nuño de, 2

Hanke, Lewis, 2, 10, 43, 71, 88, 133, 162, 174–75

Hatuey, 51

Historia de las Indias (Las Casas), 6, 51, 56, 88, 91, 93, 109, 134, 147, 168

Holy War, 19

Huacas of Peru, 146

Huancavelica, 175

Imperialism, Spanish, 8–9, 25, 27, 67, 75, 81; nineteenth-century views of, 173

Incas, 157 n. 12

230

Indianist movement, 2, 32, 36, 157
Indians: class structure among, 143; conception of, 49; decreasing population of, 195 n. 48; idealization of, 36; Lacandón, 101; narratives of, 51; of Peru, 143; resistance to conversion of, 69; as term, 187 n. 4. *See also* Natives
Indios encomendados, 50–51
Isabel, 47, 55, 58; *cédula real* of, 48

Jeronymite friars, 77–79, 151, 198 n. 41
Juan, king of Zacapulas, 100
Juderías, Julián, 171
Junta, formation of, 24–25, 59; of 1504, 25; of Burgos, 67; of Valladolid, 128–29

La Gasca, Pedro, 139
La Plata, 131, 157
Lacandón, 118
Ladrada, Rodrigo de, 134
Las Casas, Fray Bartolomé de: accomplishments of, 6; arrival in America of, 63; arrival in Ciudad Real of, 120; Dominican order and, 87; *encomienda* condemned by, 70, 72; image of, 4; interview with King Ferdinand of, 69; mythology of, 5, 178, 183; as *protector de todos los Indios*, 63, 78–79; as symbol of nonviolent reform, 180; transformation of, 64, 66; Utopian visions of, 182, 210 n. 2
Las Casas, Fray Bartolomé de, works of: *Apologética historia sumaria*, 15, 92, 134, 147; *Brevísima relación de la destruición de las Indias*, 3, 12, 20, 51, 90, 105–7, 110, 112, 137, 148, 153, 171–72; *Carta grande*, 140, 145; *Confesionario*, 121, 128, 135, 137–38, 165; *De regia potestate*, 140, 145, 147, 153; *Historia de las Indias*, 6, 51, 56, 88, 91, 93, 109, 134, 147, 168; letter to Council of the Indies, 89–91; *Memorial de remedios*, 71–75, 77; *The Only Way to Draw People to a Living Faith*, 7, 91–

92; *Principia Quaedam (Some Principles)*, 137; *Los tesoros del Perú*, 145–46; *Thirty Very Juridical Propositions*, 135–37; *Tratado comprobatorio del imperio soberano*, 135; *Tratado de las doce dudas*, 145–46, 148
Lautaro, 179
Laws of Burgos, 59–61, 68, 72, 85, 154, 161
lese-majesty, charges of, 135
liberation theology, 4, 180
Llorente, Juan Antonio, 138
Loaysa, Antonio de, 57
Loaysa, Cardinal García de, 28, 104, 117

Major, John, 26, 81
Maldonado, Alonso de, 100–102, 124
Malines, 145
Marroquín, Bishop Francisco de, 101–2, 115, 124, 126
Memorial de remedios (Las Casas), 71–75, 77
Méndez, Alonso, 142
Mendoza, Viceroy Antonio de, 100–101, 111, 165
Menéndez Pidal, Ramón, 4–5, 118, 172, 199 n. 64
Mesa, Bernaldo de, 67; seven propositions of, 67
Mexico, 40, 63, 103, 155
Mier, Servando Teresa y, 180
Minaya, Bernardino de, 99
Mita, 48
Mixteca, 159
Mixtón war, 111
Montejo, Francisco de, 118, 120
Montesinos, Antonio, 56–59, 64, 68, 88, 198 n. 37

Narváez, Pánfilo de, 65, 97, 106
Natives: deviant status of, 59; exploitation of, 55; legal status of, 56; massacre of, 65, 80; revolts by, 82, 94; rights of, 58; welfare of, 34. *See also* Indians

"Negroes," conversion of, 21

New Laws of 1542, 106, 108,113–14, 117–18, 125, 161, 166, 204 n. 25, 205 n. 34; Article 30, 115, 124; enforcement of, 116, 123–24, 154; failure of, 145, 156

Nicaragua, 97–99, 103

Noble savage, 35

Oaxaca, Mexico, 99, 111

Only Way to Draw People to a Living Faith, The (Las Casas), 7, 91–92

Order of Calatrava, 83

Order of Preachers, 87–88, 97, 102

Order of Santiago, 83

Order of the Golden Spur, 83

Ordinances for Discoveries, 6, 161

Ortiz, Luis de, 44

Ovando, Nicolás de, 38, 45–47, 49, 55, 60

Oviedo, Gonzalo Fernández de, 35, 43–44, 93, 95, 113, 128, 167, 169, 199 n. 64, 201 n. 98; *Historia general y natural de las Indias,* 128, 168; *Sumario de la general y natural historia de las Indias,* 88, 168

Pagden, Anthony, 6, 18, 20, 32, 97

Palacios Rubios, Juan López de, 26, 31, 61, 74, 88

Panamá, 52

Paria, 80, 82–83, 86, 182

Pastoralle officium, 99

Paz, Matías de, 26, 31, 74

Pereña, Luciano, 173

Perera, Canon Juan, 120

Peru, 12, 39, 63, 115, 140–42, 146, 155, 157, 161, 163, 170

Philip II, 6, 37, 75, 137, 144, 157

Pizarro, Francisco, 45, 53, 170

Pizarro, Gonzalo, 39, 115–16, 139

Pope Alexander VI, 22–24, 58; *Dudum Siquidem,* 23; *Eximiae Devotionis,* 23; *Inter Caetera,* 23

Pope Paul III, 99

Pope Pius V, 148, 177

Potosí, 175

Prince Adrian, 69

Prince Charles, 69

Principia Quaedam (Las Casas)*,* 137

Prison sentences, commutation of, 44

Puerto Rico, 52

Quiché, 100

Quintana, Dean Gil, 120, 122

Quiroga, Bishop Vasco de, 72

Reconquista, 20, 47, 110, 150

reducciones, 60, 72, 163, 179

Remesal, Antonio de, 100, 123, 158–61; *Historia general de las Indias Occidentales y particular de la gobernación de Chiapa y Guatemala,* 158

Rentería, Diego de, 66

Rentería, Pedro de, 199 n. 65

repartimiento, 48–49; practice of, 137

republic of Indians (*republica de indios*), 55

republic of Spaniards (*republica de españoles*), 55

Requerimiento of 1512, 61

Ribera, Antonio de, 139

right of nations (*iure gentium*), 29, 31

Royal Ordinance of 1526, 50

Sahagún, Bernardo de, 192 n. 64

Salamanca, 27, 38, 88, 119, 127, 132, 142, 200 n. 78

Sánchez, Luis, 157

Sandoval, Tello de, 111, 115, 126

San Juan de los Reyes, 142

San Lúcar de Barrameda, 119

San Martín, Tómas de, 139

Santiago de los Caballeros, 101

Santo Domingo, 45, 82, 84, 86, 113, 119

Santo Tomás, Domingo de, 142, 157, 192 n. 64, 209 n. 39

Sauvage, Jean le, 81

Sepúlveda, Juan Ginés de, 12, 26, 61,

232

126, 146, 168, 175; *Democrates II,* 131,
138, 205 n. 72
slavery, 147; African, 37, 74, 78, 94, 143,
197 n. 29; Indian, 37, 49, 52, 114–15,
127, 141, 197 n. 31
slave trade, 21
Some Principles (Las Casas), 137
Soto, Domingo de, 24, 27
spice trade, 41
Sublimis Deus, 99

Tabasco, 120
Tainos, 18
Tamayo, 96
Tenochtilán, 53
Tesoros del Perú, Los (Las Casas), 145–
46
Testera, Jacobo de, 104
theocratic government, 122
Theology of Liberation, 4, 180
Thirty Very Juridical Propositions (Las
Casas), 135–37
Tierra Firme, 79–81, 84, 151, 156, 199
n. 66, 199 n. 73
Tlamatinime, 53–54
Toledo, Viceroy Francisco, 72, 161–62,
170, 174–75
*Tratado comprobatorio del imperio
soberano* (Las Casas), 135
Tratado de las doce dudas (Las
Casas),145–46, 148
Treaty of Alcaçovas, 21
Treaty of Tordesillas, 23
Treinta proposiciones muy jurídicas (Las
Casas), 135–37

Tributes, 47
Trinidad, 80
Tupac Amaru I, 175
Tupac Amaru II, 179
Tuzulutlán, 97–103, 117–18, 123, 160,
167, 202 n. 117
Twelve, the, 45

Universal procurator, 10, 78, 113, 134,
213 n. 49

Valdés, Archbishop Fernando de, 126,
131
Valladolid, junta of, 12, 114, 126–31,
133, 138, 168, 175
Valle, Bishop Juan del, 157
Vela, Blasco Nuñez, 115
Velázquez, Diego de, 51, 65, 106, 168
Venezuela, 151
Vera Cruz, Alonso de la, 144, 157
Vera Paz, 123, 160
Vitoria, Francisco de, 24, 27, 31; *Relec-
ciones,* 28–29, 32

War: doctrine of just, 30; Holy, 19
White Legend, 3

Yucatán, 118–20; conquest of, 53; encomienda system in, 50

Zacapulas, 100
Zacatecas, 159
Zuazo, Alonso de, 77
Zumárraga, Bishop Juan de, 88, 102,
115, 192 n. 64

233

Daniel Castro is an associate professor of history at
Southwestern University. He is the editor of *Revolution and Revolutionaries:
Guerilla Movements in Latin America* (1999).

Library of Congress Cataloging-in-Publication Data
Castro, Daniel, 1945–
Another face of empire : Bartolomé de las Casas, indigenous rights, and
ecclesiastical imperialism / Daniel Castro.
p. cm. — (Latin America otherwise)
Includes bibliographical references and index.
ISBN-13: 978-0-8223-3930-4 (cloth : alk. paper)
ISNB-13: 978-0-8223-3939-7 (pbk. : alk. paper)
1. Casas, Bartolomé de las, 1474–1566. 2. Explorers—America—Biography.
3. Explorers—Spain—Biography. 4. Missionaries—America—Biography.
5. Missionaries—Spain—Biography. 6. Indians, Treatment of. 7. America—
Discovery and exploration—Spanish. I. Title.
E125.C4C37 2007
972'.02092—dc22
[B]   2006020435